EXCAVATIONS AT THE EARLY BRONZE AGE CEMETERY OF
TIWAL ESH-SHARQI

EXCAVATIONS AT THE EARLY BRONZE AGE CEMETERY OF TIWAL ESH-SHARQI

JONATHAN N. TUBB

WITH APPENDICES BY
JANET D. HENDERSON
AND
MARGOT M. WRIGHT

PUBLISHED FOR
THE TRUSTEES OF THE BRITISH MUSEUM
BY BRITISH MUSEUM PUBLICATIONS

© 1990 The Trustees of the British Museum
Published by British Museum Publications Ltd
46 Bloomsbury Street, London WC1B 3QQ

British Library Cataloguing in Publication Data

Tubb, Jonathan N.
Excavations at the early Bronze Age cemetery of Tiwal esh-Sharqi.
1. Jordan. Tiwal esh-Sharqi. Bronze Age cemeteries.
Excavations of remains
1. Title   II. Henderson, Janet D.   III. Wright, Margot M.
IV. British Museum, *Trustees*
933

ISBN 0-7141-1128-7

Designed by John Hawkins
Printed in Great Britain
by Henry Ling, Dorset

CONTENTS

1	*Introduction*	7
2	*The Tombs and their Contents*	
	Tombs in the north-east sector	12
	Tombs in the south-east sector	53
3	*Discussion*	88
	References	99
APPENDIX A	The Human Bones from Tiwal esh-Sharqi *Janet D. Henderson*	101
APPENDIX B	Conservation Treatments Employed at Tiwal esh-Sharqi *Margot M. Wright*	109
APPENDIX C	Distribution of Finds	111
	Plates	113

CHAPTER 1

INTRODUCTION

The large site of Tell Umm Hammad in the central Jordan Valley has been recognised as one of major significance since the survey work of Nelson Glueck in 1942. Collections made at the two elements of the site, Tell Umm Hammad esh-Sharqiya and Tell Umm Hammad el-Gharbiya, suggested to Glueck that the former had been occupied during the Late Chalcolithic to Early Bronze I periods, and subsequently in the Iron Age and the Roman and Byzantine periods. Tell Umm Hammad el-Gharbiya, on the other hand, appeared to have been occupied only during the Early Bronze IV period (Glueck's Middle Bronze I, see Glueck 1951: 318–29). A limited sounding was made at the eastern mound (Sharqiya) by James Mellaart in 1953 (see Mellaart 1962: 135–6), but it was not until 1982 that larger-scale systematic excavations were undertaken at both mounds by Svend Helms. During the course of three seasons, Helms revealed a stratified sequence of occupation at Sharqiya covering the Chalcolithic to the Early Bronze II periods ('stages' I–IV), and a very extensive Early Bronze IV occupation at Gharbiya ('stages' V–VIII) with architecture surely indicative of permanent settlement (see Helms 1984, and especially 1986).

During Helms' first season, as a result of bulldozing activities in preparation for road construction, a number of tombs were exposed in the area to the south of Tell Umm Hammad, which is known locally as Tiwal esh-Sharqi. Subsequent investigations by Helms here revealed the presence of an extensive cemetery of EBIV date, and in early 1983 a rescue excavation was launched by Helms and a team from the Department of Antiquities of Jordan. Several tombs were cleared, and the results were promptly published in a preliminary form the following year (Helms 1983).

In 1984, at the suggestion of Helms, the present writer applied for, and was generously granted, a permit to undertake a more extensive season of excavations at Tiwal esh-Sharqi on behalf of the British Museum. Seven weeks of excavations took place between March and May 1984. Geological and geomorphological studies of the physical background of the cemetery area were undertaken by Peter Dorrell of the Institute of Archaeology, London, who was also responsible for the photography and assisted with the excavations. The human remains were studied in the field by Janet Henderson (Institute of Archaeology, London), and her report is included as Appendix A in this volume. The cemetery area was surveyed and mapped by Barbara Pritzkat (University of California at Los Angeles), and her location plan appears as Figure 1 (back pocket). On-site conservation and limited restoration was undertaken by Margot Wright (Institute of Archaeology, London), and a summary of the treatments she employed is included as Appendix B. The tombs were planned in the field by Susan Thorpe (British Institute at Amman for Archaeology and History), who, in addition to serving as tomb excavator, was responsible for drawing the finds. Rupert Chapman (Palestine Exploration Fund) and Alison Betts (Institute of Archaeology, London) served as tomb excavators, and the expedition staff was completed by Ibrahim Haj Hassan, representative of the Department of Antiquities of Jordan, who assisted with the excavation of the tombs and whose presence ensured the smooth running of the season.

The writer would like to express his thanks to the Trustees of the British Museum, without the generous support of whom the Tiwal esh-Sharqi project could not have taken place. A debt of gratitude is owed to the British Institute at Amman for Archaeology and History, and in particular to its director, Andrew Garrard, for his hospitality, kindness and invaluable help. Warm thanks are also due to the Department of Antiquities of Jordan, most especially to its then Director General, Dr Adnan Hadidi, for his enthusiastic support for the project, and also for his generosity in allowing many of the tomb groups to be granted to the British Museum (see Appendix C). Special thanks are also due to Jacqui Watson (Ancient Monuments Laboratory, London) and Michael Hughes (Research Laboratory, British Museum) for their examinations and analyses of the metal objects, to David Reese (Field Museum of Natural History, Chicago) for his identifications of the shells, and to John Evans (North East London Polytechnic) for his analytical work on the four-spouted lamps. The writer would particularly like to thank Ann Searight for her tireless efforts in redrawing the site plan and preparing all the graphic material for publication.

The 1984 season of excavations at Tiwal esh-Sharqi

Tiwal esh-Sharqi is situated about 7 km south-west of Deir ʿAlla at grid reference 205172, and extends for at least 1.5 km along the north-west bank of the river Zarqa. The full extent of the cemetery has not yet been established. To the east of the modern road which cuts the site in a roughly north-south division (see Fig. 1), the northern extent is defined by the limit of the occupation site of Tell Umm Hammad esh-Sharqiya, and the southern by the cultivated fields beyond Hills 100, 102 and 111. West of the road, it seems likely that beyond the area of cultivation the cemetery curves around the occupation site of Tell Umm Hammad el-Gharbiya to the west, and extends to the south for some considerable distance. The following statement on the geomorphology of the site has been provided by Peter Dorrell:

> The bedrock underlying the site is the Lisan Marls, a series of bedded evaporites, now much cracked and faulted through contraction, slumping and earth tremors. The surface of the marl appears to have been linearly eroded in great antiquity and then covered and the erosion channels infilled by a thick deposit of silts and gravels, perhaps marking an early and more northerly course of the Zarqa. This alluvium, and the underlying marl, are now being aggressively eroded by wadis running in a south-westerly pattern to the modern Zarqa. In the older and wider re-excavated wadis, tombs appear to be aligned with their shafts on the down-slopes of the wadi side and their chambers cut into the inter-wadi ridges (with the exception of the two built graves, chambers were always cut into the marl and not just into the alluvium) while tombs exposed in the steeper and newer wadis seem to be sited randomly. This suggests that in EBIV times the morphology of the site followed the same general pattern as at present, although not so deeply cut.
>
> Ground-water which percolates through the strata emerges at seepage lines and small springs above clay-bands within the marl, but its salinity is such that drinking water for man and stock must always have been taken from the river itself. This salinity, however, is not so great as to inhibit the growth of vegetation upon the marl surface.
>
> There is an aggradation terrace some 5 metres above the present river level, now being laterally eroded by the stream. This terrace cannot be dated at the site, but if it was formed in the same way as similar terraces elsewhere in the Levant, it probably post-dates the EBIV occupation.

An initial surface survey indicated that the extent of the cemetery was extremely large, and to a degree indeterminate on the west, where much of the area lies under cultivation.

For logistic purposes, the area was divided into four sectors, North-East (NE), North-West (NW), South-East (SE) and South-West (SW), the modern agricultural road providing a convenient east-west division. On the western side, the division between north and south was established along the wide and artificially levelled wadi running south of Hills 103, 104 and 105 (see Fig. 1). The sector to the south of this (SW) had been heavily disrupted by road building and agricultural levelling operations, to such an extent that there seemed little likelihood of finding tombs there, even partially preserved. The north-

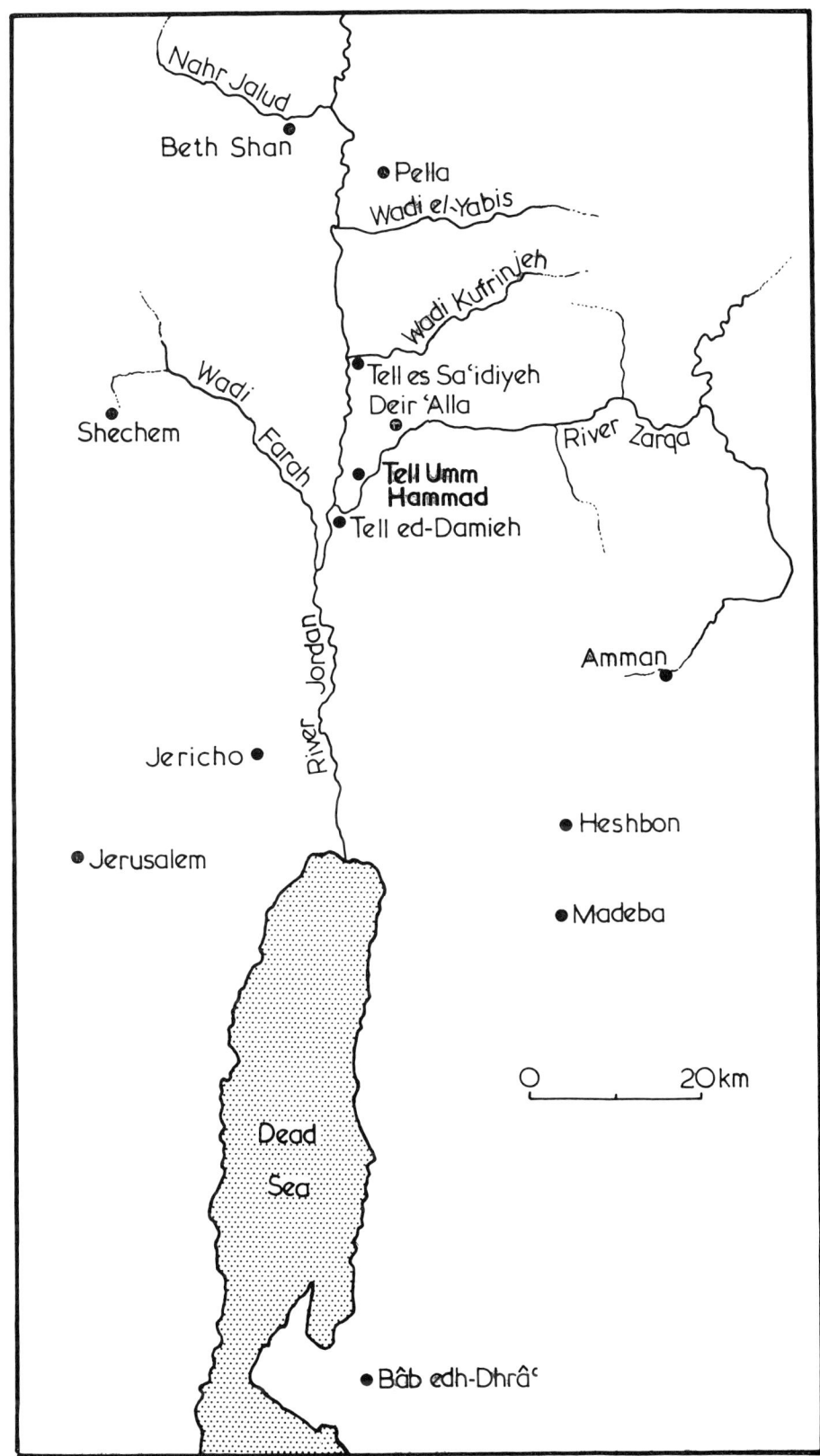

Fig. 2

west sector, including the occupation site of Tell Umm Hammad el-Gharbiya, had again, for the most part, been levelled for agricultural usage and was, at the time of the excavation, under intensive cultivation. Only the southern part of the sector, represented by Hills 103–108, had remained completely undisturbed, and three tombs were in fact located in this region, tombs NW1 and NW2 on the western slope of Hill 103, and tomb NW3 on the shallow south slope of Hill 104. All three tombs had, however, been robbed and extensively damaged in recent times. They were therefore noted but not systematically excavated, and they have not been included in the following report.

Operations in 1984 were therefore concentrated solely on the area between the Zarqa river and the modern road. Two excavation areas were here defined. The North-East area (NE) extended from Tell Umm Hammad esh-Sharqiya in the north to the wadi running approximately east-west along the southern slopes of Hills 6 and 7, and the northern slope of Hill 10 as far as the road. The area to the south, as far as the cultivated fields, was defined as South-East (SE). Tombs in each sector were numbered sequentially from 1.

Altogether, thirty-seven tombs were investigated (excluding, that is, NW1–3, see above; NE1, a non-funerary feature; and treating NE16 and NE17 as a single unit, see below), twenty-three of which produced datable finds. Some tombs produced skeletal remains only, and others, for reasons of safety, were left unexcavated beyond the definition of their shafts and entrances, or had to be abandoned during the course of excavation (NE9, NE14, NE18, SE11, SE12 and SE13). Note also that the number NE19 was not allocated.

Two of the tombs, NE8 and SE14, should more correctly be described as 'graves', and their significance within the context of the Tiwal esh-Sharqi cemetery is discussed in Chapter 3. Otherwise, the tombs were of the shaft tomb variety, a vertical shaft giving access to a chamber by way of a small entrance-way. This nomenclature, however, can only be applied in the broadest sense, for many of the tombs were found to have been cut into existing hill slopes, and in such cases the vertical element of the shaft was reduced to that of a 'semi-shaft', deep on the rear (chamber entrance side) but shallow on the down-slope (see especially tomb NE14 for a classic example of this type of tomb approach). It is assumed, nevertheless, that the approach to such tombs was still essentially vertical, in the manner of those tombs cut from level surfaces. In other cases, however, particularly with regard to the smaller tombs, it would seem likely that the direction of approach was horizontal rather than vertical, the removal of a triangular 'wedge' from the hill slope having produced in effect a 'horizontally cut threshold'. Obviously, on hill slopes where substantial erosion has occurred the distinction between these two ostensibly similar, but conceptually rather different approach methods cannot be detected. Indeed, as was discovered during the excavation, erosion had in many instances been so severe that not only had all traces of the external approach to the chamber been completely lost, but the chamber itself had been largely destroyed, leaving little more than a shallow curving ledge or 'scoop'.

Some of the tomb chambers were so very small that it would seem unlikely that they had been provided with either a semi-shaft or a horizontally cut threshold. Instead, it is suggested that these tiny tombs were entered directly from the hill slope, and were sealed with a stone placed on the surface.

With the possible exception of this last-mentioned category, the tomb-builders were seeking the level of hard, white marl into which they could cut their chambers with some assurance that the roofs would remain secure. For tombs which were located on the side-slopes of existing wadis, this was a relatively straightforward process: the marl level could (and indeed still can) be seen outcropping. Advantage was therefore taken of the morphology by cutting the semi-shaft or threshold on the down-slope, and then excavating the chamber beneath the inter-wadi ridge. When tombs were cut from a level surface, it seems that a broad sounding was first made in order to locate the level of hard marl, and only when this had been established was the shaft proper sunk vertically from that level (see especially Chapter 2, tomb NE9). The eventual collapse of the chambers of such tombs might well itself have contributed to the formation of some of the more recent gullies (see Chapter 2, tombs SE1–3).

Generally speaking, the tombs at Tiwal esh-Sharqi had been skilfully cut. The chamber walls, although in some cases somewhat irregular, were well smoothed and the floors were consistently even and level. Tool-marks were observed to some degree in the shafts and chambers of most of the tombs. Where they were best preserved, as in the shaft of tomb SE3,

Introduction

they showed as straight furrows up to 30 cm in length and 2–3 cm wide, semicircular in section and running almost vertically. Since no pick-like tool could have been driven into the marl for these distances, the tools used were presumably spikes or rods, hammered down into the rock and then used as levers to prise away blocks or fragments of marl. Within the chambers, the marks ran obliquely, and some at least were slightly curved and shorter, suggesting the use of picks.

The individual characteristics and features of the tombs are fully described in Chapter 2. No attempt has been made to construct a typology of tomb architecture, for clearly, within the context of the cemetery as a whole, the thirty-seven tombs examined during the 1984 season represent an almost insignificant proportion of the potential total, and such a typology would therefore be of very little value.

CHAPTER 2

THE TOMBS AND THEIR CONTENTS

In this chapter, the tombs excavated in the north-east sector (prefixed NE) are described first, followed by those in the south-east sector (SE). Locations are given with reference to the overall site plan, Fig. 1, which is to be found in a pocket at the end of the volume. 'Orientation' refers to the tomb itself, and not to the individual(s) found within it. In the case of the shaft tombs, the position of the chamber is indicated first: thus, a tomb which is described as 'west-east' has its chamber on the west and its shaft on the east.

Tomb contents are numbered according to their plotted positions recorded on the accompanying plans. Pottery descriptions are given in accordance with the conventions laid out in the 'Gezer Field Manual': W.G. Dever and H.D. Lance (eds), *A Manual of Field Excavation: Handbook for Field Archaeologists* (New York, 1978).

Tombs in the north-east sector

TOMB NE1
Surface Hill 2

This was the first feature encountered on the level surface of Hill 2 following the removal of the upper 20 cm of topsoil by a mechanical excavator (see below, tomb NE8). It appeared as a roughly circular feature, approximately 1.0 m in diameter, showing as dull reddish-brown against the pale brown weathered top-marl. The fill consisted of loose, finely divided soil with few inclusions. At a depth of about 40 cm, the cylindrical 'shaft' terminated in a roughly flat base.

Whatever this feature might have been, it was clearly not a tomb shaft as originally supposed. No artifacts, nor bones were encountered in the fill, and no suggestion as to its function can be offered. Since numbers had already been assigned to several other tombs, NE1 was retained for this non-funerary feature.

TOMB NE2   Pl. IIA
East slope Hill 6
Orientation: S–N

As in the case of the other tombs on the east slope of Hill 6 (tombs NE4, NE5, NE6, NE7 and NE24), the chamber of tomb NE2 was dug into an existing slope, and would not have been approached by means of a true shaft. Instead, it would have had a horizontally cut threshold leading to a vertically cut entrance, an entrance set directly on the hill slope, or a vertically cut semi-shaft (see Chapter 1). For tomb NE2, however, this information had been almost com-

Tombs in the north-east sector

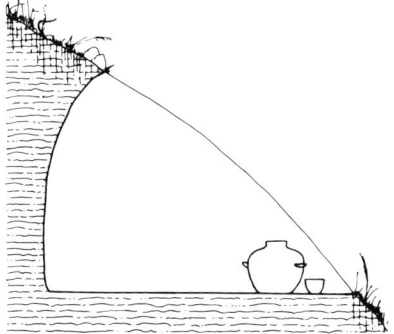

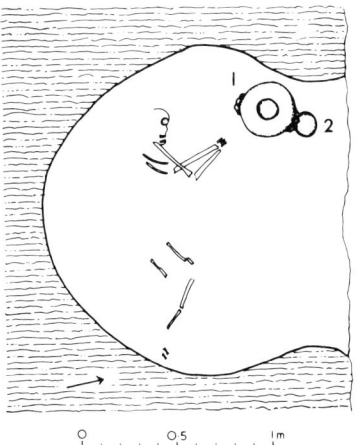

Fig. 3 Tomb NE2

pletely lost through erosion, and although approximately 80 per cent of the floor of the chamber was preserved, only the slightest trace of the approach was found, suggesting perhaps that it might have been a circular, horizontally cut threshold similar to that of tomb NE4. The dimensions of the roughly circular chamber base could be estimated with reasonable accuracy as 1.70 × 1.60 m. The upper part of the chamber had been lost through erosion, but the curvature of the most fully preserved rear wall suggested that the original height of the chamber would have been about 1.20 m.

When excavated, the preserved lower part of the chamber was found to be filled with crushed and broken marl blocks, derived from the roof of the tomb, mixed with washed soil from the upper slope. Below this was found a thin, irregular layer of finely divided brown soil, representing the silting of the chamber prior to the collapse of the roof. This in turn covered the tomb deposit, which consisted of the fragmentary remains of a single individual, lying in a flexed position on the left side, head to the west, facing north. The arms were extended in front of the face, and close to where the hands would have been were found two pottery vessels, a ledge-handled storejar (NE2.1) and a small cup (NE2.2), both standing upright. The poorly preserved skeletal

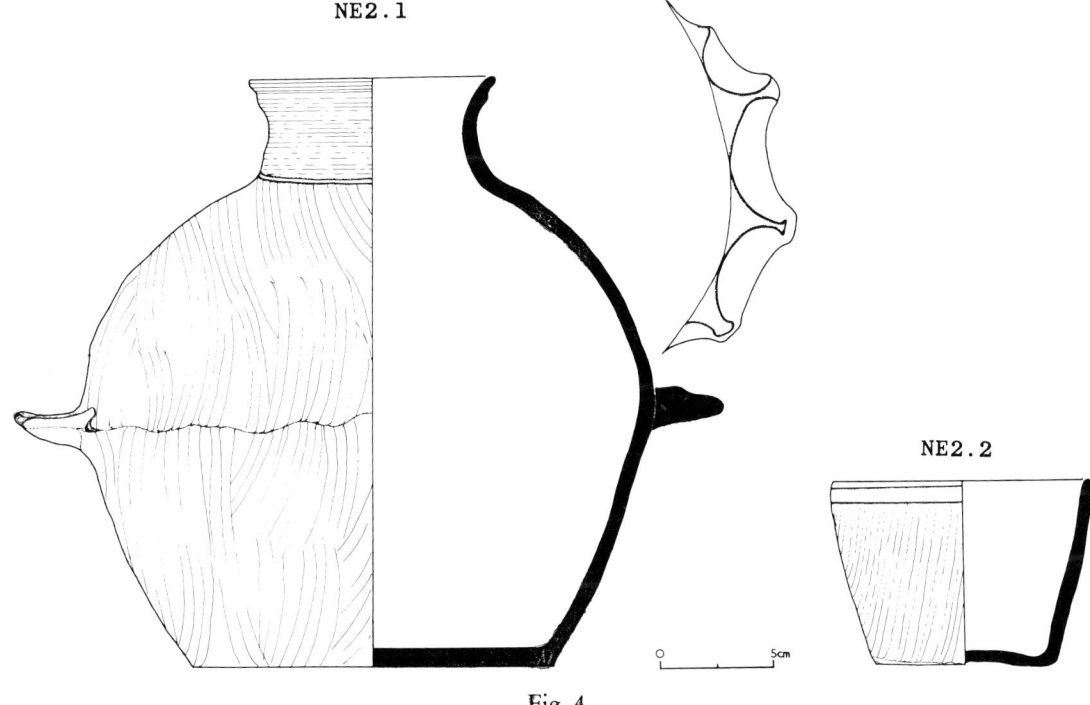

Fig. 4

remains were of a juvenile (sex indeterminable), aged 12–15 years.

Contents

NE2.1   Ledge-handled storejar

Technique: Handmade with wheelmade rim. *Paste*: 7.5YR 'pinkish grey' 7/2; many very small sand, few medium sand and ceramic; no core; hard. *Surface* (Interior): as paste. (Exterior): 2.5Y 'white' 8/2 wash; irregular vertical combing; low cordon at base of neck.

NE2.2   Cup

Technique: Handmade. *Paste*: 7.5YR 'pink' 7/4; many small-medium sand, some large wadi gravel and ceramic; no core; hard. *Surface* (Interior): as paste. (Exterior): as paste; light horizontal combing on rim for depth of 10 mm, vertical combing below to base.

TOMB NE3
East slope Hill 2
Orientation: W–E

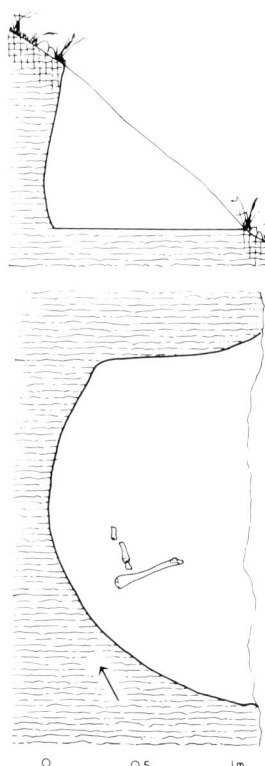

Fig. 5 Tomb NE3

This extensively eroded tomb consisted of part of the floor and rear wall only. No traces remained of the approach, which would have been on the slope side giving horizontal access to the chamber. Originally, the chamber would probably have been almost circular, and approximately 1.80 m in diameter. The height would have been in excess of 85 cm. The excavated fill, consisting of decayed and washed marl, covered the partial and fragmentary remains of a single adult, possibly female. No finds were recovered.

TOMB NE4
East slope Hill 6
Orientation: S–N

This relatively well-preserved tomb, situated immediately to the north of tomb NE2, had a roughly circular horizontal threshold giving access to the chamber by means of a sub-rectangular entranceway, approximately 85 cm high by 75 cm wide. The blocking of the entrance was found intact, and consisted of large wadi stones. Beyond the entrance, the floor of the chamber was found to be some 25 cm below the level of the threshold. The chamber was oval in plan, measuring 1.68 × 2.32 m at its base, and was, on average, 1 m high.

Tomb NE4 was one of the few tombs excavated in which the roof had not collapsed. The floor of the tomb was covered with a thin (10 cm) layer of silt, with only a small number of marl fragments from the roof. Although the roof was intact, however, the deposit was extremely poorly preserved, and showed signs of having been extensively flooded by intrusive rainwater. The fragmentary remains of a single adult female were found, as far as could be judged lying in a flexed position on her left side, head to the west, facing north. A single stone bead (NE4.1) was found in a position suggesting that it had been placed or worn close to the waist.

Contents

NE4.1   Bead

White stone; bored from both ends with conical drill.

TOMB NE5
East slope Hill 6
Orientation: S–N

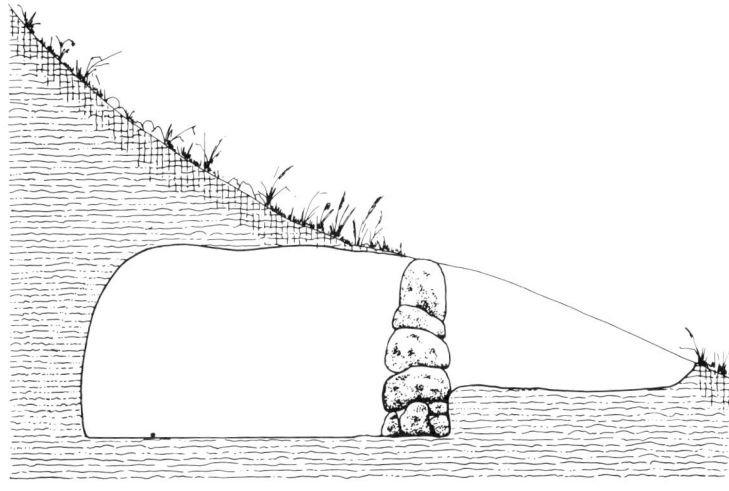

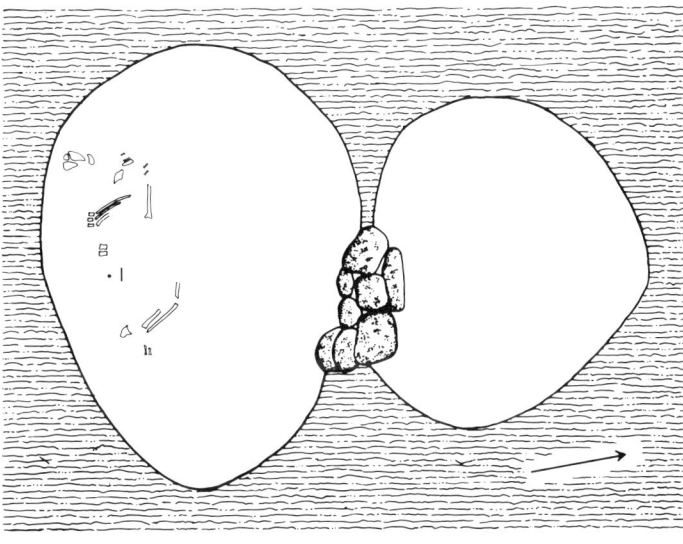

Fig. 6 Tomb NE4

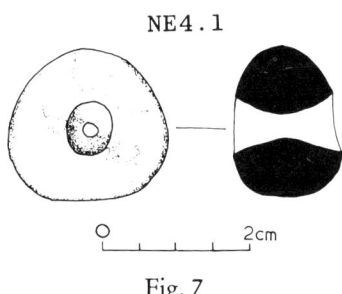

Fig. 7

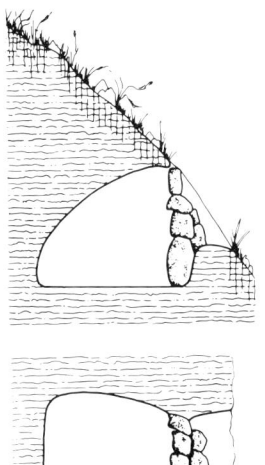

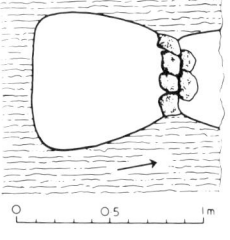

Fig. 8 Tomb NE5

Access to this small tomb was again probably by means of a horizontal threshold cut into the slope of the hill. Although for the most part eroded away, this threshold would appear to have been rectangular. The entrance to the chamber was sealed with wadi stones, and removal of this blocking showed that it was nearly square, being very slightly arched at the top and measuring 40 cm wide by 45 cm high. Beyond the entrance, the floor of the chamber was found to be 20 cm lower than the threshold, the lowermost course of the blocking being supported by the vertical face of the step. The chamber itself was sub-rectangular in plan and very small, measuring only 65 × 60 cm. The roof of the tomb was intact, and was, at its maximum (at the front), 60 cm above the floor.

Despite the preservation of the roof, the interior of the tomb was filled to within 15 cm of the top with water-laid silt. The bottom 10 cm of this was quite hard and compacted, and contained a few bone fragments which were all that survived of the original deposit. Clearly the tomb had been subjected to severe disturbance by water flooding in. From the few bones recovered, it would seem that the burial was that of a single juvenile, aged 2–3 years. No finds were recovered.

TOMB NE6
East slope Hill 6
Orientation: S–N

This largely eroded tomb was represented by a part of its chamber floor and rear wall only. No traces of the entrance remained, but the chamber would probably have been approached by means of a horizontally cut threshold, as in the case of NE5 which lies immediately adjacent to it. In fact, the plan of the preserved part of the chamber is very similar to that of NE5, suggesting a close relationship between the two tombs.

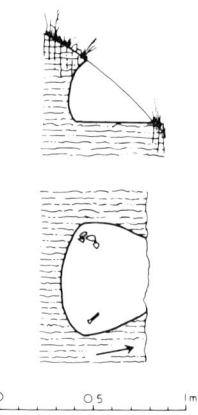

Fig. 9 Tomb NE6

The partial chamber was filled with crushed and weathered marl, mixed with soil washed from the slope. On the floor were found a few bone fragments, indicating that the burial was that of a single juvenile, aged 6 months to 1 year. No finds were recovered.

TOMB NE7
East slope Hill 6
Orientation: S–N

The presence of tomb NE7 was indicated by its large blocking stones, which had eroded out on the slope of the hill. Excavation revealed that the tomb was of similar design to tombs NE4 and NE5, with a horizontally cut threshold leading to the chamber.

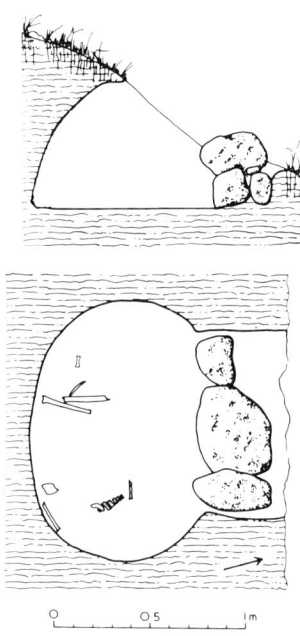

Fig. 10 Tomb NE7

Only a small part of this threshold had survived, but enough to suggest that it was probably square or rectangular, 94 cm wide. Most of the roof of the chamber and the top of the entrance-way into it had been eroded away. Only two courses of the blocking stones were found, and these consisted of large river boulders wedged tightly together. Removal of the blocking showed that the entrance-way into the chamber was 94 cm wide, occupying that is the full width of the threshold. Although its top was not preserved, by analogy with NE4 and NE5, where the blocking extended to the roof of the chamber, the height of the entrance-way would have been about 55 cm. The interior of the chamber was found to be 20 cm lower than the threshold, and the blocking stones were seen to be supported on the inner face of this step. The chamber was roughly oval, measuring 1.34 × 0.85 m.

The interior of the tomb was filled with marl blocks and decayed marl debris from the collapse of the roof. Little silting had occurred prior to this collapse, and the funerary deposit lay directly below the fallen marl on the floor of the tomb. The bones were only partially preserved and fragmentary, having been severely crushed and disrupted by the collapse of the roof and subsequent weathering. The remains of two individuals were identified, both adults, one female and the other possibly female. There was no evidence to suggest that these two individuals were not interred at the same time. No finds were recovered.

TOMB NE8
Surface Hill 2
Orientation: S–N

Pl. IIIA-B

'Tomb' NE8 was the first of the stone-built graves to be discovered during the 1984 season. The relatively level surface of Hill 2 had been identified by Helms in 1983 as one from which tombs had been dug (1983: fig. 4, tombs 1, 3 and 4). In 1984, therefore, a mechanical excavator was brought in to remove the top 20 cm of topsoil and eroded marl in order to reveal the presence of tomb shafts which, it was hoped, would show up as dark soil features against the paler weathered marl. It was in fact as a result of this process that the shafts of tombs NE9, NE20 and NE25 were located. During the course of the operation, the blade of the mechanical excavator struck a very large flat stone which, on examination, proved to be one of three such slabs lying in a row *in situ*, covering what appeared to be a small oval stone-built grave.

In order to undertake the excavation of this grave, the two southernmost capstones were removed, leaving the third, northern one in place for purposes of photography. All three slabs were of roughly dressed limestone, and were approximately 10–15 cm

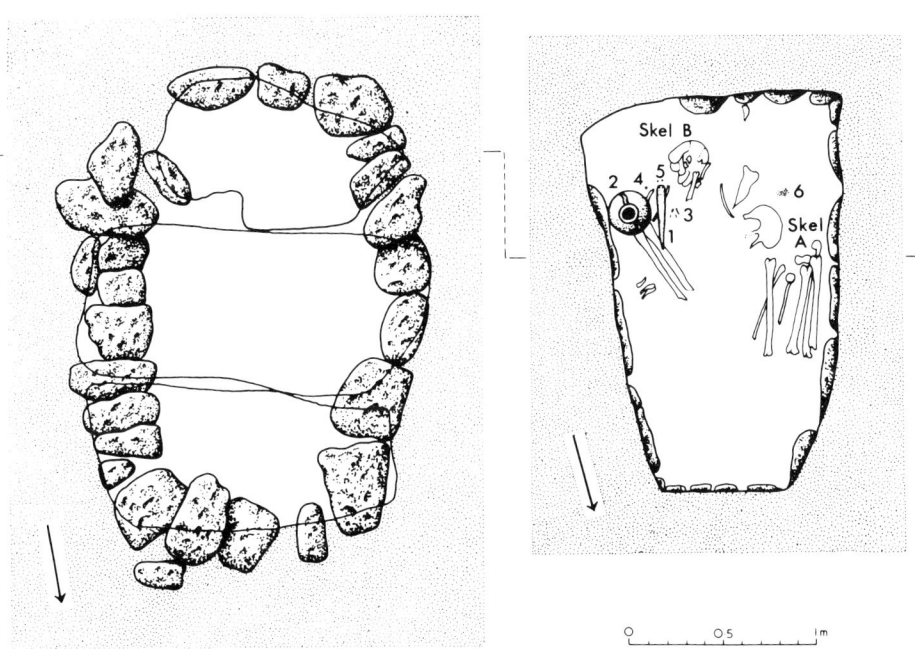

Fig. 11 Tomb NE8

thick. The two southern slabs had been shaped to be more or less rectangular, and measured 1.55 × 0.74 m (southernmost) and 1.80 × 0.78 m (central): the northern capstone, either by design or accident, was less regular and smaller, measuring only 1.30 × 0.76 m.

Removal of the two southern slabs revealed the plan of the top course of boulders lining the grave itself. This was at first seen to be roughly oval, but as excavation proceeded, it became clear that this uppermost course had suffered slight displacement, and that the original plan of the grave, as preserved by its lower portion, was sub-rectangular with a slight widening at the southern end. The grave consisted of three to four courses of river boulders, neatly set into the sides of a well-cut and well-prepared sub-rectangular pit. The matrix into which the grave had been set was not the hard banded marl into which the shaft-tomb chambers had been excavated, but the decomposed and crumbly surface of the marl, which is loose and quite soft. In preparing the grave, therefore, the stones had been pressed into the sides of the pit by as much as 50 per cent. The spaces in between the projecting faces had then been packed with earth to provide a smooth interior surface. It is clear that it had not been the intention of the grave-builders to produce a solid walled structure, but rather to line a rectangular pit with stones. Even quite large gaps left between stones were therefore of little consequence, and the stones, although quite regularly placed, were not truly coursed as in structural dry-stone building.

The stones themselves had not been dressed in any way and varied in size from between 10 cm to 30 cm. The floor of the grave was quite plain, consisting of a well-levelled and beaten surface.

The interior fill of the grave consisted of two distinct layers. The upper, which extended from beneath the capstones to a depth of about 30 cm, was composed of loose, soft brown soil with few inclusions. Below this was a much denser, compact layer of orange silt, which increased in hardness as it approached the floor of the grave. The lower part of this layer was laminated, showing clear evidence of puddling and sedimentation.

The south-east corner of the grave showed evidence of a slight disturbance in that a few of the stones from the lower part of the south wall had been dislodged and had tumbled into the grave. Apart from this disturbance, which was almost certainly caused by animal activity, NE8 was found intact and there was nothing to suggest that it had been robbed, either anciently or in recent times.

Excavation of the grave deposit revealed the remains of two individuals. The skeletal remains were poorly and only partially preserved, the poor condition resulting from the proximity of the grave to the surface, and the incompleteness possibly due to the intrusive animal activity noted above or, in the case of skeleton B, to the nature of the burial practice, which was apparently secondary (see Appendix A below). The two individuals had, nevertheless, been buried at the same time. Skeleton A was found against the west wall in what was judged to have been a tightly flexed position. Examination suggested that it was that of an adult male, whose stature could be estimated as 1.70 ± 0.879 m. A group of twenty-six small beads of various materials was found close to the fragmentary skull (NE8.6), and it is interesting to observe that several of these had not been properly finished, in that their holes had only been partially drilled.

The second skeleton (skeleton B) was found on the south-east side of the grave, and was that of a male aged between 25 and 35 years. Again the bones had been badly disturbed, but their general disposition suggested that the individual had been buried in a flexed position on his right side. A copper dagger (NE8.1) was found close to the right femur, and this had four rivets in position on the hilt. A further two rivets (NE8.5) were found, side by side, approximately 15 cm in line from the dagger hilt, and, as stated in Chapter 3 (p. 95), this observation provides a suggestion as to how the handles were fixed to such weapons (see also daggers from tombs NE25 and SE1). A single, small stone bead (NE8.4) was found close to the skull, and close to this were four isolated copper rivets (NE8.3), presumably included as a grave offering in their own right. Also associated with skeleton B was a loop-handled amphoriskos (NE8.2), found standing upright in the south-east corner of the grave.

Contents

NE8.1   Dagger

Arsenical copper. Four rivets in position on hilt.

NE8.2   Loop-handled amphoriskos

Technique: Handmade with wheelmade rim. *Paste*: 2.5YR 'light reddish brown' 6/4; many small-

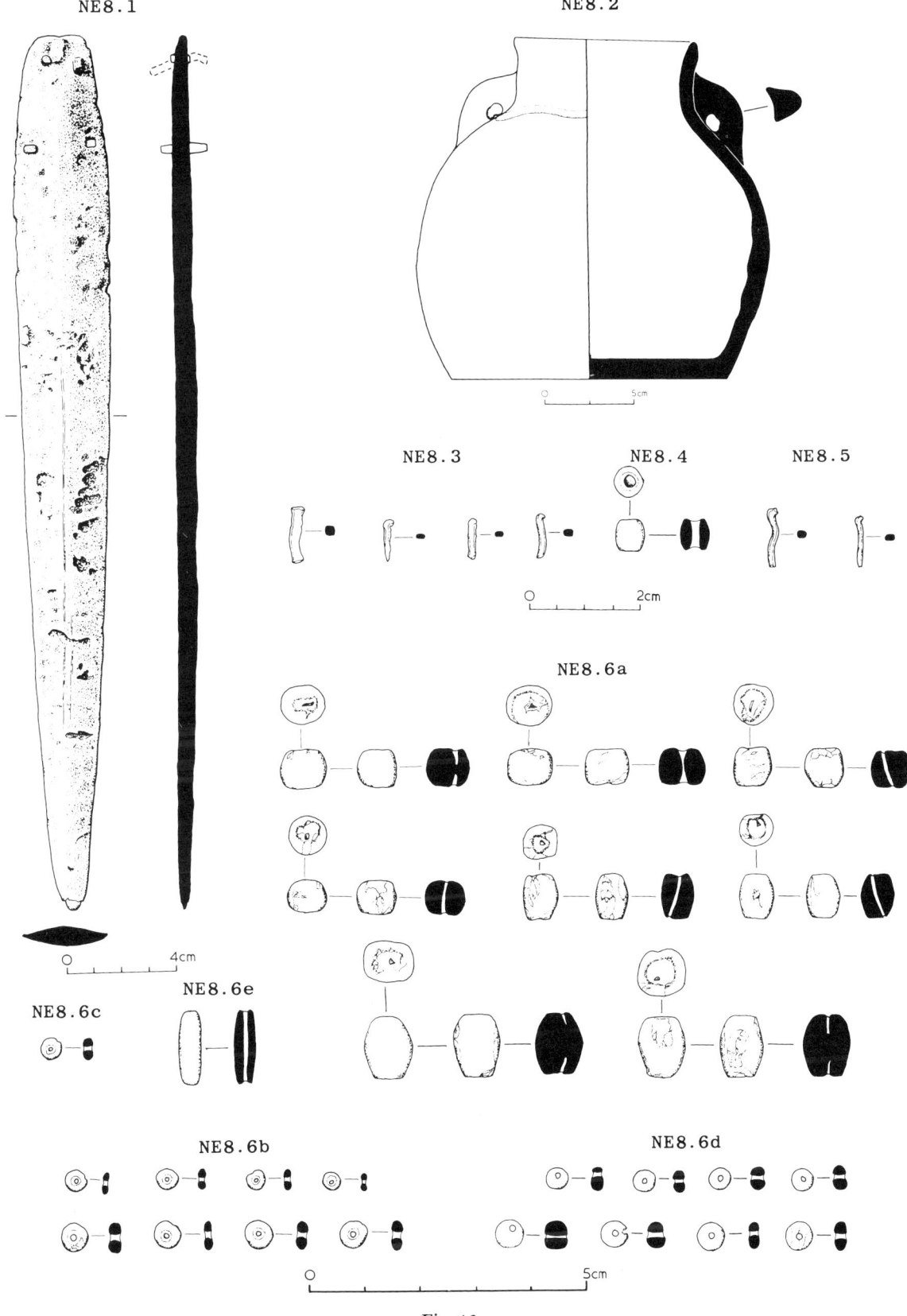

Fig. 12

medium sand and ceramic, some large sand and lime; no core; hard. *Surface* (Interior): as paste. (Exterior): 7.5YR 'pinkish white' 8/2 wash.

NE8.3   Four rivets

Copper/copper alloy.

NE8.4   Bead

Hard orange translucent stone; bored from both ends with cylindrical drill.

NE8.5   Two rivets

Copper/copper alloy.

NE8.6   26 beads   (Pl. XIB)

a. 8 very crude quartz; unfinished – holes not completely drilled.
b. 8 carnelian.
c. Green stone.
d. 8 bone (tooth).
e. Composition.

TOMB NE9   Pl. IVA
Surface Hill 2
Orientation: S–N

The shaft of tomb NE9 was revealed during the topsoil clearance operation of Hill 2 described above (see tomb NE8). On the surface it appeared as a greyish-brown oval or, more correctly, 'tadpole'-shaped feature against the pale brownish-cream decayed top-marl. Orientated east-west, it measured approximately 5 m by 1.50 m, widening to 2.50 m at the west end. Excavation revealed that the whole area of this feature had been dug down to a depth of just over 1.0 m, terminating in a roughly level surface and corresponding with the top of the hard, undecayed marl. It was from this surface, at the west end, that the shaft proper had been cut. Clearly, the tomb-builders had been fully aware of the potential hazards involved in digging a shaft through the topsoil and unstable decayed marl, and, in order to minimise the risk of collapse of the upper shaft, had cleared a sizeable approach platform. Having decided upon the location of the tomb shaft proper, it seems that they widened the western end of this platform, allowing space for a surrounding 'safety ledge'. This undertaking surely accounts for the unusual 'tadpole' shape of the uppermost shaft.

The shaft proper first appeared as a roughly oval cutting, approximately 1.90 by 1.50 m and orientated north-south. The excavated fill consisted of compact grey soil with many small white marl chips. At a depth of 1.80 m below the surface, the north and west sides of the shaft had been stepped in to produce a shallow ledge, 10 cm wide, presumably to serve as a foothold. At 2.57 m below surface, a further reduction of the shaft had been made, leaving a step, again on the north and west sides where it extended to widths of 60 cm and 20 cm respectively. The lowest section of the shaft, therefore, was roughly square, and measured 1.25 by 1.20 m. The bottom of the shaft was reached at a depth of 2.95 m below the surface.

The entrance to the chamber was found on the south-west side, and was covered, although not completely sealed, by a single large stone, measuring approximately 60 × 60 × 28 cm. The removal of this stone revealed a small, neatly cut, arched entrance-way, 44 cm wide at its base and 55 cm high. The entrance-way gave access to a funnel-shaped passage,

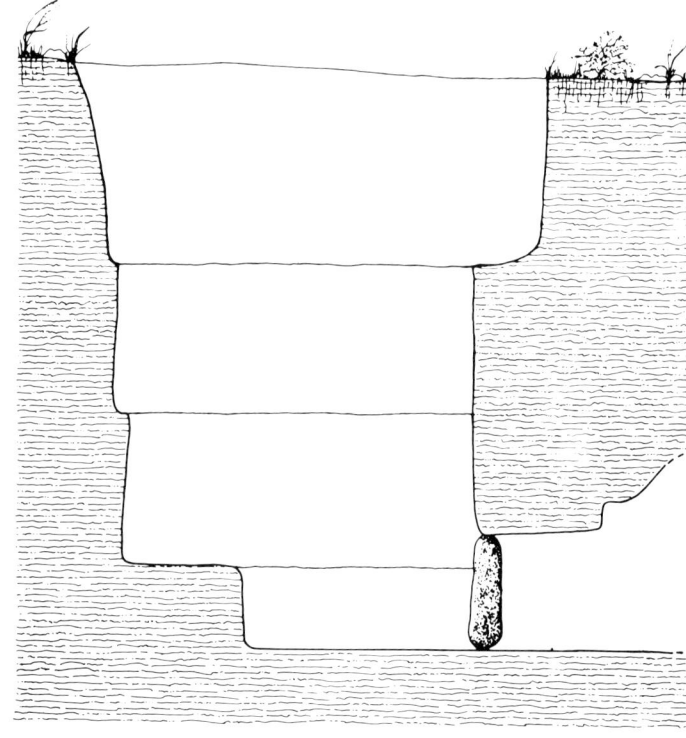

Fig. 13a Tomb NE9 Section A–B

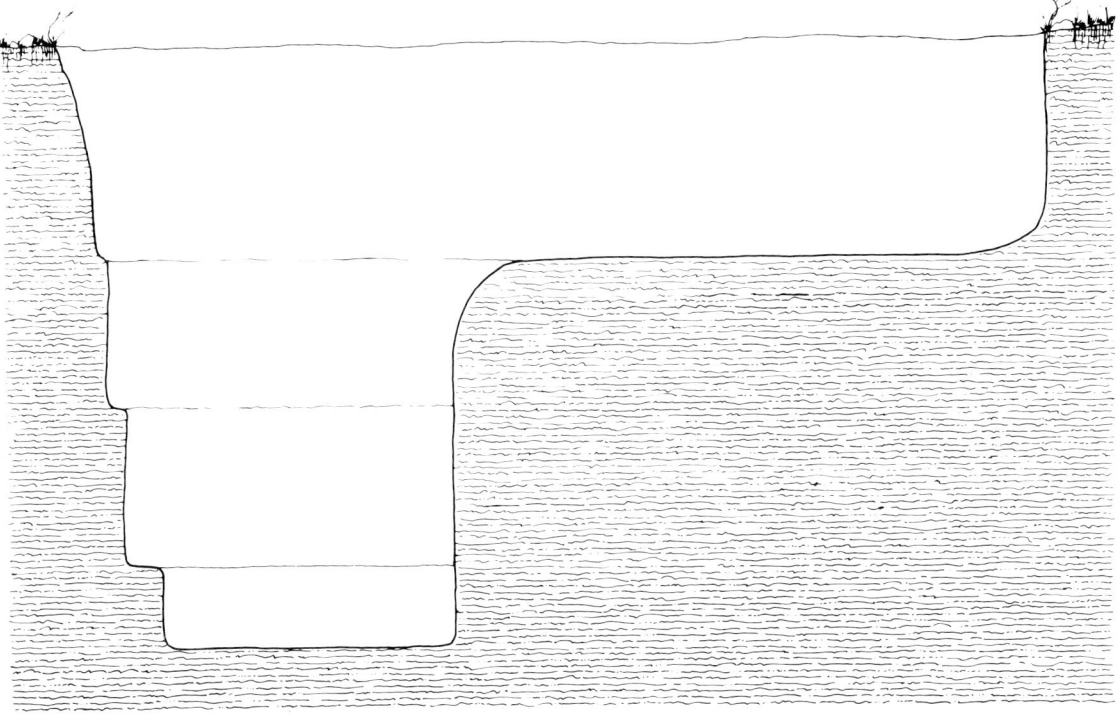

Fig. 13b Tomb NE9 Section C–D

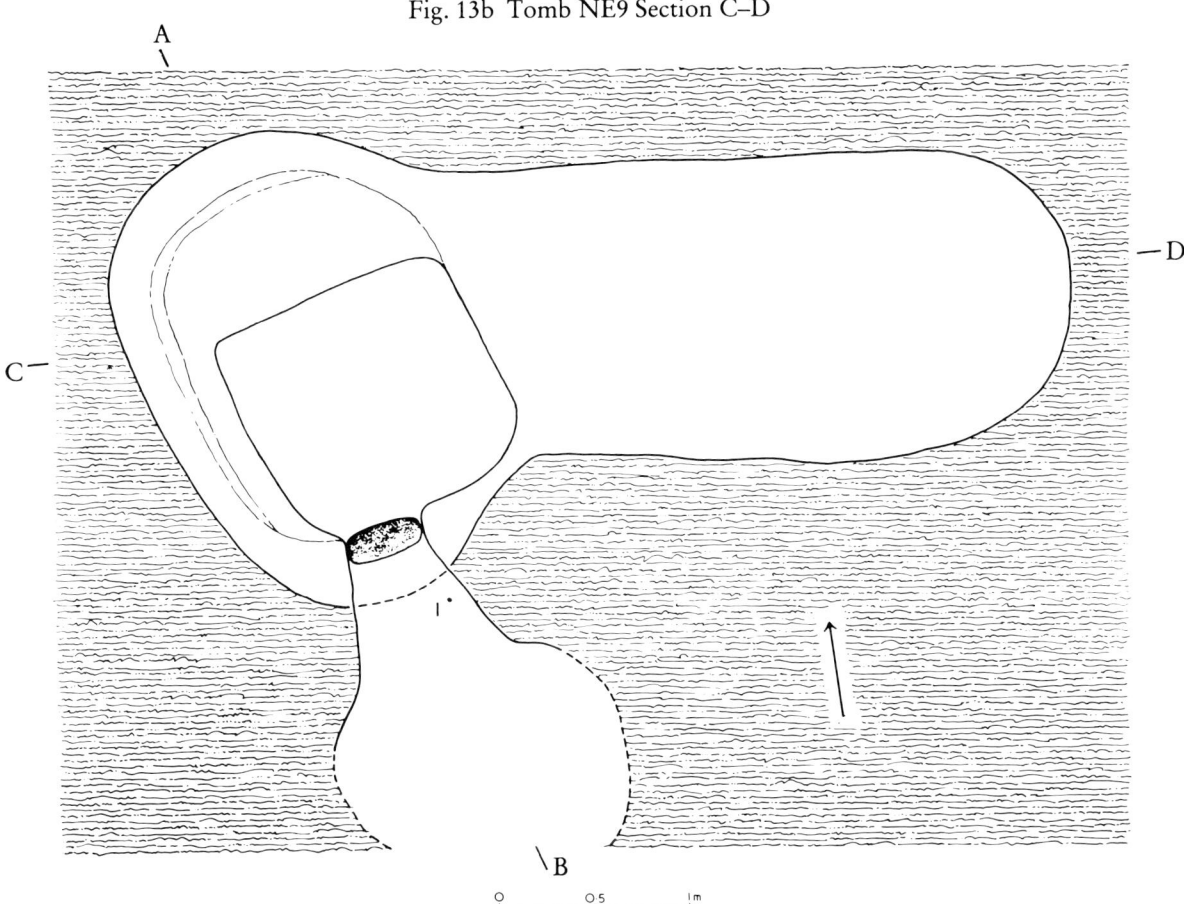

Fig. 13c Tomb NE9

85 cm long and widening towards the chamber. The whole of this passage was filled with a dense deposit of reddish-brown silt. The end of the passage was defined by a marked change in the angle of curvature of its side walls and roof, indicating the beginning of the chamber itself. The interior fill at this point could be seen to consist of the same compact silt, but mixed with sizeable blocks of marl, showing clearly that the roof of the chamber had collapsed. As removal of the fill proceeded, the floor of the chamber was established, and was found to be on the same level as the base of the shaft. The curvature of the side walls, and that of the roof, suggested that the chamber was quite small – circular with a diameter of about 1.50 m and with a domed roof. Unfortunately, before these details could be verified, a major collapse occurred within the chamber, rendering further excavation impossible on the grounds of safety.

Very little of the funerary deposit was encountered within the 20 cm of the chamber excavated before the collapse. A few bone fragments were retrieved which were sufficient only to establish that the individual was adult. A single stone bead (NE9.1) was found on the floor, close to the east wall of the chamber.

A large sherd from a cup (NE9.2) was found on the west side of the shaft, lying on the 1.80 m ledge. Although of course it cannot be positively demonstrated that this piece has any connection whatever with the funerary deposit of NE9, its position, apparently deliberately placed on the step, suggests that it might have been associated in some way with the tomb-builders. One might speculate that it came from a drinking cup, accidentally broken during the digging of the tomb, or from a vessel intended for inclusion in the chamber, but which again had been somehow broken before deposition. In any event, it should almost certainly be seen as contemporary with the primary chamber deposit.

Contents

NE9.1   Bead

Stone: cream with pinkish tinge. Bored from both ends with cylindrical drill.

NE9.2   Cup

Technique: Handmade with wheelmade rim. *Paste*: 5YR 'light reddish brown' 6/4; many small sand,

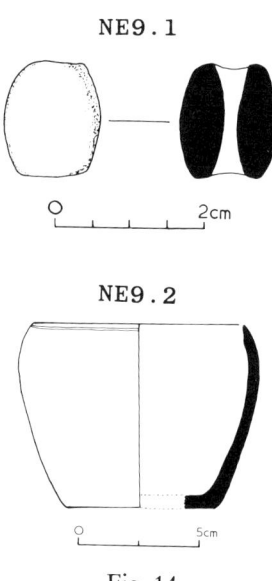

Fig. 14

ceramic and lime; no core; hard. *Surface* (Interior): 10YR 'white' 8/2 wash. (Exterior): as interior; band of fine combing around rim; vertically smoothed below rim to base.

TOMB NE10   Pls IVB and VA
West slope Hill 4
Orientation: E–W

The west slope of Hill 4 almost certainly existed as such at the time of tomb cutting, and, like the tombs on the east slope of Hill 6, those found here (tombs NE10–14, 18) would probably have been approached either by means of a semi-shaft, shallow on the down-slope, or by a horizontally cut threshold. This is particularly clear with regard to tomb NE10. A surface clearance operation of the hill slope revealed a series of interruptions in the marl strata, one of which proved to be the shaft of tomb NE10. Excavation resulted in the clearance of a rectangular semi-shaft, fully preserved on all four sides and measuring 1.05 by 2.15 m. The rear (east) face of the shaft was preserved to a height of some 1.70 m. More importantly, the front (west) face was completely preserved, the top edge showing a deliberate rounding, quite different from the type of truncation that occurs with erosion. This front face was only 10 cm high, providing little more than a shallow step down from the hill slope to the level of the chamber entrance.

On the south side of the shaft, at a distance of about 1.20 m from the step, the entrance to a small, subsidiary chamber was found. This is described below as tomb NE10A.

The entrance to the principal chamber, on the steep east side of the shaft, was roughly rectangular and arched at the top, and measured 86 cm in height and 52 cm in width. As found, its blocking was intact and consisted of a single large stone, approximately square (47 × 44 cm) and 7.5 cm in thickness. Above and around the stone, the entrance had been sealed using a dense clay packing. Removal of the blocking revealed that the roof of the chamber had unfortunately collapsed, the whole interior space being filled with massive blocks of marl. Preliminary examination of a small area just within the entrance-way suggested, however, that a considerable degree of silting had occurred prior to the roof collapse. The possibility existed, therefore, of finding a reasonably well-preserved funerary deposit, protected within or below the silt layer. Excavations were consequently continued, with utmost caution, in order to remove the collapsed marl fill.

The sides and rear wall of the chamber were found to be well preserved, the ground plan showing a long, narrow, sub-rectangular form, 5.10 m in length, with a maximum width of 1.85 m. The entrance-way height continued for a distance of about 1.0 m into the chamber, creating a low tunnel, beyond which a near vertical cutting had been made to elevate to the chamber roof. The roof of the chamber has been reconstructed, on the basis of surviving angles of curvature at the east and west ends, as slightly domed, achieving a maximum height of 1.75 m towards the centre.

The funerary deposits themselves were found within a thick (30 cm) silt layer which extended from the bottom of the collapsed roof material to the floor of the chamber. Fairly hard and compact, this silting had clearly resulted from the seepage of water through the chamber roof. Considerable disturbance had been caused by this water. The excavated bones and pottery vessels showed evidence of having been washed around and redeposited at random points about the chamber. The original position of one interment may however be indicated by the cluster of vessels found in the north-east corner of the chamber (NE10.4–10). Some of these were quite large and heavy (especially the round-based storejar NE10.7 and the ledge-handled jar NE10.4) and would not have shifted to the same extent as the smaller vessels. In addition, it was in this area, close to the east wall, that a concentration of bones, including skull fragments, was found. These, constituting skeleton A, were identified as those of a male, aged between 20 and 25 years. A second concentration of bones was found near to the south wall, approximately 2.0 m from the entrance. These remains, referred to as skeleton B, were identified as those of a juvenile (sex indeterminable), aged 5–10 years. No grave goods were found in close proximity to skeleton B. Whilst the seven pottery vessels (NE10.4–10) can reasonably be attributed to skeleton A, the remaining three (NE10.1–3), which were found in a line almost equidistant between the two skeletons, could be assigned to either. There was nothing in the manner of the entrance to suggest a secondary sealing, and it must therefore be assumed that the two interments were made at the same time.

Contents

The pottery vessels from tomb NE10 are illustrated and described below. It should be noted that the funnel (NE10.10) was found inside the loop-handled amphoriskos (NE10.5). The significance of this observation is discussed below with regard to the possible function of these vessels (see Chapter 3).

NE10.1   Four-spouted lamp

Technique: Handmade, upper part finished on wheel. *Paste*: 5YR 'reddish yellow' 7/6; many small-medium lime, sand and ceramic; no core; hard. *Surface* (Interior): as paste. (Exterior): 10YR 'very pale brown' 8/3 wash; fire-blackened on one spout only.

NE10.2   Four-spouted lamp

Technique: Handmade, upper part finished on wheel. *Paste*: 7.5YR 'pink' 7/4; many small-medium sand and ceramic; no core; hard. *Surface* (Interior): as paste. (Exterior): as paste; fire-blackened on two adjacent spouts; faint combing around rim.

NE10.3   Loop-handled amphoriskos

Technique: Handmade with wheelmade rim. *Paste*: 10YR 'very pale brown' 8/3; many very small – small

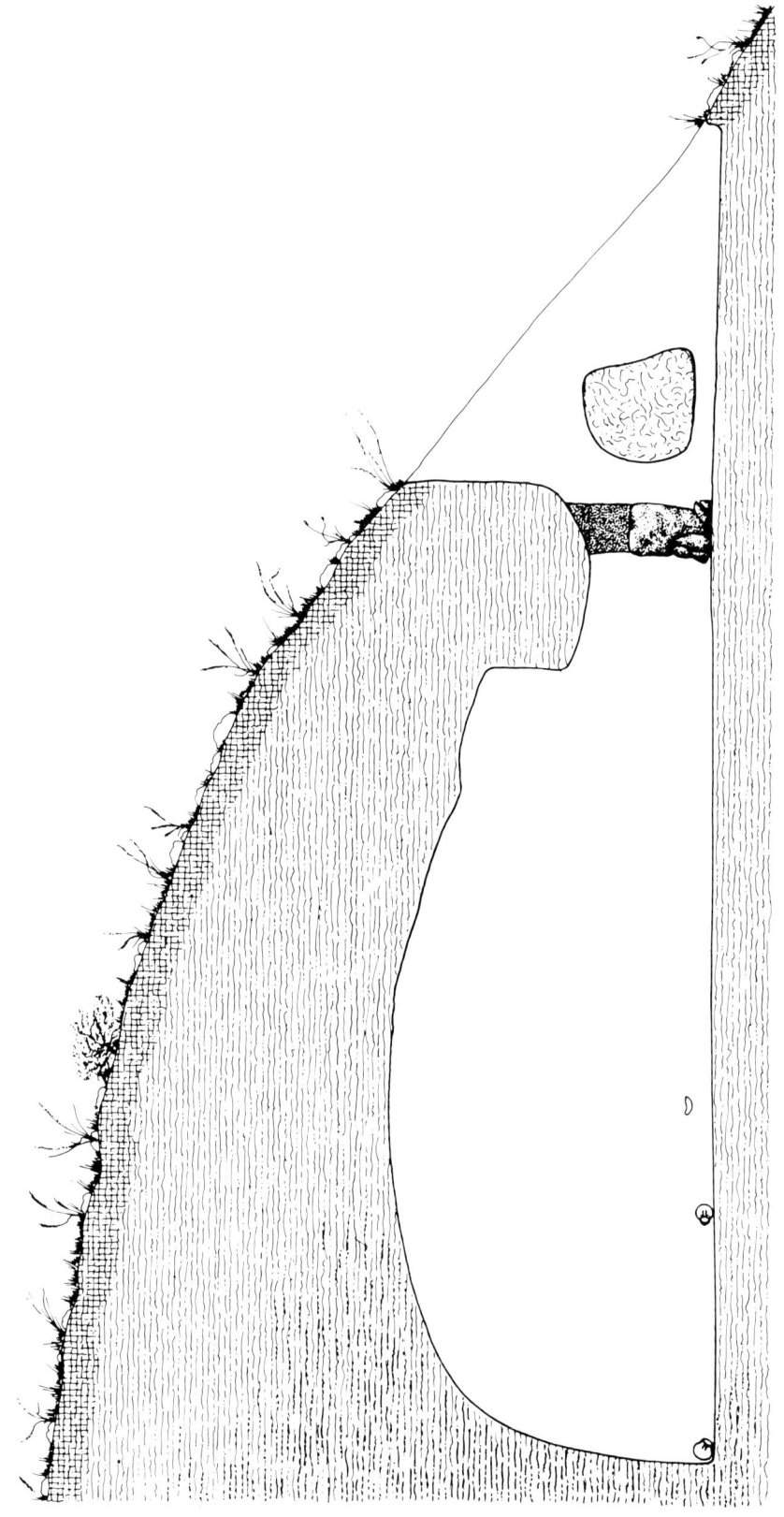

Fig. 15a Tomb NE10

Fig. 15b Tomb NE10

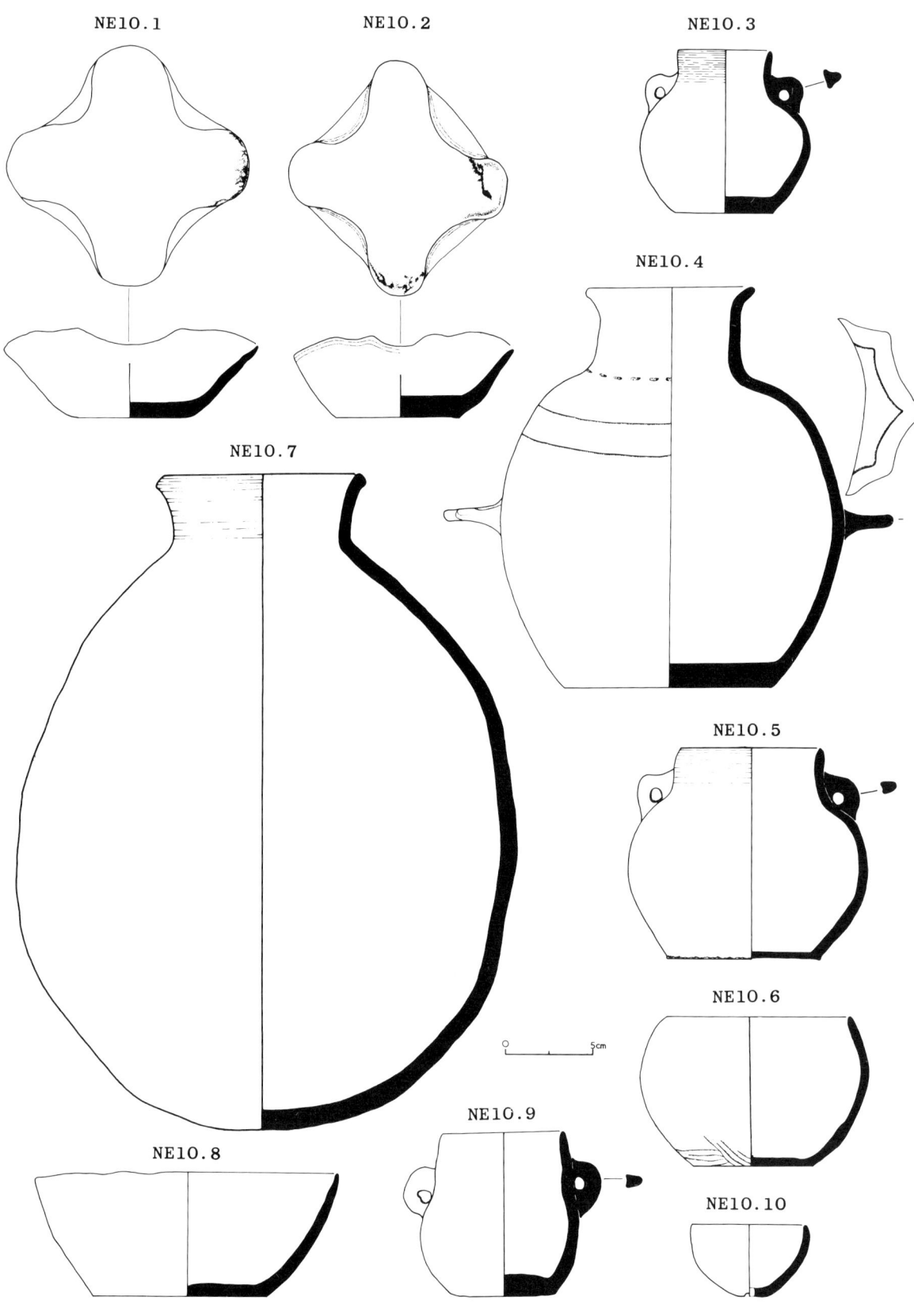

Fig. 16

sand and ceramic; no core; hard. *Surface* (Interior and Exterior): as paste.

NE10.4   Ledge-handled storejar

Technique: Handmade with wheelmade rim. *Paste*: 2.5Y 'light grey' 7/2; very many small-medium sand and ceramic, some medium lime; no core; hard. *Surface* (Interior): as paste. (Exterior): as paste; two incised lines on shoulder; band of punctate incisions at base of neck.

NE10.5   Loop-handled amphoriskos

Technique: Handmade with wheelmade rim. *Paste*: 2.5YR 'red' 5/6; many small-medium wadi gravel, ceramic and lime; light grey core; hard. *Surface* (Interior and Exterior): 2.5Y 'white' 8/2 wash.

NE10.6   Bowl

Technique: Handmade, rim finished on wheel. *Paste*: 7.5YR 'reddish yellow' 7/6; very many very small sand, some medium ceramic and lime; no core; hard. *Surface* (Interior): as paste. (Exterior): as paste; wet-smoothed.

NE10.7   Round-based storejar

Technique: Handmade with wheelmade rim. *Paste*: 10YR 'very pale brown' 8/3; very many very small-small sand and ceramic, some large ceramic; no core; hard. *Surface* (Interior): as paste. (Exterior): as paste; wet-smoothed.

NE10.8   Bowl

Technique: Handmade, rim finished on wheel. *Paste*: 7.5YR 'reddish yellow' 7/6; very many small-medium sand, ceramic and lime; no core; hard. *Surface* (Interior): 10YR 'very pale brown' 8/4 wash. (Exterior): as paste; wet-smoothed.

NE10.9   Loop-handled amphoriskos
          ('mug' amphoriskos)

Technique: Handmade. *Paste*: 7.5YR 'reddish yellow' 8/6; very many very small sand and ceramic; no core; hard. *Surface* (Interior): as paste. (Exterior): as paste; wet-smoothed.

NE10.10   Perforated cup

Technique: Handmade. *Paste*: 5YR 'reddish yellow' 7/6; many small-medium sand and ceramic; no core; hard. *Surface* (Interior and Exterior): as paste.

TOMB NE10A
West slope Hill 4
Orientation: S–N

During the excavation of tomb NE10, an irregularity in the marl strata was observed on the south side of the shaft. Investigation revealed that this irregularity was in fact a blocking of crushed marl cement, sealing the entrance to a small chamber. Removal of this blocking showed that the entrance was irregularly rectangular, and quite small (60 cm by 65 cm). The base of the entrance was approximately 15 cm above the base of the shaft. Inside the chamber, the floor was lower than the base of the entrance, again by about 15 cm.

The chamber itself was small, roughly circular in plan (80 cm by 1.0 m), and had an almost level roof. The interior fill consisted of a loose deposit of fallen decayed marl from the roof (40–50 cm in depth), below which was a dense and compact layer of silt, 40 cm thick and similar in character to that encountered in the chamber of NE10. Below and partially within the silt layer were found the remains of a juvenile (sex indeterminable), aged 5–10 years. Again, the bones were in fragmentary condition, and had suffered severely from the effects of water and from redeposition. A single large loop-handled amphoriskos (NE10A.1) was found close to the entrance on the west side of the chamber, and its position, standing perfectly vertical on the floor, suggests that it had not shifted since the time of its placement.

The relationship between tombs NE10 and NE10A is difficult to establish with certainty. No evidence in the form of secondary re-excavation of the shaft fill was found, nor indeed would this be expected since it seems likely that the shaft of NE10 had been left open and exposed. Certainly the nature of the fill, showing a textural gradation with depth, suggests a natural process of in-filling over a period of time rather than a deliberate back-filling. In any case, given the slope of the hill, it would have been difficult to achieve an effective back-fill. Without doubt, NE10 was the principal chamber, and as such would obviously have been constructed first. The question remains as to when the chamber of NE10A was cut. It could have been cut immediately after the completion of the main chamber, or immediately after that chamber had been sealed. Given the amount of space available inside NE10, however, this would seem somewhat improbable. Also, it is difficult to understand why the base of the entrance of NE10A was set some 15 cm above the base of the shaft, especially when the intention had been to make the floor of the chamber lower than the base of the entrance. The resultant sill would have been difficult to execute, and unnecessary.

It seems far more likely that at the time of construction of NE10A, the base of the shaft had silted up by approximately 15 cm, and that the entrance had been established on the same level as this existing, albeit not original, surface. It is therefore suggested that NE10A was dug into the shaft of NE10 at a later date, the time difference being represented by an unquantifiable layer of silting, 15 cm in depth.

The plan and elevation of tomb NE10A are shown with those of tomb NE10.

Contents

NE10A.1   Loop-handled amphoriskos

Technique: Handmade with wheelmade rim. *Paste*: 10YR 'very pale brown' 7/3; very many very small sand, few small-medium ceramic and lime; no core; hard. *Surface* (Interior): as paste. (Exterior): as paste; wet-smoothed.

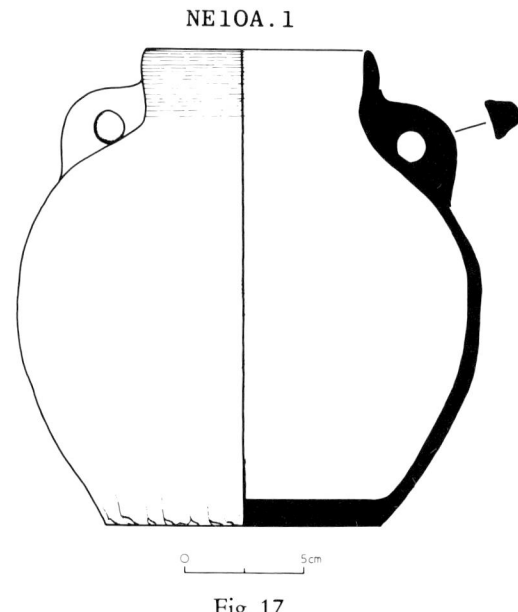

Fig. 17

TOMB NE11
West slope Hill 4
Orientation: E–W

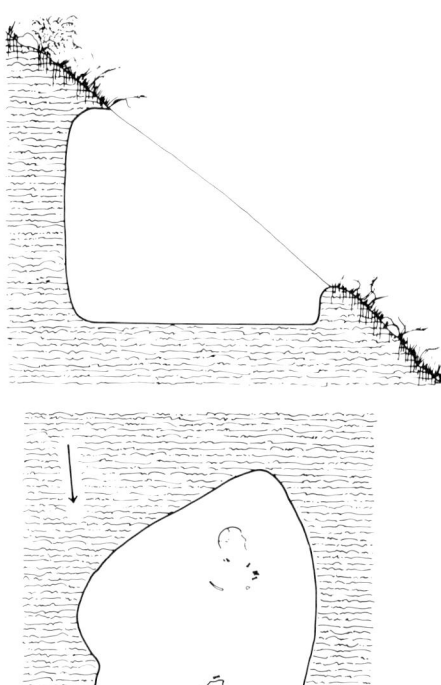

Fig. 18 Tomb NE11

Situated south of tomb NE10, tomb NE11 had suffered considerably from erosion, and although the complete floor plan of the chamber was preserved, nearly all of the roof and chamber approach had been lost.

No trace of the entrance was preserved, but part of a 13 cm high kerb, stepping down to the chamber floor, was found on the west (slope) side, showing that the tomb had either been approached by means of a semi-shaft or by a horizontally cut threshold (most probably the latter, given the very small size of the chamber). The chamber was irregular in plan, approximating most closely to triangular, and measured 1.30 m (north-south) by 1.20 m (east-west). From the preserved curvature at the top of the rear wall, the height of the chamber can be estimated as approximately 1.10 m, and the angle of inclination of the in-curve would suggest a level rather than a domed cutting. Into the west wall, close to the back of the chamber, a small semicircular niche had been cut, 35 cm above the floor surface. This niche was 30 cm wide across the front and 14 cm deep.

The excavated fill of tomb NE11 consisted of decayed marl rubble mixed with greyish-brown hard soil. Only a thin (4–5 cm) layer of reddish-brown silt was found at the base of this deposit, resting on the floor of the chamber, which suggests that the roof had collapsed shortly after interment.

The fragmented and incomplete remains of a single individual were found on the floor of the chamber. Although in extremely poor condition, the skeletal remains showed that the body had been buried in a fully articulated condition, and enough was preserved to indicate that it was in a flexed position, lying on its left side, orientated south-north, facing west. A number of finger bones were found close to the fragmentary skull, suggesting that the arms had been drawn up with the hands covering the face. The skeleton was identified as that of a juvenile (sex indeterminable), aged 5–10 years.

A stone pendant (NE11.1) and a tubular stone bead (NE11.2) were found close to the skull in positions suggesting that they had been worn around the neck.

Contents

NE11.1   Pendant   (Pl. XIA)

Greyish-black stone, veined with white; suspended elliptical hole.

NE11.2   Bead

White stone (calcite).

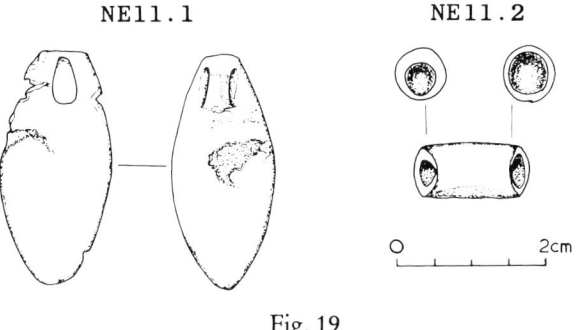

Fig. 19

TOMB NE12
West slope Hill 4
Orientation: E–W

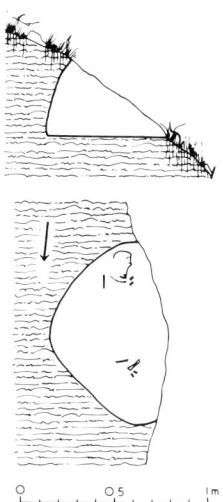

Fig. 20 Tomb NE12

This small tomb, situated between tombs NE13 and NE14, had suffered extensively from the effects of erosion. Only a part of the chamber had survived, consisting of the lower parts of the side and rear walls and about 75 per cent of the floor. No traces of the approach or entrance were found, but given the very small size of the chamber, it is possible that this tomb had been cut directly into the hill slope without shaft or threshold. From the surviving floor, the chamber would appear to have been originally roughly circular in plan, approximately 90 cm in diameter. The curve of the rear wall suggests a domed roof, achieving a maximum height of little more than 55 cm.

The excavated fill consisted of decayed, collapsed marl and topsoil. A very thin layer of reddish-brown silt (less than 4 cm) lay between this deposit and the chamber floor, again suggesting that very little time had elapsed between interment and the collapse of the roof. The fragmented and partial skeletal remains of a single individual were found. Despite its poor state of preservation, it was possible to determine that the body had been buried in an articulated condition, flexed on its left side, head to the south, facing west. The individual was identified as a juvenile, aged 3–5 years. On the north side of the chamber, there was evidence of an animal burrow which had disturbed the lower part of the skeleton. It would seem likely

Tombs in the north-east sector

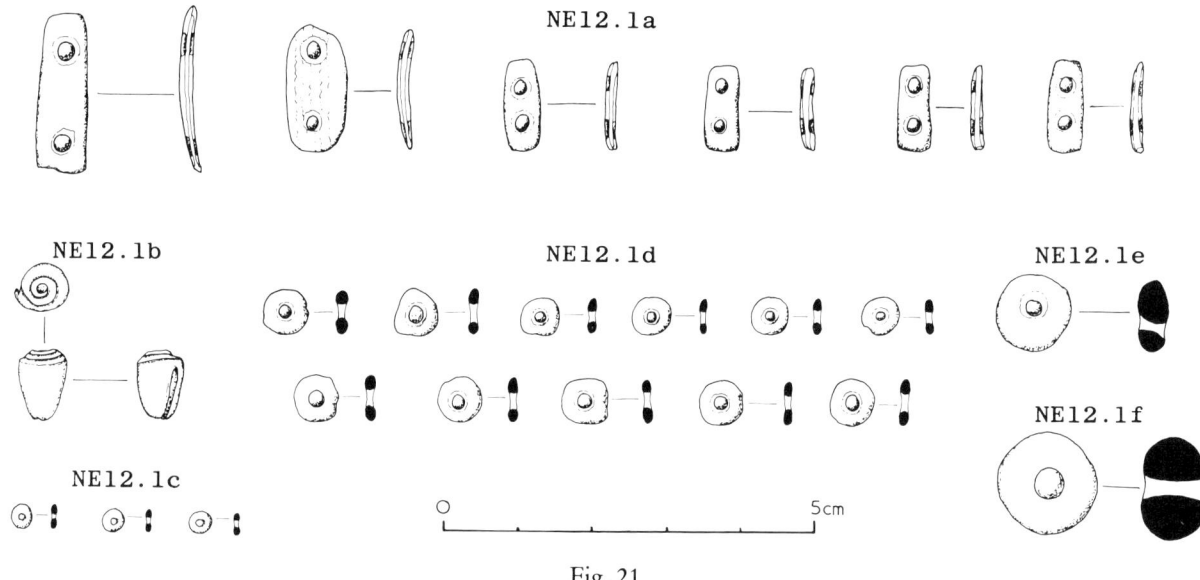

Fig. 21

that the animal in question (probably a rodent) had removed many of the smaller bones, and this would help to account for the incomplete condition of the skeleton. An attractive necklace of shells, spacers and beads was found at the base of the skull (NE12.1).

Contents

NE12.1   Necklace   (Pl. XIc)

a. 6 limestone sub-rectangular double spacers.
b. 19 pierced shells (*conus*).
c. 49 pale bluish-green composition cylindrical beads.
d. 11 limestone annular beads.
e. Alabaster annular bead.
f. White stone compressed spherical bead.

The holes of *a*, *d*, *e* and *f* are bored from both ends with a conical drill. The holes of *c* are cylindrical, and the beads were probably formed around a rod.

TOMB NE13
West slope Hill 4
Orientation: E–W

Like tomb NE12, to which it is adjacent, tomb NE13 was only partially preserved. No traces of the approach or entrance had survived, and only parts of the chamber floor (perhaps 50 per cent), rear and side walls remained. Like tomb NE12, the chamber was probably originally circular, with a diameter of about

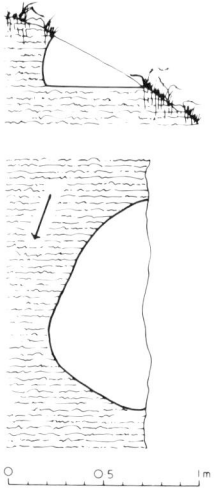

Fig. 22 Tomb NE13

105 cm. Judging by the curvature of the rear wall, it was most likely domed with a maximum height of 40–50 cm.

The excavated fill consisted of decayed collapsed marl and topsoil above a thin (less than 3 mm) layer of reddish-brown silt. A few fragments of bone were found in and below this silt layer, but these could be identified only as human. No associated grave goods were found.

TOMB NE14
West slope Hill 4
Orientation: E–W

The well-preserved shaft of tomb NE14 was encountered during the slope clearance operation of Hill 4 mentioned above with regard to tomb NE10. It provides the clearest and best example of the semi-shaft method of approach used for tombs cut into an existing hill slope. Trapezoidal in plan, it measured 2.70 m in length (maximum) by 1.15 m at the eastern (chamber) end, and 0.83 m at the western (hill-slope) end. The rear (eastern) face was preserved to a height of 3.20 m, and had clearly been truncated by erosion. The shallow slope (western) face was fully preserved, the uppermost edge showing a deliberately executed smoothing and rounding. At 12 cm below this top edge, the shaft had been stepped in by 15 cm, leaving a drop of a further 46 cm to the base.

On either side of the shaft, ledges had been cut, 10–12 cm deep and 60 cm in height. These extended from the rear (eastern) face, where they flanked the chamber entrance, for distances of respectively 2.0 m along the south side and 1.70 m along the north side, in both cases terminating in carefully rounded, vertical jambs. The function of these ledges is suggested by their height and positioning. It would seem likely that they served as supports for a roof-covering of timber, or perhaps reeds. The effect produced, therefore, would have been that of a low tunnel connecting the thus diminished shaft to the chamber entrance (see also tombs NE10 and SE11 for similar features).

The entrance to the chamber, on the rear face of the shaft, was 60 cm wide at its base, had roughly vertical sides with an arched top, and reached a maximum height of 56 cm at the centre. The upper part of the entrance was sealed with a cement of crushed marl. Below this were the remains of two courses of deep orange-brown mud bricks. Each course consisted of two bricks only. The upper two bricks showed signs of having been damaged, and were not preserved to their full height. The lower bricks were, however, fully preserved, and measured 30 cm wide by 24 cm deep by 14 cm high. The bricks in each course had been laid directly on top of one another, and had been mortared together and to the sides, using what appeared to be a mixture of crushed marl and sand. The nature of the blocking, showing two different materials, and the clearly observed damage to the upper course of mud bricks, strongly suggests that the chamber had been re-used, the mud-brick representing the remains of the original sealing, and the crushed marl cement the reblocking following a re-entry.

Removal of the blocking gave access to a low tunnel which preserved the dimensions of the entrance for a further 80 cm. This tunnel was found to be completely filled with large blocks of fallen marl, apparently not from the tunnel itself, the roof of which was intact, but rather from the chamber beyond. Unlike tomb NE10 (above), there appeared to be no silt layer between this marl collapse and the floor.

Having cleared the tunnel of marl debris, excavation proceeded into the chamber proper. This, on first appearance, seemed to be relatively stable. For, although the chamber contained large quantities of fallen marl blocks, these were concentrated towards the rear, spilling forwards into the tunnel and leaving the side walls relatively clear. It was also apparent that although the rear (eastern) half of the roof had collapsed completely, the front (western) half was intact. For a distance of about 40 cm into the chamber, the removal of the collapsed fill proceeded without mishap, and from this small internal vantage point it was possible to establish the approximate dimensions of the chamber. It was seen to be sub-circular, quite small, with a maximum diameter of 2.0 m. The rear wall could not, of course, be reached, and this has been reconstructed on the plan. The rear part of the roof had collapsed, but from the surviving, well-preserved front part it could be seen to be steeply domed, with a maximum height of 1.45 m at the centre of the chamber.

Unfortunately, attempts to clear further back into the chamber resulted in a major roof fall. The previously intact western end of the chamber roof collapsed, bringing down an enormous quantity of marl debris. In addition, large cracks began to appear

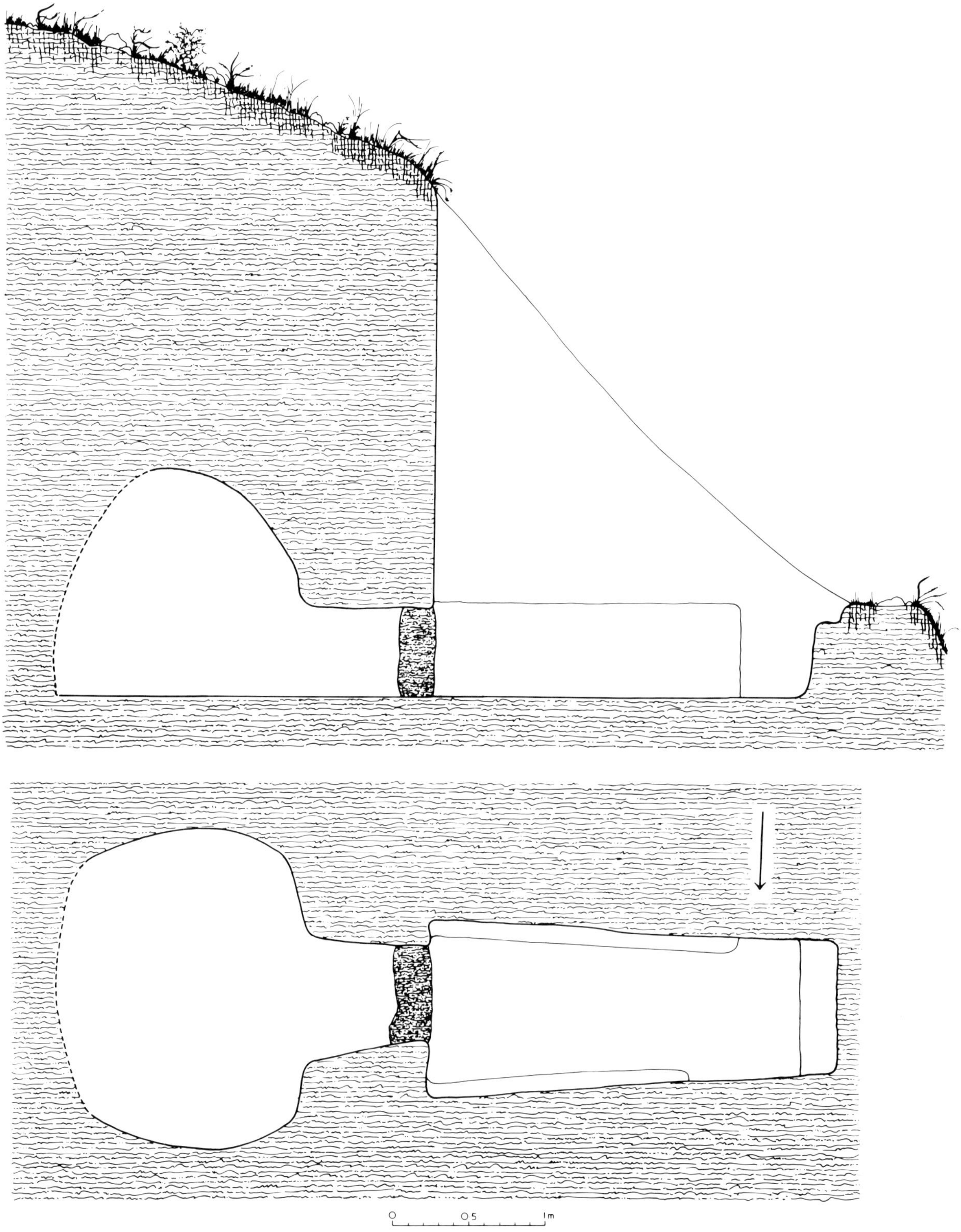

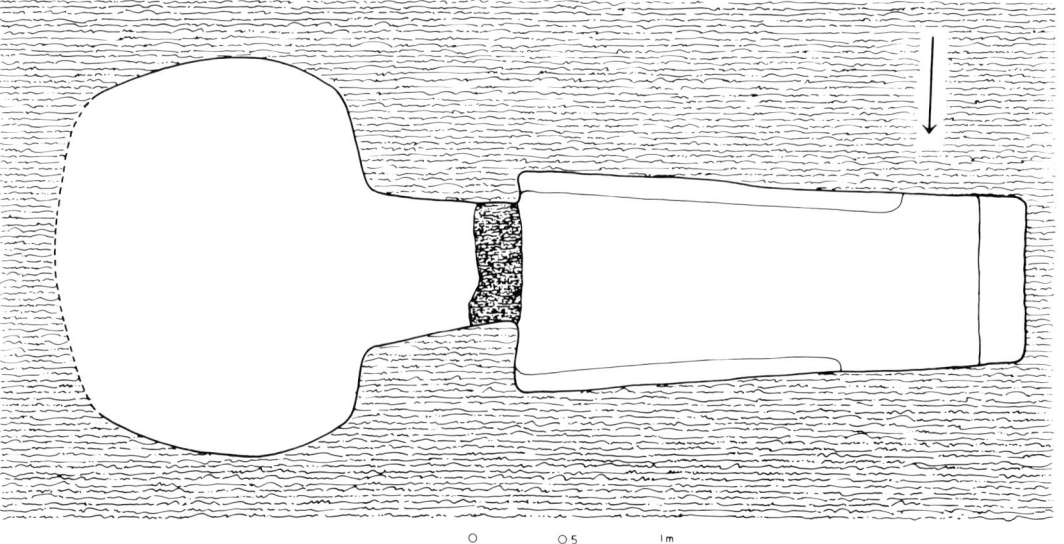

Fig. 23 Tomb NE14

in the roof and sides of the tunnel. The situation was clearly far too unstable to allow further excavation, and, regrettably, this structurally interesting tomb had to be abandoned. The chamber floor had been reached in only a very limited exposure, and neither skeletal remains nor grave goods were encountered.

TOMB NE15   Pl. VB
East slope Hill 1
Orientation: W–E

The east slope of Hill 1 almost certainly did not exist in its present form at the time of tomb cutting. It owes its present form to the effects of extensive bulldozing, undertaken in order to provide an access route from the bed of the river Zarqa to the modern paved road. That Hill 1 originally had a slope on the eastern side and was not simply continuous with Hill 4 on a level plateau is, however, clear from the disposition of tombs on the west slope of Hill 4. These (tombs NE10–14, above) had obviously been cut into an existing western hill slope which must, therefore, have opposed an eastern facing slope on the other side of a wadi. In other words, the bulldozing operation had involved widening the wadi by making use of the existing terrain, and seems to have been directed towards the eastern side only. Any tombs situated on the original east slope of Hill 1 would have been destroyed completely. More beneficially, however, the bulldozer exposed a number of tombs which had originally been cut from the level surface of Hill 1, some distance away from the slope. Two such tombs were NE15 and the bilobate tomb NE16/17, which, despite their appearance at the time of excavation, must be regarded as having been, at the time of their cutting, vertical shaft tombs.

The shaft of tomb NE15 was defined during a scraping operation of the present eastern slope of Hill 1. It first appeared as a grey-brown rectangular feature against the paler yellowish-brown decayed surface marl. Removal of the somewhat clayey fill initially produced a long rectangular plan, 2.35 m by 0.85 m. At a depth of 28 cm below the surface on the eastern (slope) side, a broad step, 33 cm wide, was encountered, below which the shaft continued for a further 62 cm, terminating in an extremely well-levelled base. On the western side, the top of the entrance to the chamber was found at a depth of only 1.0 m below surface, and, surprisingly, the bottom of the entrance was found to be at 1.80 m below surface; that is some 55 m above the base of the shaft as revealed at the eastern end. Indeed, the surface from which the entrance had been cut was itself found to be a step, 55 cm wide, below which the shaft continued down for a further 56 cm.

This rather peculiar structure, in effect producing an elevated chamber entrance, can only be explained by reference to the small side chamber, NE15A, located on the north side of the shaft. The small semicircular entrance (48 cm high by 52 cm wide) to this chamber had been established on the same base level as the bottom of the shaft. It might be assumed from this that two phases of usage had taken place, the original base of the shaft in fact being represented by the two steps at either end (although not of equal height), and that a subsequent recutting had removed the central part, deepening the shaft to allow for the insertion of a second chamber. However, there was nothing in the filling of the shaft to suggest that any such recutting had taken place. The deposit was homogeneous, and appeared to be sedimentary in nature, indicating that the shaft had been left open to silt up naturally. Given this circumstance, there would have been little reason to have deepened the shaft, as the entrance to the side chamber could just as well have been cut from the same surface as that of the principal chamber. It must, therefore, be assumed that the unusual structure of the approach to tomb NE15/15A was deliberately planned in that way, and represents a single coherent phase of usage.

The shaft fill contained a number of undiagnostic body sherds which had clearly been washed in during the silting-up process. In addition, a complete perforated cup or funnel (similar to NE15.8) was found in the fill, and although this has been assigned a tomb inventory number, NE15.1, it must be appreciated that it cannot in any way be related to the funerary deposits of either the principal chamber, NE15, nor indeed to the side chamber, NE15A, and must again be seen as having washed into the shaft subsequent to the sealing of the chambers.

The sealing of the entrance to the side chamber, NE15A, was found intact, and consisted of a thick (*c*.35 cm) 'plug' of dense reddish clay. Removal of this blocking revealed a low chamber (maximum height 55 cm), the roof of which was intact, but which was filled completely with water-laid silt. Excavation and clearance of this silt produced the plan of a small oval chamber, 1.60 m by 1.10 m. No finds were en-

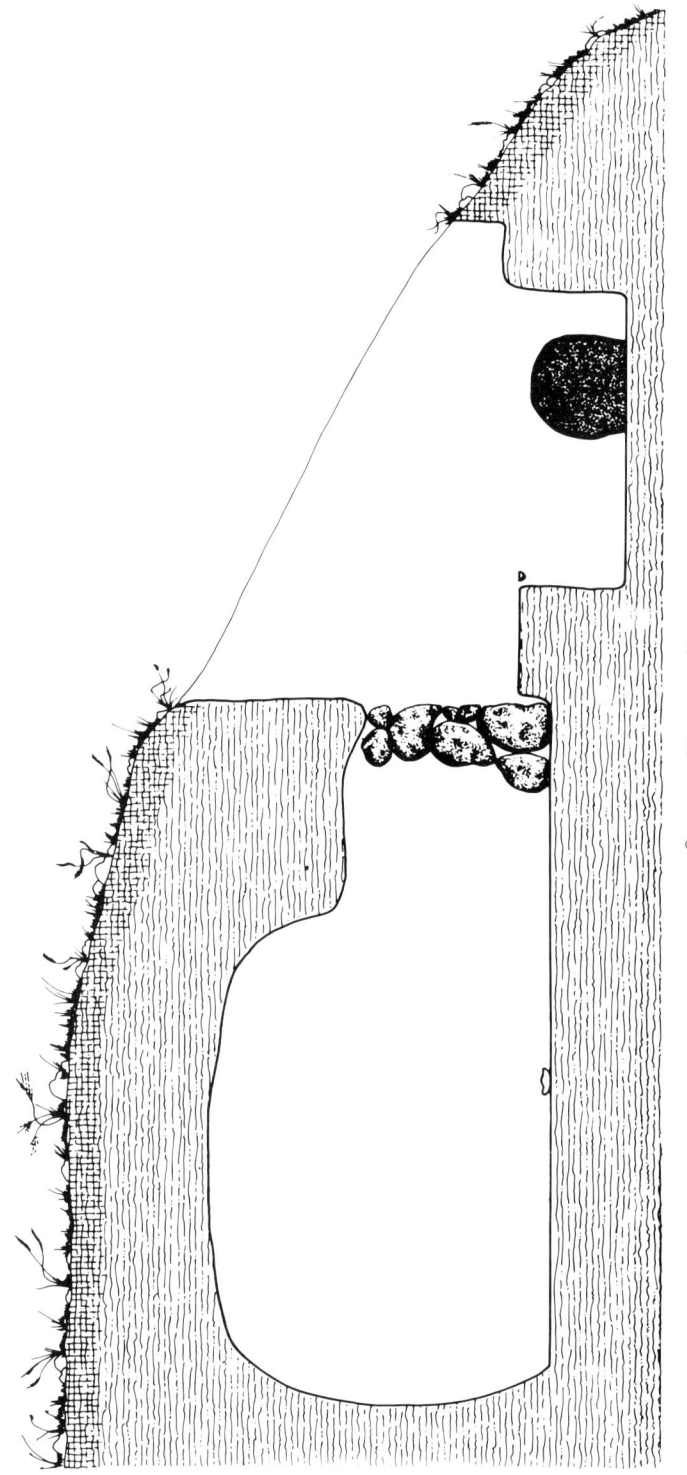

Fig. 24a Tomb NE15

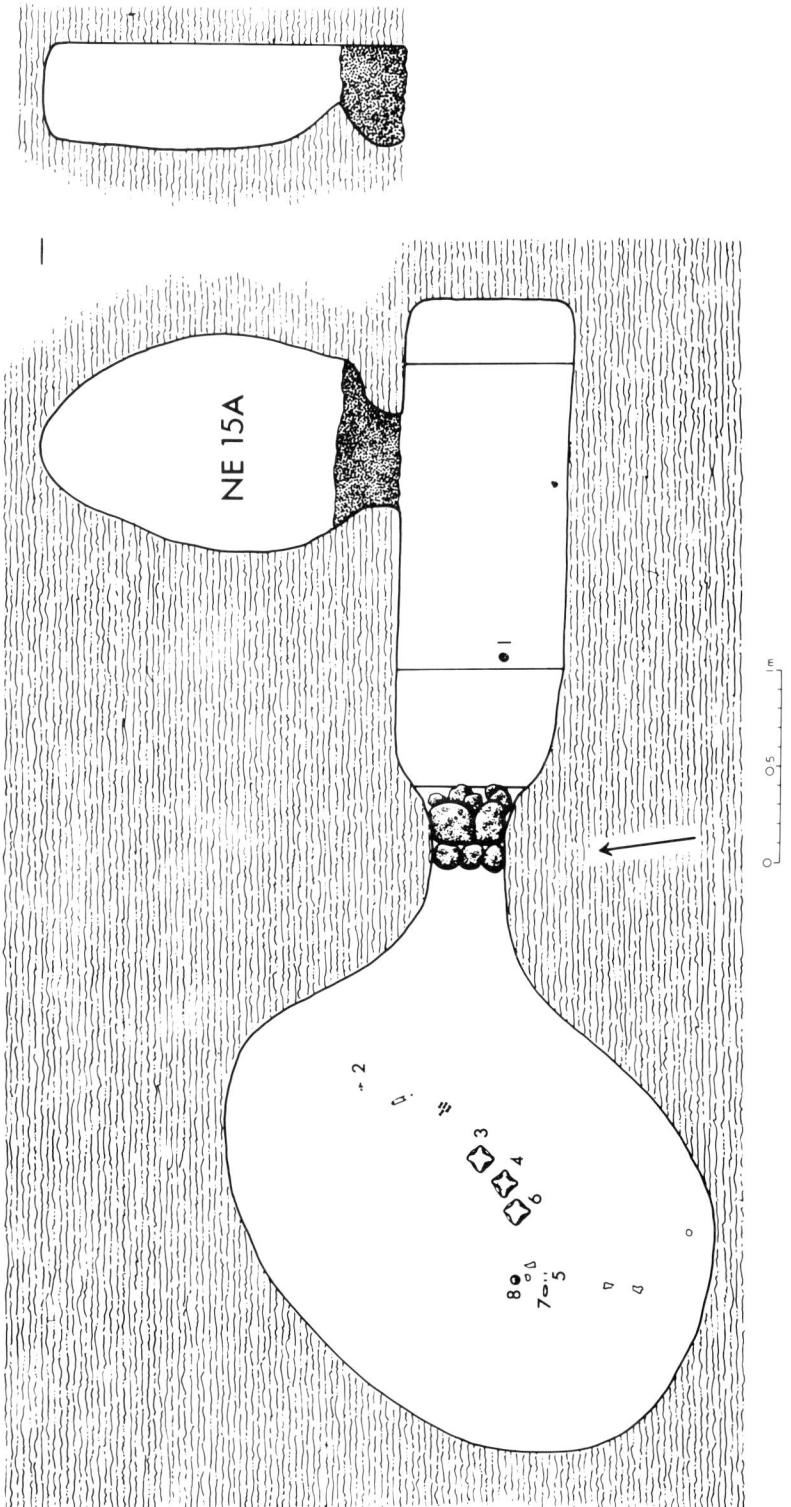

Fig. 24b Tomb NE15

countered, nor were there any traces of skeletal remains. It would seem somewhat unlikely that a chamber had been prepared and sealed without any interment having taken place, and it would be more reasonable to suppose that an individual had indeed been buried in the chamber but that the skeleton had subsequently suffered complete disintegration. This would not be surprising in view of the location of the chamber. For, situated at the bottom of a shaft which is thought to have been left exposed, the chamber, despite the clay sealing, would undoubtedly have been subjected to prolonged and regular flooding (as was in fact suggested by the extensive silt deposit). It would therefore not be unreasonable to expect any bones, particularly those of an infant or juvenile, for which the small size of this chamber would seem appropriate, to have disintegrated entirely.

The entrance to the principal chamber, NE15, was also found with its blocking intact. In this case, large boulders, up to 35 cm in diameter, had been used, with smaller stones filling the spaces. Having removed this blocking, it was possible to establish the dimensions of the entrance itself. This was found to be roughly rectangular, slightly and irregularly arched at the top, with a height of 85 cm and a maximum width of 51 cm. Beyond the entrance, the floor had been cut 17 cm deeper than the threshold, and it was against the inner face of this step that the blocking stones had been laid. Otherwise, the dimensions of the entrance-way had been preserved for a further 60 cm, to form a low tunnel. Beyond this point, the side walls curved outwards, in a gradual expansion, developing into those of the chamber proper. The low height, however, had been maintained for a further 45 cm, terminating in a more abrupt transition to the chamber roof.

Although the tunnel was fully intact and relatively clear of debris, consisting only of a 20–30 cm deep deposit of rather compact greyish silt, the chamber itself was seen to be completely filled with fallen marl blocks, decayed marl debris and topsoil, still, however, resting on the same silt layer as in the tunnel. Since it was clear that the original roof had completely collapsed, and given the proximity of the top of the chamber to the existing ground surface of Hill 1, it was decided in this case to remove the debris from above. This initially involved the removal of about 70 cm of soil from an area judged to be directly above the tomb chamber. Below the upper 20 cm of topsoil, the limits of the excavation were readily established, for the collapse of the chamber had itself created a disturbance and depression into which soil, much looser and darker in colour than the surrounding decayed top-marl, had slipped and accumulated. The approximate dimensions of the chamber could therefore very quickly be estimated, but there proved to be a further 50 cm of loose brownish-grey soil to be removed before the surviving tops of the incurving chamber walls became visible. This debris, which clearly came from the roof, was seen to overlie a thick deposit of silt, somewhat greyish in colour and identical with that encountered in the entrance tunnel.

The silt layer proved on excavation to be in excess of 30 cm in depth, indicating that a long period of time had elapsed between interment and the collapse of the roof. When excavation was complete, it was possible to establish fully the plan and dimensions of the chamber. It was roughly circular in plan, with a diameter of approximately 2.50 m, and had a slightly domed roof which reached a maximum height of 1.78 m towards the centre of the chamber (as estimated from the surviving angles of curvature).

The funerary deposits were contained within and below the 30 cm silt layer which lay between the floor and the collapsed debris from the roof. The remains of two individuals were found, both in extremely fragmentary condition. The bones were scattered around the chamber, and had clearly been extensively washed around, presumably as a result of regular and repeated intrusions of rainwater. Although it was impossible to identify the original positions of the interments, it was at least evident that the burials were contemporary, for the chamber showed no signs of re-use or re-entry. The two individuals were identified as a female, aged 25–35 years, and a juvenile (sex indeterminable), aged 5–10 years.

The evidence for regular intrusion of water into the chamber could also be adduced from the nature of the silt layer itself, which showed a varved structure indicative of seasonal pooling. To what extent the grave goods were in their original positions is difficult to estimate. Certainly, the finding of three four-spouted lamps (NE15.3, 4 and 6) in an east-west row in the centre of the chamber suggests a deliberate and original placement. Indeed, it is reminiscent of tomb NE10 (above), where three vessels (two of which were also lamps) were found in a row equidistant between the two individuals.

To the west of the three lamps was found a small copper blade (NE15.7). Two copper rivets (NE15.5)

Tombs in the north-east sector

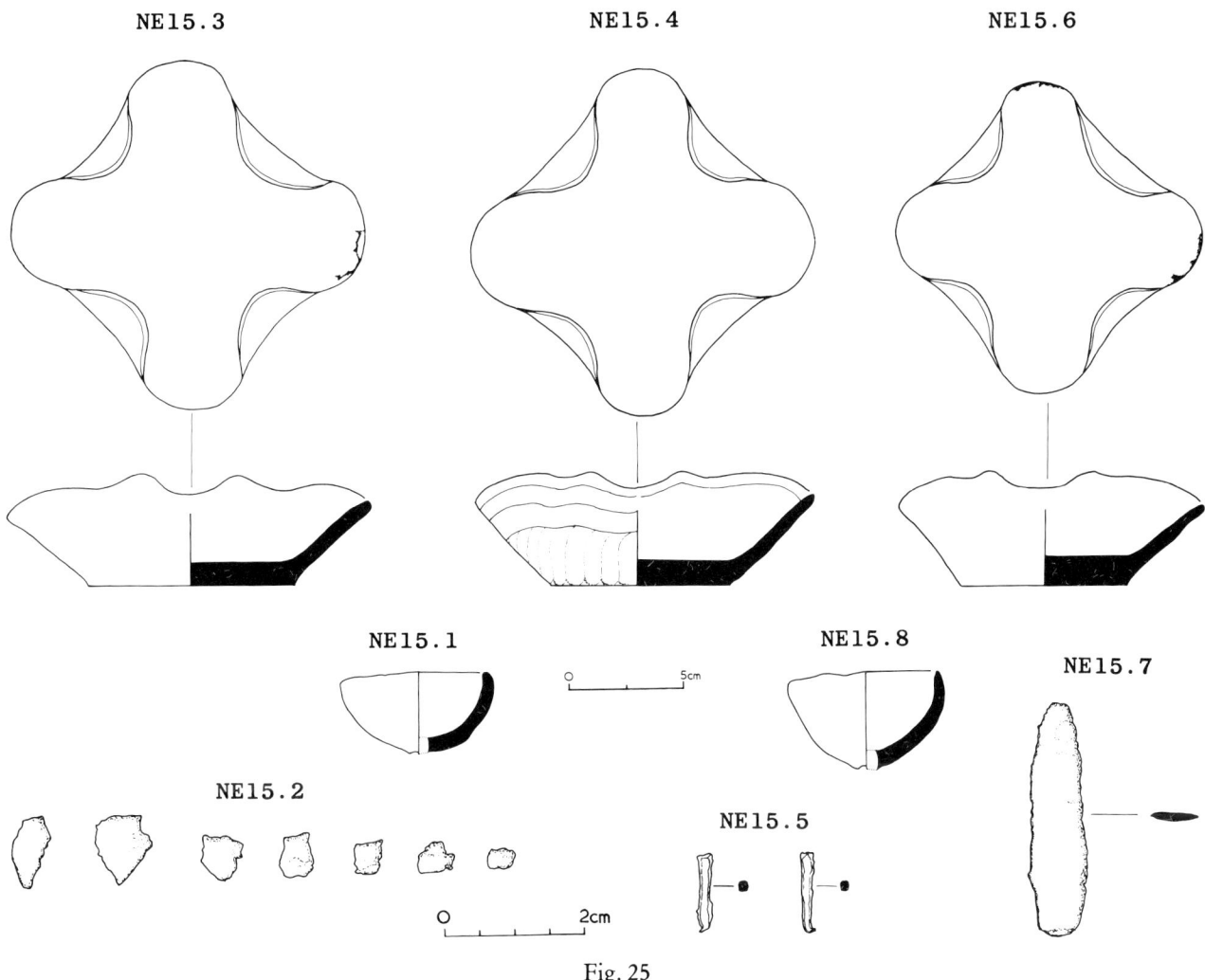

Fig. 25

were found directly in line with the distal end of this blade, at distances of 1 cm and 4 cm away. As in the case of the daggers found in tombs NE8, NE25 and SE1, the positioning of the rivets suggests the method by which the handle might have been attached to the blade (see below, Chapter 3).

Close to the copper blade was found a small perforated cup or funnel (NE15.8), similar in every respect to that found in the shaft fill (NE15.1). Finally, towards the north side of the chamber were found eight small fragments of sheet copper (NE15.2), but, despite many attempts, no coherent form could be made from these.

Contents

NE15.1   Perforated cup (from the shaft fill)

Technique: Handmade. *Paste*: 10YR 'very pale brown' 7/3; very many very small sand and ceramic; light grey core; hard. *Surface* (Interior and Exterior): 2.5Y 'white' 8/2 wash.

NE15.2   Metal sheet

Copper/copper alloy (8 fragments).

NE15.3   Four-spouted lamp

Technique: Handmade, upper part finished on wheel. *Paste*: 5YR 'pink' 7/4; many small-medium lime, some medium wadi gravel; no core; hard. *Surface*

(Interior and Exterior): as paste; slight blackening on one spout only.

NE15.4   Four-spouted lamp

Technique: Handmade, upper part finished on wheel. *Paste*: 5YR 'reddish yellow' 7/6; many small-medium sand, ceramic and lime, some large sand and lime; no core; hard. *Surface* (Interior and Exterior): as paste; no blackening.

NE15.5   Two rivets

Copper/copper alloy.

NE15.6   Four-spouted lamp

Technique: Handmade, upper part finished on wheel. *Paste*: 5YR 'pink' 8/4; many small-medium sand and ceramic, some large lime and wadi gravel; no core; hard. *Surface* (Interior and Exterior): 7.5YR 'pinkish white' 8/2 wash; slight blackening on one spout only.

NE15.7   Knife blade

Copper/copper alloy.

NE15.8   Perforated cup

Technique: Handmade. *Paste*: 2.5Y 'white' 8/2; very many very small sand and ceramic, some small-medium wadi gravel; no core; hard. *Surface* (Interior and Exterior): as paste.

TOMB NE16/17   Pl. VIA
East slope Hill 1
Orientation: W–E

This interesting bilobate tomb, lying directly to the south of tomb NE15, was discovered during the surface scraping operation of the east slope of Hill 1 described above. Initially, two depressions were found high up on the slope, which were recognised, on analogy with tomb NE15, as representing two collapsed tomb chambers. At this stage, there was no indication that these shared a common entrance, and not unreasonably, therefore, two tomb numbers were assigned, NE16 to the southern chamber, and NE17 to the northern. Subsequent investigations on the lower slope, east of the chambers, revealed that there was in fact one single entrance leading to both chambers. Nevertheless, it was decided to retain the two numbers as a convenient means of referring to the two parts of what was clearly a double, or bilobate, tomb.

The bulldozing operation described above (see tomb NE15) had severely damaged the approach to the tomb. Almost no traces of the shaft had survived (only enough to show that it had possessed one), but the rear part of the entrance-way itself was found to be reasonably well preserved. This was low and arched, 56 cm wide at the base, and with a maximum height of 75 cm at the centre. As found, the entrance was open, any blocking having presumably been dislodged by the bulldozer. There were, however, substantial traces of red clay adhering to the sides and top of the entrance, indicating that this material had been used in either the primary or secondary sealing (see below).

As in the case of tomb NE15, because of the obvious proximity of the chambers to the present ground surface, it was decided to clear them from above. The interior fill consisted of large marl blocks from the roofs, decayed marl debris and topsoil. Below this was a silt layer, 10–12 cm in depth and uniformly distributed throughout the tomb. Similar in character to the deposit encountered in tomb NE15, this silt is most likely to have been laid down as a result of seasonal pooling of intrusive rainwater. On completion of excavation of this layer, the structure and dimensions of the tomb could be established.

Beyond the entrance-way there was no tunnel as in the case of tomb NE15; instead, there was direct access, in the first instance, to the more southerly chamber, NE16. This was irregularly oval in plan, developing from a gradual expansion of the entrance-way, and was 2.65 m long by 1.65 m wide (maximum). The roof had completely collapsed; however, based on the surviving curvature of the rear (western) wall and that of the east wall above the entrance-way, it would seem that it had been domed, perhaps reaching a maximum height of about 1.55 m towards the centre of the chamber.

Access to the northern chamber, NE17, was by means of a tall arch cut from the northern wall of NE16, beginning some 90 cm from the entrance-way. This arch, which had clearly never been sealed in any way (nor indeed would that ever have been the intention), was 1.08 m wide and 1.15 m high at the centre, where it was seen to correspond to the full roof height of NE17. Beyond the arch, the chamber of NE17 was found to be irregularly oval in plan,

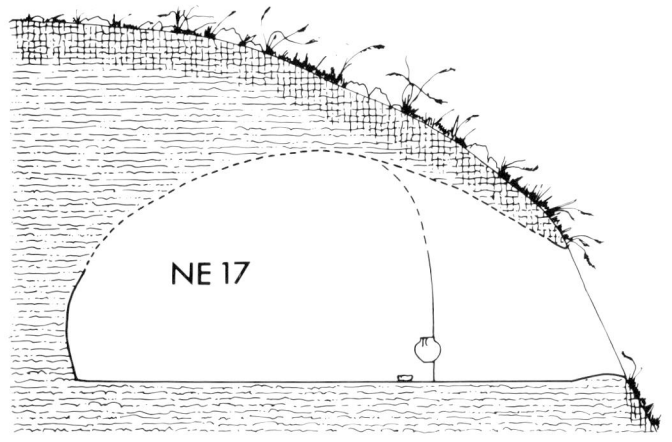

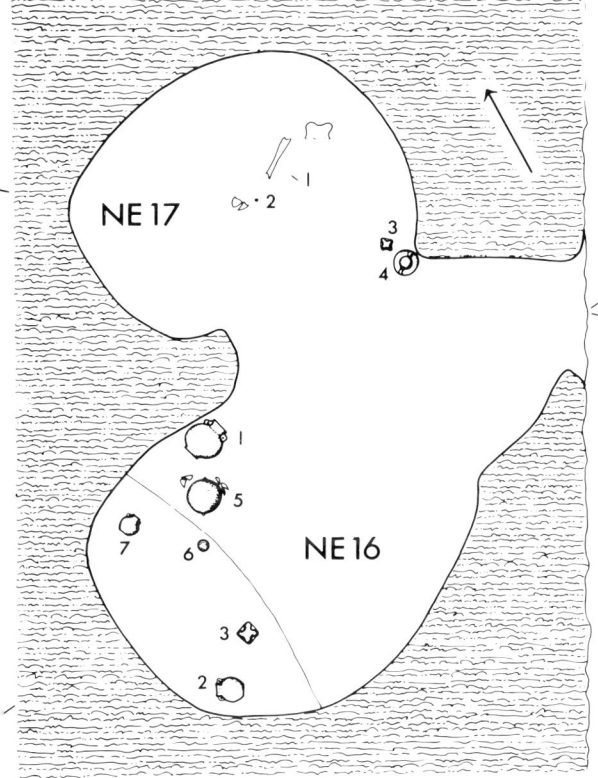

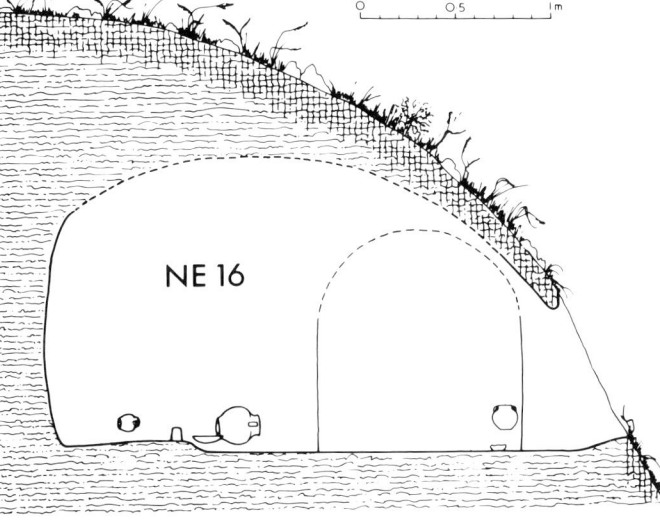

with dimensions of 1.40 m north-south, and 1.70 m east-west. The roof, like that of NE16, had also collapsed, but its maximum height would not have been greater than that of the connecting arch, that is 1.15 m.

The above description makes it clear that although tomb NE16/17 had been conceived of as functionally bilobate, in terms of construction the northern chamber, NE17, had been developed from the southern NE16, and that the latter had, therefore, almost certainly been cut first.

The funerary deposits were found to be contained within and below the silt layer separating the marl roof collapse from the chamber floors. In NE16, poorly preserved fragments of bone were found scattered at random around the chamber, but were generally lying on or close to the floor surface. These could only be identified as those of a human adult. Considerable disturbance had clearly occurred as a result of intrusive water, and this was reflected also in the distribution of the grave goods. Close to the south wall at the western end of the chamber was found, on its side, a loop-handled amphoriskos (NE16.2), which had inside it a small perforated cup or funnel (NE16.4). Slightly to the north of this was a four-spouted lamp (NE16.3). These vessels were found to be lying directly on the floor of the chamber. Close to the centre of the tomb was a small cup (NE16.6), lying upside-down but again resting directly on the floor surface. It is possible that these vessels were in more or less their original positions, for the floor surface on which they lay, at the west end of the chamber, was slightly elevated (by about 5 cm), which would have made any pots placed here somewhat less susceptible to disturbance by water than those which had been set in the lower, north-eastern part. Certainly, the three remaining vessels discovered on the north side of the chamber were found resting at different levels within the silt layer, suggesting that they had been carried up with the gradual elevation of the deposit. These were a loop-handled amphoriskos (NE16.1), found hard against the north wall, a flat-based bowl (NE16.5) and another small loop-handled amphoriskos (NE16.7).

A similar situation was encountered in the northern chamber, NE17. The fragmentary remains of a single individual were found scattered throughout the upper 5 cm of the silt layer, but with a concentra-

Fig. 26 Tomb NE16/17

tion towards the north-central part of the chamber. These were identified as those of an adult, probably female. A copper pin (NE17.1) and a carnelian bead (NE17.2) were found associated with this bone scatter. Towards the south side of the chamber, and close to the arch connecting with NE16, was found, high up in the silt layer, a loop-handled amphoriskos (NE17.4). Close to this, and directly on the floor surface, was a four-spouted lamp (NE17.3), associated with a scatter of charcoal. The lamp was badly broken, and appeared to have been crushed in antiquity: certainly its poor condition could not have been due to the collapse of the chamber roof, which had left the much higher and more exposed loop-handled amphoriskos (NE17.4) unaffected and intact.

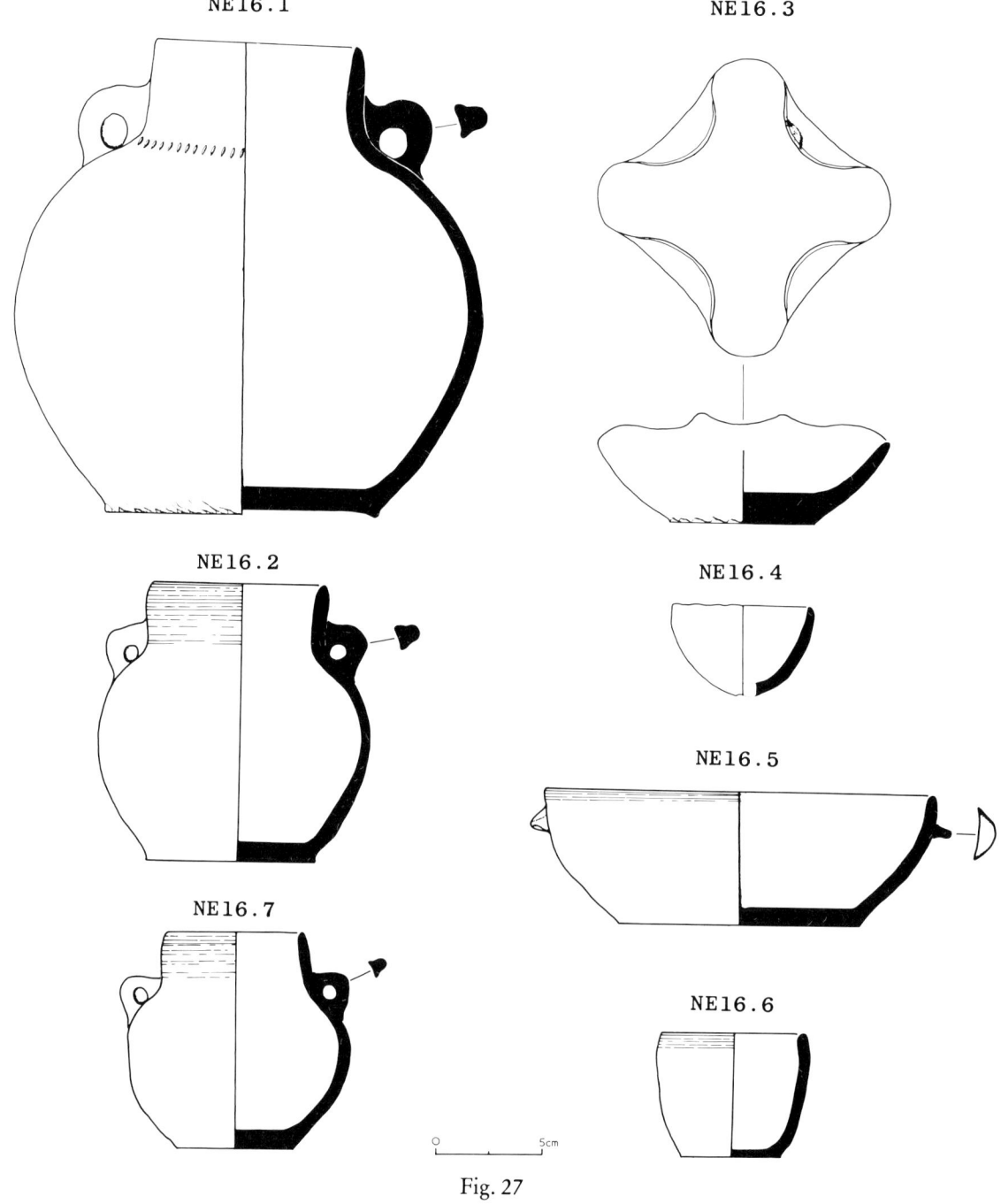

Fig. 27

This lamp is important, for its position and condition indicate the chronology of the tomb's usage. For, although it may be assumed that NE16/17 was conceived as an integral structure and was cut in one basic operation, it need not follow that both chambers were used contemporaneously.

The fact that the lamp, NE17.3, had been crushed *in situ* strongly suggests that it had been disturbed and trampled after its initial placement. This would, in itself, imply two phases of usage of the tomb. However, there was no evidence to suggest that there had been two such phases in NE17, for the remains of only one individual were found there. It follows, therefore, that if two phases of usage had occurred, these must correspond to a chronological distinction between the two chambers. It can therefore be reasonably argued that a first usage of the tomb is represented by the deposit in NE16. In support of this, it should be noted that some of the vessels (NE16.2–4, 6) and the majority of the skeletal remains were found directly on the floor surface. It would seem likely that the lamp, NE17.3, was also placed in the tomb at this time, and that, despite its position just within chamber NE17, it should more correctly be assigned to NE16. At a later stage, after a certain amount of silting had occurred, the tomb was reopened and a second interment placed in NE17. During the course of this process, the lamp became trampled and damaged. It might be significant to point out here that none of the skeletal remains, nor any of the grave goods associated with NE17, were found directly on the floor surface, which supports the theory that they had originally been placed on a pre-existing layer of accumulated silt. It is unfortunate of course that no additional evidence in support of this reconstruction could be adduced from the sealing of the tomb entrance, which, as stated, was no longer in place at the time of excavation.

Contents

NE16 (Pl. XIIIc)

NE16.1   Loop-handled amphoriskos

Technique: Handmade with wheelmade rim. *Paste*: 10YR 'very pale brown' 8/3; many small-medium sand, ceramic and lime, few large lime; no core; hard. *Surface* (Interior): as paste. (Exterior): as paste; faint traces of vertical combing on body; tooth impression at base of neck.

NE16.2   Loop-handled amphoriskos

Technique: Handmade with wheelmade rim. *Paste*: 7.5YR 'reddish yellow' 8/6; many small-medium sand and ceramic, some medium lime; no core; hard. *Surface* (Interior and Exterior): as paste.

NE16.3   Four-spouted lamp

Technique: Handmade, upper part finished on wheel. *Paste*: 5YR 'reddish yellow' 6/6; many small-medium sand, ceramic and lime; no core; hard. *Surface* (Interior and Exterior): 10YR 'very pale brown' 8/3 wash; no blackening.

NE16.4   Perforated cup

Technique: Handmade. *Paste*: 7.5YR 'pink' 7/4; many small-medium sand and ceramic, some medium lime; no core; hard. *Surface* (Interior and Exterior): as paste.

NE16.5   Bowl

Technique: Handmade, upper part finished on wheel. *Paste*: 7.5YR 'reddish yellow' 8/6; very many very small sand, some medium lime, sand and ceramic; no core; hard. *Surface* (Interior and Exterior): 10YR 'very pale brown' 8/3 wash.

NE16.6   Cup

Technique: Handmade, upper part finished on wheel. *Paste*: 7.5YR 'reddish yellow' 8/6; many very small-small sand and ceramic, some medium lime; no core; hard. *Surface* (Interior): as paste. (Exterior): as paste; wet-smoothed.

NE16.7   Loop-handled amphoriskos

Technique: Handmade with wheelmade rim. *Paste*: 7.5YR 'reddish yellow' 7/6; many small-medium wadi gravel, sand and ceramic, some medium lime; no core; hard. *Surface* (Interior): as paste. (Exterior): as paste; wet-smoothed.

NE17

NE17.1   Awl

Copper/copper alloy.

NE17.2 Bead

Carnelian; bored from both ends with cylindrical drill.

NE17.3 Four-spouted lamp

Technique: Handmade. *Paste*: 7.5YR 'light brown' 6/4; many medium sand and ceramic, few medium lime; no core; hard. *Surface* (Interior and Exterior): as paste; blackened on two adjacent spouts.

NE17.4 Loop-handled amphoriskos

Technique: Handmade with wheelmade rim. *Paste*: 10YR 'very pale brown' 7/3; many small-medium sand and ceramic; no core; hard. *Surface* (Interior and Exterior): 2.5Y 'white' 8/2 wash.

TOMB NE18
West slope Hill 4
Orientation: E–W

Towards the end of the excavation season, a small depression, roughly triangular in shape, was observed on the west slope of Hill 4, slightly to the south of tomb NE11. At first, this was assumed to be the heavily eroded, partial chamber of a small tomb, similar to tomb NE12 (above). As excavation of the filling of topsoil and broken marl debris proceeded, however, it became clear that the feature represented not a tomb chamber of this sort, but rather the shaft or semi-shaft of what was likely to be a larger tomb, possibly similar to tomb NE10. By this late stage, however, neither time nor resources were available to undertake the investigation of a tomb of this sort, and so, regrettably, the excavation of tomb NE18 had to be discontinued.

TOMB NE19

Number not allocated

TOMB NE20
Surface Hill 2
Orientation: W–E

The shaft of this tomb was located during the surface clearance of Hill 2, described above (see tomb NE8). It appeared on the surface as a greyish-brown oval-shaped feature against the paler, brownish-cream weathered top-marl. Orientated north-east by south-west, it measured some 4.90m by 1.0m.

Excavation revealed that the whole area of this extensive surface feature had been cut down to a depth of about 80cm (in terms of the existing surface), terminating in a well-flattened surface at the

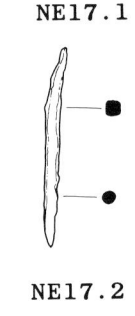

NE17.1

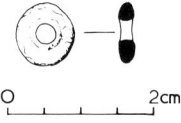

NE17.2

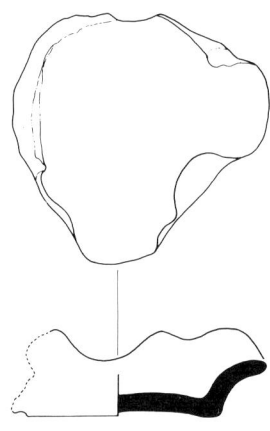

NE17.3

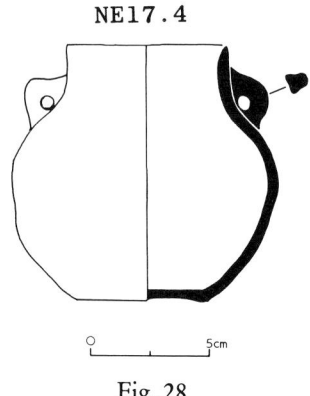

NE17.4

Fig. 28

level of the transition from the weathered top-marl to the undecayed solid marl. It was from this surface, at the eastern end, that the tomb shaft proper had been continued in depth.

As in the case of tomb NE9 (above), it would seem that this initial cutting had been undertaken as a type of probe to locate the level of undisturbed marl, obviously with the knowledge that such structurally solid material was necessary for the establishment of a sound chamber.

The continuation shaft, at the east end of the 'probe', was sub-rectangular in plan, maintaining the curvature of the original oval at the eastern end but being more or less straight on the western side. Its base was reached at only 1.90 m below surface, that is 1.10 m below the base of the initial 'probe' cutting.

The excavated shaft fill consisted of fairly loose, greyish-brown soil, containing many small whitish-cream chips of marl, and, in terms of the fill, there appeared to be no distinction between the two elements of the shaft. As in the case of tomb NE9, the material, with its high marl content, suggests a process of deliberate back-filling after interment.

With the removal of the fill, the structure of the shaft could be seen to be closely similar in many respects to the semi-shaft of tomb NE14 (above). It was long and narrow, and somewhat irregular, measuring approximately 2.40 m by 85 cm. The entrance to the tomb chamber appeared on the short western side as a low arched, almost semicircular opening, 60 cm high and 75 cm wide across the base. Flanking the entrance, on either of the long sides, were ledges 15 cm deep and 60 cm in height (corresponding with the maximum height of the entrance-way). These ledges, which had been left as projections during the cutting of the shaft, extended from the chamber entrance for distances of 1.30 m along the south side and 1.20 m along the north, in both cases terminating in carefully rounded vertical jambs. As in the case of tomb NE14 (and SE11 below), it would seem possible that these ledges served as footings for a roof covering of timber or reeds to provide a low approach tunnel to the chamber entrance.

As found, the entrance to the chamber was only partially blocked with large stones, many of them, it was later discovered, having fallen back into the chamber. These stones were quite large, in the order of 35 cm by 20 cm by 15 cm. No additional material appeared to have been used to seal or mortar the stones in position. Removal of the blocking showed that the floor of the chamber had been cut some 50 cm deeper than the threshold (base of the shaft), and that it was against the inner face of this deep step that the lowest courses of blocking stones had been laid.

When first observed, the appearance of the chamber beyond the entrance was quite extraordinary. For although the roof, apart from a small central portion, was relatively well preserved, most of the floor had subsided, leaving a large central depression encircled by a 'shelf' which represented all that remained of the original floor. Further examination of this rather peculiar situation revealed that the chamber floor had in fact collapsed through the roof of another chamber which lay directly below. This underlying chamber, tomb NE25 (see below), had presumably been cut after the completion of tomb NE20, since, although it is just conceivable that the roof of NE25 could have been formed without bringing down the floor of NE20, it would certainly have been impossible to stand, or put any weight, on the floor of NE20 without falling straight through into NE25, had that tomb already existed.

The original floor of NE20 was, as previously stated, represented only by a narrow shelf, approximately 35–40 cm wide, running around the perimeter of the central depression. This bore a 15–20 cm thick layer of fairly compact, orange-brown silt, mixed with a few, generally small, pieces of marl from the roof. At the eastern (entrance) end of the chamber, somewhat more of the floor survived, and here, in addition to the silt and marl fragments, lay a number of blocking stones, which had fallen into the chamber or had perhaps been dragged in by the collapse of the floor.

The chamber itself was approximately, and irregularly, circular in plan, measuring 3.00 m north-south by 2.70 m east-west. The roof was gently domed, reaching a maximum height of 1.50 m at the centre of the chamber (assuming the floor to have been level).

Investigation of the interior of the chamber involved the excavation of the deposits associated with the surviving floor, coupled with the careful removal of the upper filling of tomb NE25, which, it was inferred, might contain elements of the NE20 tomb deposit which had fallen through the floor.

Two vessels, a loop-handled amphoriskos (NE20.2) and a four-spouted lamp (NE20.3), were found on the remnants of the floor on the south side

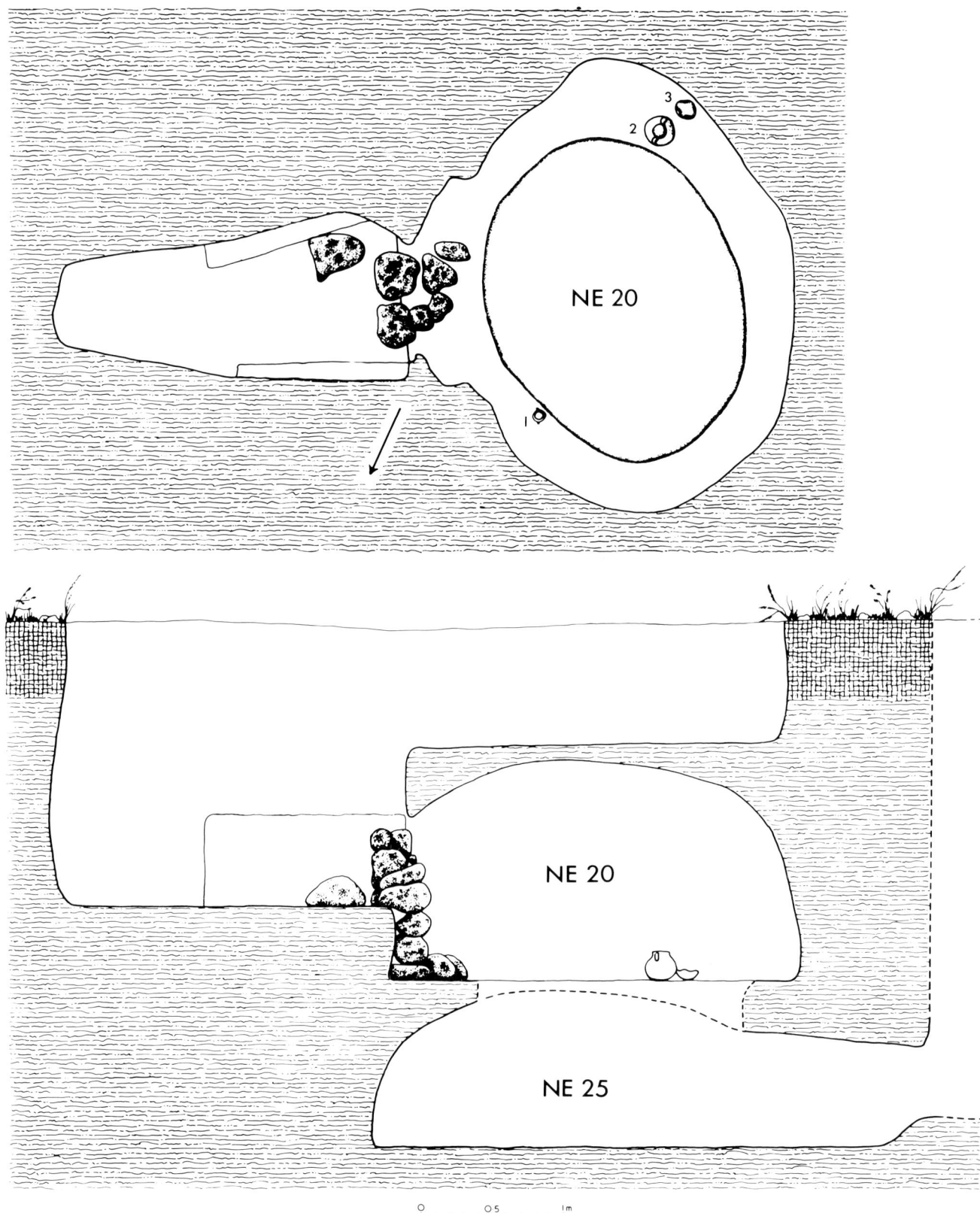

Fig. 29a Tombs NE20 and NE25

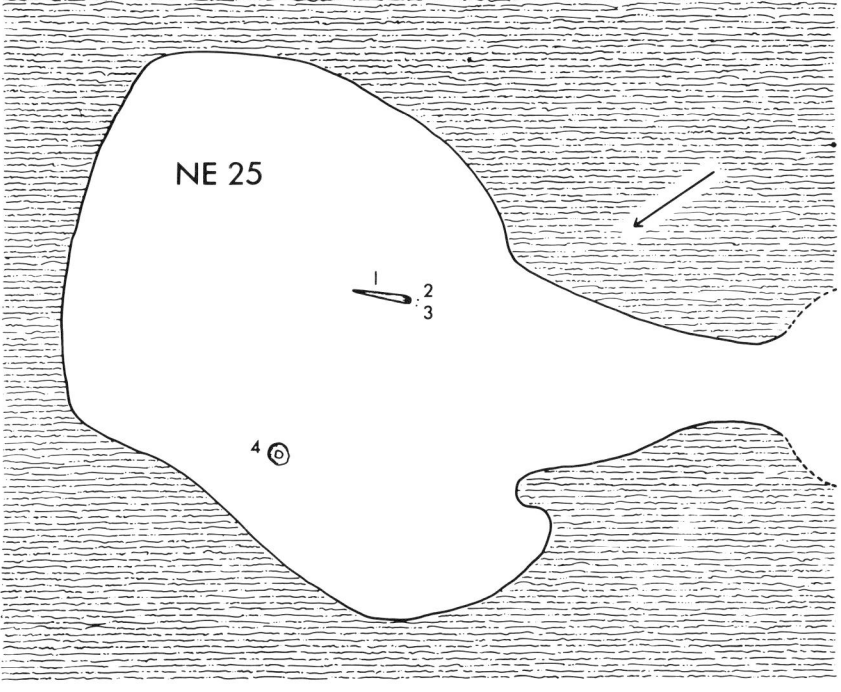

Fig. 29b Tomb NE25

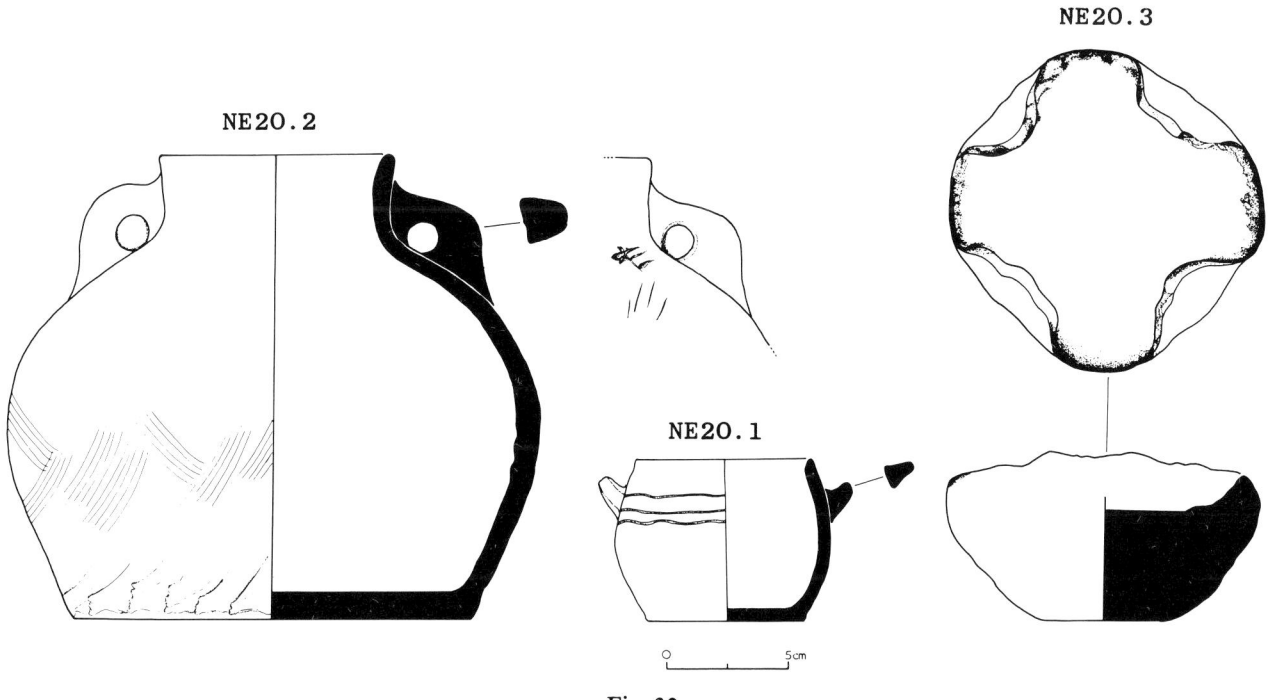

Fig. 30

of the chamber. These were almost certainly in their original positions. The upper fill of tomb NE25 contained a few fragments of bone which must surely have derived from tomb NE20. These, unfortunately, could only be identified as human. Also found within this upper layer of collapsed fill was a small cup (NE20.1), which again must be attributed to the funerary deposit of tomb NE20.

Contents

NE20.1   Cup

Technique: Handmade. *Paste*: 7.5YR 'reddish yellow' 7/6; very many small-medium sand and lime, few medium ceramic; no core; hard. *Surface* (Interior): as paste. (Exterior): as paste; incised lines on body.

NE20.2   Loop-handled amphoriskos

Technique: Handmade. *Paste*: 10R 'light red' 6/6; some medium-large lime and ceramic; no core; hard. *Surface* (Interior): as paste. (Exterior): 7.5YR 'pink' 8/4 wash; coarse diagonal combing on body; incised potter's mark on shoulder.

NE20.3   Four-spouted lamp

Technique: Handmade. *Paste*: 5YR 'pink' 7/4; few large lime; no core; hard. *Surface* (Interior and Exterior): as paste; blackened all around rim.

TOMB NE21
North slope Hill 2
Orientation: W–E

Judging from the disposition of the tombs and their orientations, it would seem reasonable to assume that the north slope of Hill 2 existed at the time of tomb cutting. Certainly, three of the four tombs found there during a surface scraping operation (NE21, 23 and 24) would appear to have been dug into an existing hill slope (the situation with regard to NE22 may be slightly different, see below). In such a position, they would probably have been approached either by means of a semi-shaft, shallow on the downslope, or directly from a horizontally cut threshold, in the same way as those tombs located on the east slope of Hill 6 or the west slope of Hill 4 (above).

Unfortunately, however, in the case of tomb NE21, all evidence relating to the approach to the chamber had been lost through erosion, and all that was found was part of the chamber itself, consisting of about 50 per cent of the floor together with associated remnants of the rear and side walls. From these surviving remains, it can be suggested that the chamber was originally very small and sub-circular, with an approximate diameter of 75 cm. The curvature of the rear wall indicated that the roof would have been quite steeply domed, reaching a maximum height of perhaps 50 cm.

The excavated fill consisted of decayed marl debris from the collapse of the chamber roof, mixed with topsoil. Below this was a thin (5 cm) layer of fine yet compact orange-brown silt, representing a phase of water-laid deposition prior to the collapse of the roof.

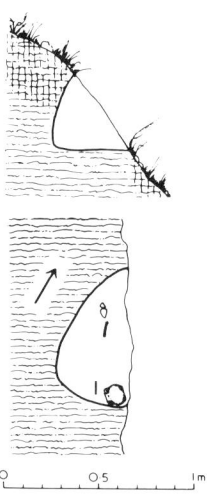

Fig. 31 Tomb NE21

Within this layer were found the fragmentary, partial and poorly preserved remains of a single individual, which were identified as those of a juvenile (sex indeterminable), aged 1–2 years. The positions of the few surviving bones suggested that the body might have been interred with its head towards the west. A loop-handled amphoriskos (NE21.1) was found on the south side of the chamber, slightly elevated above the floor surface within the silt layer.

Contents

NE21.1   Loop-handled amphoriskos

Technique: Handmade with wheelmade rim. *Paste*: 10YR 'dark grey' 4/1; many small wadi gravel, ceramic and lime; no core; hard. *Surface* (Interior): as paste. (Exterior): 5Y 'light grey' 7/2 wash.

Tombs in the north-east sector

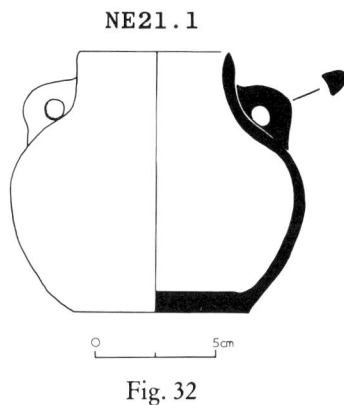

Fig. 32

TOMB NE22   Pl. IIB
North slope Hill 2
Orientation: S–N

Tomb NE22 was the only tomb discovered during the 1984 season which demonstrably dated to a period other than Early Bronze Age IV, containing as it did grave goods clearly attributable to the Proto-Urban period. Like the later EBIV tombs (NE21, 23 and 24), tomb NE22 was undoubtedly dug into what was then an existing hill slope. Certainly, there is no reason to believe that the wadi between the north slope of Hill 2 and the south slope of Hill 1 had formed during the seven hundred or so years separating the two periods. Nevertheless, a certain amount of erosion would surely have taken place during this intervening time, a factor which, when taken into account with the generally good state of preservation of the tomb chamber, must indicate that tomb NE22 had been dug substantially deeper or further back into the hill slope than the later tombs. In such a circumstance, the approach to the chamber might have been somewhat different from the usually encountered semi-shaft or horizontally cut threshold. For either of these methods would have involved the cutting away of an extremely large wedge of material from the hill slope, leaving an approach which would have been very long indeed. It would seem more likely, therefore, that in the case of this tomb the chamber would have been approached from a true vertical shaft, dug down, nevertheless, into the side of the hill. This remains speculation, however, for unfortunately no traces of the approach, nor of the chamber entrance had survived, these having been totally lost through erosion. As found, during the surface scraping operation of the north slope of Hill 2, tomb NE22 was represented by a roughly rectangular feature, which on excavation proved to be the fully preserved lower part of the chamber only.

The shaft and chamber entrance would probably have been located on the north (down-slope) side, but as stated, there were found to be no surviving traces of these. Indeed, it is interesting to note that the chamber wall on this north side was found preserved to a height of 25 cm, indicating that the entrance (and base of the shaft) would have been quite high in relation to the chamber floor. A number of stones, presumably from the original entrance blocking, were in fact found in the interior fill, but, interestingly, these were situated towards the centre of the chamber. This observation, coupled with the absence of any positive evidence for an entrance on the north side, raises the possibility that access to the chamber might instead have been gained by means of a vertical shaft opening directly through the roof.

The chamber itself had been finely cut. The trapezoidal ground plan had been realised with great precision, and the walls and floor were perfectly

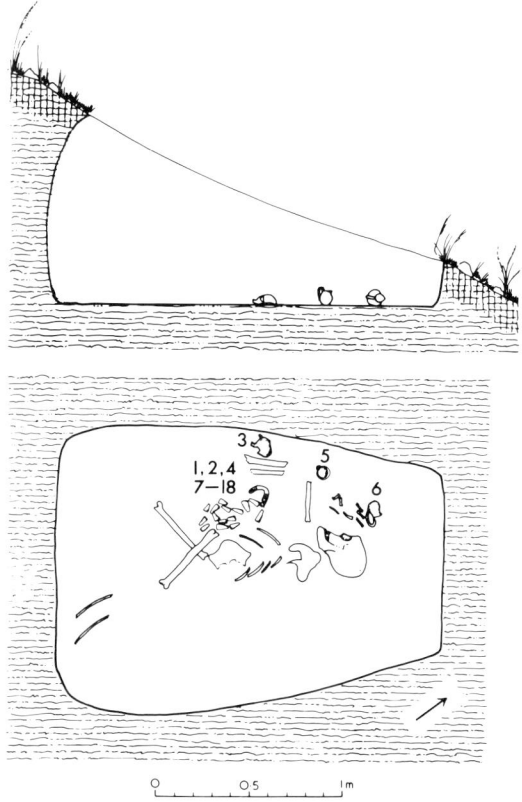

Fig. 33 Tomb NE22

NE22.1, 2, 4, 7-18

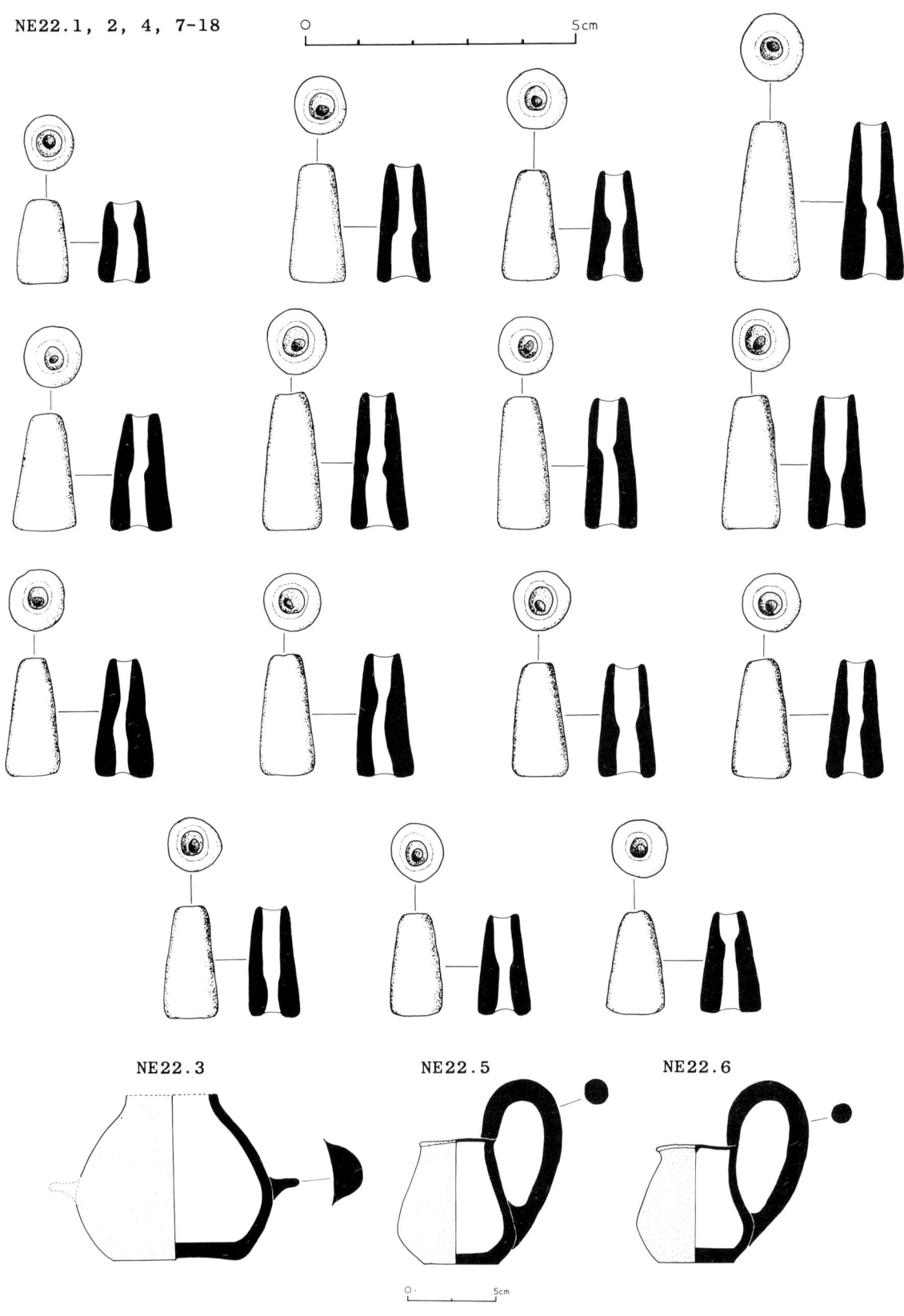

NE22.3   NE22.5   NE22.6

Fig. 34

smooth and regular. Attention had been paid to the corners, which had been carefully carved to produce smoothly rounded angles. From the surviving elevations, the walls of the chamber would appear to have been almost vertical, and only that of the best-preserved southern side showed traces of an incurve defining the transition to the roof. The chamber was quite small, measuring 2.00 m north-south by 1.25 m at the southern end and 0.90 m at the narrower northern end. To judge from the sharpness of the angle of curvature at the top of the southern wall, the roof would probably have been nearly flat, or only slightly domed, producing a maximum chamber height in the order of 1.00 to 1.10 m.

As excavated, the fill of the chamber consisted, for the upper part, of soft, reddish-brown soil with discontinuous layers of silt. Below this was found a dense layer, 15–20 cm thick, of marl debris, derived presumably from the collapse of the chamber roof. Between this and the floor of the chamber was a 10–12 cm thick layer of compact brown silt, and it was within and below this material that the funerary deposits were found.

Altogether, the remains of three individuals were found, but only one of these was represented by a coherent skeletal assemblage. Occupying a more or less central position within the tomb was found a generally articulated, yet incomplete skeleton (skeleton A), which, on analysis, proved to be that of a male aged 25–30 years. The body had been placed in a flexed position on the right side, orientated north-south and facing west. The right arm was drawn up in front of the face, with the hand clasping the handle of a loop-handled juglet (NE22.6). It was possible to estimate the stature of this individual as $1.72 \text{ m} \pm 0.0879$ ($c.5'7''$).

In addition to the bones associated with or attributable to skeleton A, a number of others were also encountered which could not be related to it. These were found predominantly on the south and east sides of the chamber, where they appeared as disarticulated concentrations. Examination revealed that these bones could be resolved into two further individuals, one an adult female and the other a juvenile (sex indeterminable), aged 10–15 years. Although referred to as skeletons B and C respectively, it should be noted that the distinction is artificial, and does not represent the situation in the tomb itself, in which the bones of the two skeletons were found jumbled together.

The relationship between the three individuals can be suggested by reference to their relative conditions, and it would seem likely that there had been at least two (possibly three) phases of interment. For the disarticulated and confused state of the bones of skeletons B and C must be seen as having resulted from a secondary disturbance, the cause of which can most plausibly be explained by the subsequent interment of a further individual, represented by skeleton A. Such a sequential relationship is further indicated by the disposition of the bones of skeletons B and C, which were found close to the sides of the chamber, as if displaced there by the need to create a space in the centre of the tomb for the placement of skeleton A. Whether skeletons B and C represent contemporary or successive burials cannot be established.

Apart from the clear association of the loop-handled juglet, NE22.6, with skeleton A, no other certain attributions can be made with regard to the remaining grave goods. A second loop-handled juglet, NE22.5, was found close to the western wall of the chamber, and just to the south of this was a small, broken and incomplete ledge-handled jar (NE22.3). This latter fragmentary vessel was found amidst a concentration of bones attributed to skeletons B/C, and this association, together with its poor state of preservation, suggests perhaps that it should be related to the earlier phase of interment. The most interesting find from tomb NE22 was undoubtedly the collection of fifteen conical calcite beads (NE22.1, 2, 4, 7–18), which were found on the west side of the chamber. These were lying in what must have been their original pattern, consisting of three rows of five (see Pl. IIB: note that two of the beads in the central row were removed before the photograph was taken). Although these beads were found close to the lower jaw of skeleton B, the fact that they had clearly not been disturbed in any way would make it seem more likely that they should be associated with the later interment, represented by skeleton A. The beads were in fact found quite close to the pelvis of skeleton A, and it might be suggested, therefore, that they constituted not a necklace, but rather a type of waist ornament.

Contents

NE22.1, 2, 4, 7–18   Beads
　　　　　　　　　　　(possibly from a belt)

Calcite; bored from both ends with cylindrical drill.

NE22.3   Ledge-handled jar

Technique: Handmade. *Paste*: 5YR 'reddish yellow' 7/6; some medium sand and ceramic, few organic; light grey core; hard. *Surface* (Interior): as paste. (Exterior): 2.5YR 'red' 4/6 slip, burnished.

NE22.5   Loop-handled juglet

Technique: Handmade. *Paste*: 7.5YR 'light brown' 6/4; many small-medium sand and ceramic, few large ceramic; light grey core; hard. *Surface* (Interior): as paste. (Exterior): 2.5YR 'red' 5/6 slip, vertical burnishing.

NE22.6   Loop-handled juglet   (Pl. XIIIA)

Technique: Handmade. *Paste*: 7.5YR 'pink' 7/4; many small-medium sand, ceramic and lime; light grey core; hard. *Surface* (Interior): as paste. (Exterior): 2.5YR 'red' 5/6 slip, vertical burnishing.

TOMB NE23
North slope Hill 2
Orientation: S–N

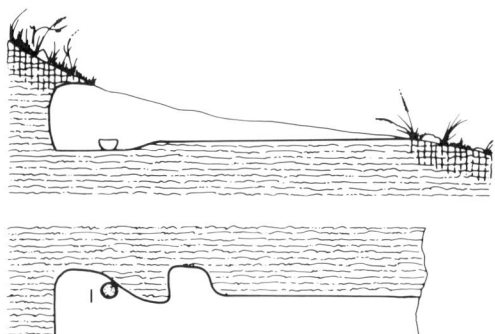

Fig. 35 Tomb NE23

This small tomb of unusual form was found just to the south of tomb NE21. The slope of the hill was quite shallow at this point, and although the tomb had sustained some damage through erosion, the ground plan was found to be well preserved. Removal of the fairly small amount of loose fill and collapsed marl debris revealed a long narrow approach, 1.05 m by 50 cm, at the far (southern) end of which had been cut two opposing niches, roughly rectangular in plan and measuring 20 cm by 16 cm on the west side and 25 cm by 15 cm on the east. Beyond these niches, the approach developed into the chamber proper, the transition marked by a slight constriction and a barely perceptible lowering of the floor surface (less than 5 cm).

The chamber itself was extremely small and bell-shaped in plan, measuring 55 cm in length and 58 cm across the rear wall. The roof was well preserved at the rear of the chamber, and appeared to have been cut horizontally rather than domed. The height of the roof was only 34 cm above the floor.

No blocking was found separating the approach from the chamber, and the excavated fill produced no evidence to suggest that there had been any at this point. This lack of a sealing can perhaps be explained by assuming that, in this case, the chamber had been entered by means of a horizontally cut tunnel and the blocking had originally been set directly over the opening on the hill slope. This method of entry is indeed indicated by the structure of the approach itself, for the long narrow form is hard to reconcile with the concept of either a semi-shaft or a horizontally cut threshold, and is far more suggestive of a tunnel.

The chamber contained a few scattered and fragmentary bones, which could only be identified as those of a juvenile (sex indeterminable), aged 5 years or less. A small pottery cup was found against the south wall, lying directly upon the floor surface.

Contents

NE23.1   Cup

Technique: Handmade, upper part finished on wheel. *Paste*: 7.5YR 'light brown' 6/4; very many very small sand and ceramic; no core; hard. *Surface* (Interior): as paste. (Exterior): 10YR 'white' 8/2 wash; light horizontal combing around rim, vertical combing below to base.

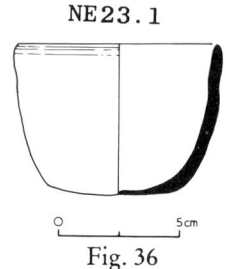

Fig. 36

TOMB NE24
East slope Hill 6
Orientation: W–E

This extensively eroded tomb was found just to the south of tomb NE7 (see above). Unlike that tomb, however, very little had survived, and tomb NE24 was represented only by a part of its chamber (perhaps 80 per cent), together with remnants of its rear and side walls. No traces of the approach or entrance had been preserved, but a single large stone found in the interior fill of the chamber suggested that it had been provided with a stone blocking.

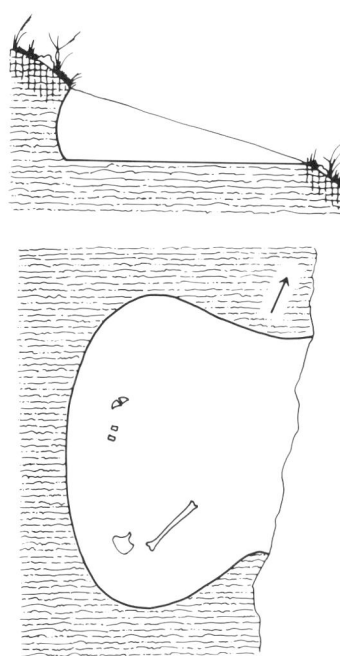

Fig. 37 Tomb NE24

The chamber itself was irregular in plan, most closely approximating to oval, and measured 1.60 m north-south by 1.25 m east-west (reconstructed). Judging by the surviving curvature of the rear wall, the roof would probably have been domed, with a maximum height of about 50 cm towards the centre of the chamber.

The excavated fill consisted of topsoil and decayed marl debris, resting on an 8–10 cm thick layer of finely divided but compact reddish-brown silt. This silt had been laid down, probably as a result of seasonal water intrusion and pooling, prior to the collapse of the chamber roof. Beneath the silt and lying on the chamber floor were found the fragmentary remains of a single individual. Sufficient was preserved to indicate that the body had been buried in an articulated condition, and had probably been placed in a flexed position, orientated north-south and facing east. Unfortunately, the remains could only be identified as those of an adult (sex indeterminable). No grave goods were found.

TOMB NE25
Surface Hill 2
Orientation: NE–SW

(The plan and section of this tomb are included on Figs 29a and b, with tomb NE20)

Tomb NE25 was discovered during the course of excavation of tomb NE20, the chamber floor of which had collapsed into the immediately underlying chamber of another tomb. For the reasons given above (see discussion of tomb NE20), it would seem probable that this lower tomb, NE25, postdated tomb NE20 in construction.

Having completed the excavation of tomb NE20 proper, and having carefully isolated and removed those deposits which formed the upper filling of tomb NE25 but which nevertheless clearly belonged to tomb NE20 (see above), the remaining fill of the chamber of tomb NE25 was removed. This consisted mainly of loose greyish-brown soil and decayed marl debris. Beneath this, the chamber floor was encountered directly, with no intervening layer of silt. This strongly suggests that very little time had elapsed between interment in tomb NE25 and the collapse of the chamber roof, which was undoubtedly caused by the instability created by the construction of tomb NE20.

When fully cleared, the plan of the chamber could be seen to be extremely irregular, and can only be described as amorphous. It was quite large, measuring 2.50 m north-south by 3.20 m east-west. Part of the roof was found to be preserved on the north side, where it appeared as gently doming towards the centre of the chamber. The maximum height would have been approximately 1.05 m.

Access to the chamber was on the south-west side. The chamber was connected to the entrance by means of a low, rather long, tunnel, similar in many respects to that encountered in tomb NE15 (see above). This was 70–75 cm in height, and level with the top of the

Tombs in the north-east sector

entrance, but had been cut about 20 cm lower than the entrance threshold, corresponding with the level of the chamber floor. In plan, this connecting tunnel was funnel-shaped, initially preserving the dimensions of the entrance but then gradually widening northwards towards the chamber, at the transition to which it reached its maximum width of 1.15 m.

The entrance-way itself had vertical sides and was arched at the top. It measured 48 cm in height and 40 cm across the base. No blocking was found sealing the entrance, but had this consisted of stones, these might well have fallen back into the base of the shaft, which was not excavated beyond a small probe undertaken merely to establish its presence. Although it was therefore known to exist, it proved impossible, in fact, to identify the top of the shaft on the ground surface.

The funerary deposits associated with tomb NE25 were found to be extremely poorly preserved. A scatter of bone fragments was found towards the centre of the chamber, but the position and orientation of the deceased could not be recognised, and the remains could only be identified as those of an adult (sex indeterminable). Associated with the bone scatter was found a copper dagger (NE25.1) with four rivet holes and rivets still in position. Two further rivets (NE25.2–3) were found side by side approximately 12 cm in line from the dagger hilt. As with the daggers found in tombs NE8 (above) and SE1 (below), the positioning of the rivets suggests the method by which the handle might have been attached to the blade (see Chapter 3). The only other object found in the tomb chamber was a stone digging-stick weight (NE25.4). This might have been intended as a funerary gift, but on the other hand it might simply have been a tool used and discarded during the cutting of the tomb and left behind.

Contents

NE25.1   Dagger

Arsenical copper; four rivets in position on hilt.

NE25.2–3   Two rivets

Copper/copper alloy.

NE25.4   Digging-stick weight

Orange sandstone.

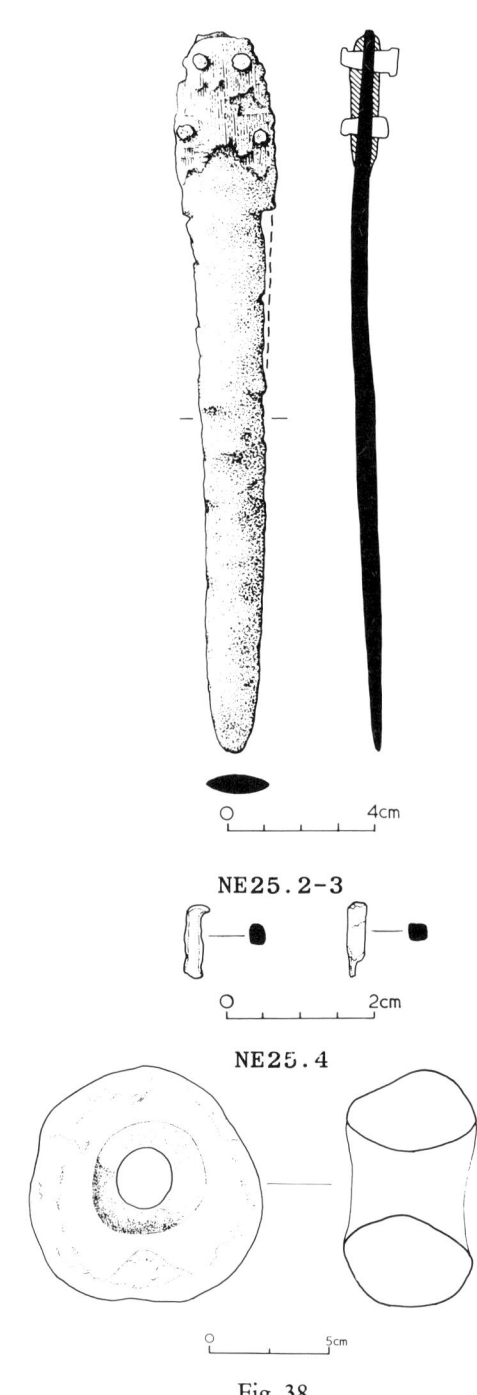

Fig. 38

Tombs in the south-east sector

TOMB SE1 Pl. VIIA–B
West slope Hill 114
Orientation: W–E

From the disposition of the tombs found on the west slope of Hill 114 (Pl. VIB), and from their relative orientations, it is clear that the wadi at present separating Hills 113 and 114 did not exist in antiquity, and that these two hills, at the time of tomb cutting, formed a single continuous whole. The process of collapse of the tomb chambers situated here might well itself have contributed to, or been directly responsible for, the formation of the wadi. Especially relevant in this respect is tomb SE3, the chamber of which, to judge from the scale and proportions of the shaft and entrance, must have been monumental in size (see below).

A surface scraping of the somewhat steep western slope of Hill 114 revealed three significant interruptions in the marl strata, the most southerly of which proved to be the collapsed chamber of tomb SE1.

Initially, a large, roughly circular feature was isolated, showing as dull greyish-orange against the pale brownish-cream solid marl. Excavation revealed that the feature was composed of heavily weathered, decayed marl rubble, the removal of which began to uncover the fully preserved lower part of a tomb chamber. Beneath the decayed marl rubble, larger slabs of marl appeared, which had derived, presumably, from the collapse of the chamber roof. Mixed with the marl slabs were dense prismatic blocks of clay. These had come from a broad (50 cm) band of clay, clearly visible running through the marl strata above the preserved chamber, and into which the chamber roof must, therefore, have been partly cut. Below this mixed deposit and overlying the chamber floor was a thin (5–10 cm) layer of compact reddish-brown silt. The insubstantial depth of this silt deposit perhaps suggests that only a short period of time had elapsed between interment and the collapse of the chamber roof. The silt was clayey and appeared to have been water-laid, presumably as a result of intrusive rainwater.

The chamber of tomb SE1 was sub-circular in plan and quite large, with a maximum diameter of 4.0 m (north-west–south-east). Parts of the roof were preserved on all sides, and these suggested that it had been gently domed, reaching a maximum height of about 1.35 m towards the centre of the chamber.

The entrance to the chamber was on the east side, and six large river boulders were found in position forming the blocking. These did not extend to the arched top of the entrance, and the sealing here had been completed with a packing of dense greyish-blue clay. When the blocking was removed, it became apparent that the same material had been used to cement in the spaces between the stones on the exterior (shaft-side) face. The entrance itself had been neatly cut, and was small and arched, measuring 90 cm in height and 80 cm across the base. There was no threshold, the base of the entrance having been cut on the same level as that of the chamber floor.

The fill from the lower part of the shaft was carefully removed in order to ascertain its plan and dimensions. The fill was fairly compact, and consisted of pale greyish-brown soil containing many small chips of marl. This suggests that, following the sealing of the entrance, the shaft had been back-filled using the material removed during its excavation. Further evidence for this process of back-filling may be adduced from the presence in the chamber, in the area immediately in front of the entrance-way, of a thin (less than 1.5 cm thick) layer of material, identical to that encountered in the shaft. This material had presumably seeped through gaps in the entrance sealing, fanning out beyond it, into the chamber itself. That it had been deposited as a result of deliberate back-filling is suggested by the fact that it lay directly above the chamber floor and below the layer of silt. It must, therefore, have been deposited very soon after the sealing of the entrance, before the silt had had time to accumulate.

The base of the shaft was apsidal in plan, measuring 1.25 m east-west and 1.40 m along the straight western side. The remainder of the shaft was not cleared, but the top was located on the surface of Hill 114, where it appeared as an approximately square feature (side 70 cm), pale greyish-brown against the somewhat more yellowish topsoil. The depth of the preserved shaft could, therefore, be calculated as 6.15 m. A discrepancy in vertical alignment between the excavated bottom and the exposed top of the shaft suggests that it must have been cut on a slight slope, inclining westwards from top to bottom. Additionally, it would seem likely that the shaft had been stepped in some way, probably on the eastern side, as shown on the reconstructed elevation.

The funerary deposits of tomb SE1 were found within and below the thin layer of silt covering the chamber floor. The fragmentary remains of two individuals were found, both in extremely poor condition. Water disturbance had clearly been responsible for extensive damage to the skeletal remains, and no information could be adduced concerning the postures or orientations of the deceased, nor of the type of practice (primary or secondary) involved. The two individuals were represented by two clusters of bones, one towards the north-east side of the chamber (skeleton A) and the other close to the wall on the north-west side (skeleton B). Skeleton A was identified as that of an adult, probably female, and skeleton B that of an adult, probably male. In the absence of any evidence to the contrary, it must be assumed that these two individuals had been interred at the same time.

With regard to the grave goods, although it would seem unlikely that the positions of the copper objects had changed since the time of their placement, it is clear that most of the pottery vessels had been moved from their original positions by the action of water. In all cases except that of the ledge-handled storejar (SE1.15), the vessels had been carried up to various levels within the silt layer as it gradually built up. It is therefore of course impossible to attribute the various finds to either skeleton A or skeleton B.

Altogether, three ledge-handled storejars were found, one of which (SE1.15), as mentioned above, was standing upright, close to the wall on the south-west side of the chamber, in what might have been its original position. To the north of this vessel, close to the centre of the west wall, was found a second example (SE1.2), lying on its side. The third storejar (SE1.1) was found, also lying on its side, on the north-west side of the chamber, close to skeleton B, with which it might possibly have been associated. Between storejars SE1.15 and SE1.2, two further vessels were found close to the chamber wall, a loop-

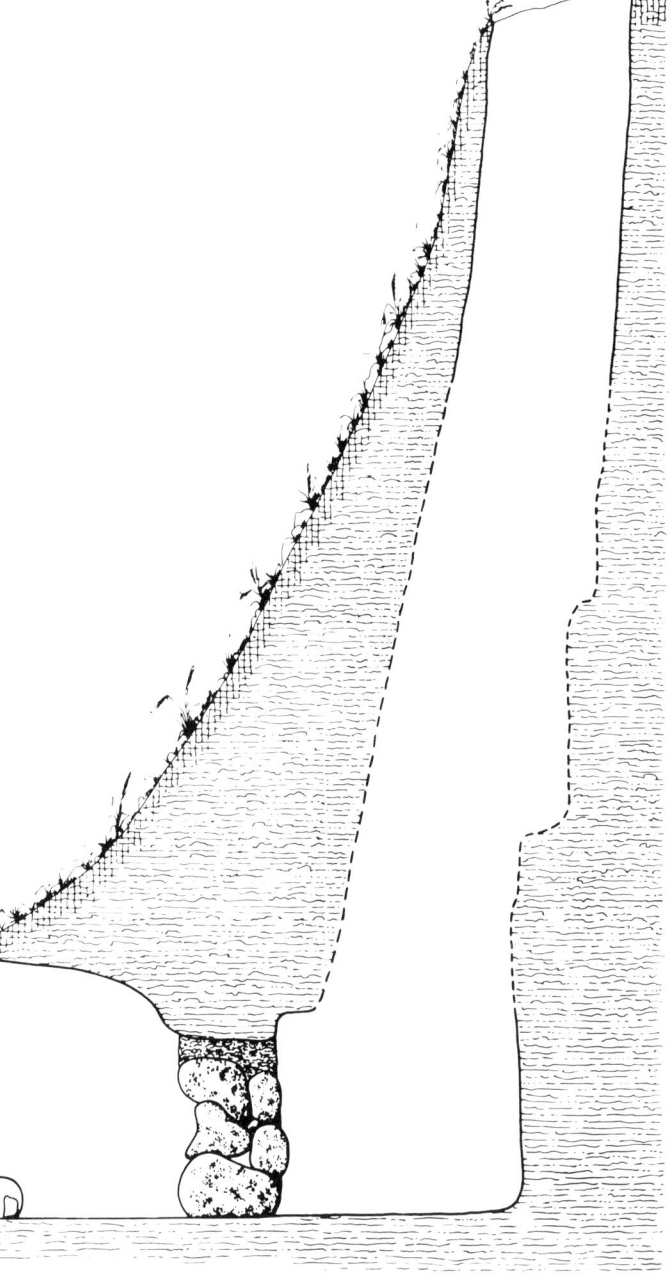

Fig. 39a Tomb SE1

Tombs in the south-east sector

handled amphoriskos (SE1.4) and a small cup (SE1.3). Both these vessels were lying on their sides, as was a second cup (SE1.5), which was found to the east of the above vessels, towards the centre of the tomb. On the east side of the chamber, just to the south of the entrance, were two four-spouted lamps (SE1.8 and SE1.11). These were found upright, but within the silt layer above the floor surface.

Close to the centre of the chamber was found a bronze dagger (SE1.6) with four rivets in position on the hilt. As in the cases of the daggers from tombs NE8 and NE25 (see above), two additional rivets were found, side by side, approximately 12 cm in line from the hilt, and as stated below (Chapter 3), this observation provides a suggestion as to the method of handle attachment. Just to the south of the dagger were found two further metal implements, a javelin (SE1.12) and a small awl (SE1.14), and together with these were two disc-shaped carnelian beads (SE1.13).

On the north side of the chamber, a small, roughly semicircular feature was found cut into the wall at floor level. Measuring only 20 cm in height and 18 cm across the base, it was at first assumed to be a type of niche. Excavation of the compact silty fill revealed within it a lamp of a most unusual design (SE1.7), in essence a four-spouted lamp, but with a lower hollow chamber connecting to a side-spout. Another example of this hitherto unrecorded type of lamp was recovered from tomb SE9 (see below), and the two vessels are discussed in greater detail in Chapter 3.

Continued excavation of the 'niche' demonstrated that it was in fact more in the nature of a 'window', forming a link between tomb SE1 and a second tomb chamber lying directly to the north (called tomb SE1A).

Contents

SE1.1   Ledge-handled storejar

Technique: Handmade with wheelmade rim. *Paste*:

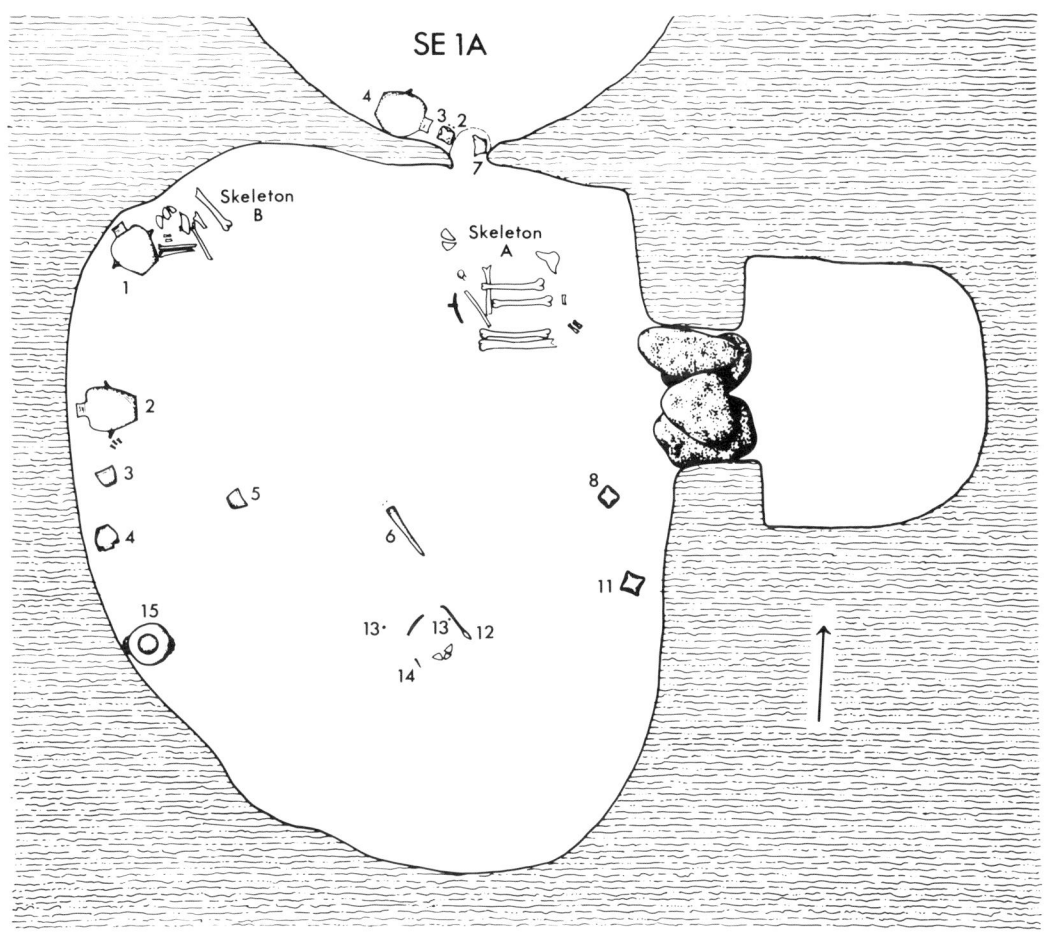

Fig. 39b Tomb SE1

Fig. 40a

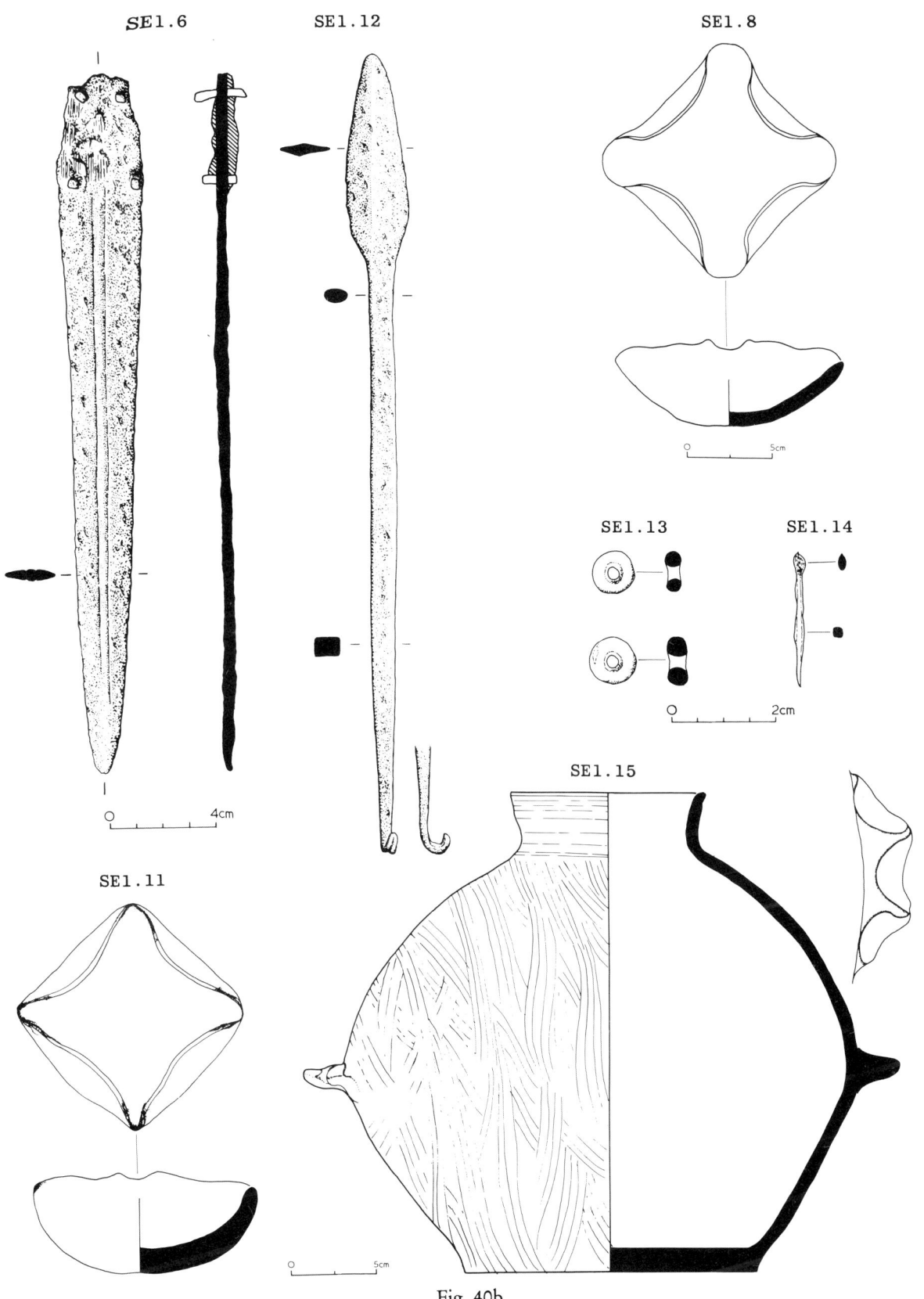

Fig. 40b

2.5YR 'red' 5/6; many small-medium sand, ceramic and lime; light grey core; hard. *Surface* (Interior): as paste. (Exterior): 2.5Y 'white' 8/2 wash; band of denticulate moulding at base of neck; diagonal combing on body.

SE1.2   Ledge-handled storejar

Technique: Handmade with wheelmade rim. *Paste*: 2.5YR 'red' 5/6; very many very small sand and lime, some small ceramic; no core; hard. *Surface* (Interior): as paste. (Exterior): 2.5Y 'white' 8/2 wash; diagonal combing on body.

SE1.3   Cup

Technique: Handmade, upper part finished on wheel. *Paste*: 7.5YR 'pink' 8/4; many small-medium sand, ceramic and lime; no core; hard. *Surface* (Interior and Exterior): 10YR 'white' 8/2 wash.

SE1.4   Loop-handled amphoriskos

Technique: Handmade with wheelmade rim. *Paste*: 2.5YR 'light red' 6/6; very many very small wadi gravel, ceramic and lime; no core; hard. *Surface* (Interior): as paste. (Exterior): 2.5Y 'white' 8/2 wash.

SE1.5   Cup

Technique: Handmade, upper part finished on wheel. *Paste*: 5YR 'reddish yellow' 7/6; many very small sand, some small ceramic and lime; no core; hard. *Surface* (Interior): as paste. (Exterior): 10YR 'white' 8/2 wash; vertically shaved.

SE1.6   Dagger   (Pl. XIIc)

Bronze; four rivets in position on hilt. Two additional rivets found in close proximity (not numbered separately).

SE1.7   Side-spouted lamp   (Pl. XIV)

Technique: Handmade. *Paste*: 2.5YR 'light red' 6/6; many medium-large sand and ceramic, few medium lime; no core; hard. *Surface* (Interior): as paste. (Exterior): 5YR 'pink' 8/3 wash; blackened on all four spouts of upper bowl.

SE1.8   Four-spouted lamp

Technique: Handmade. *Paste*: 7.5YR 'pink' 7/4; very many small-medium sand and ceramic, some medium lime; grey core; hard. *Surface* (Interior and Exterior): as paste; extensively blackened all around rim.

SE1.11   Four-spouted lamp

Technique: Handmade. *Paste*: 5YR 'reddish yellow' 7/6; very many small-medium sand, ceramic and lime; no core; hard. *Surface* (Interior and Exterior): as paste; blackened on all four spouts.

SE1.12   Javelin   (Pl. XIIA)

Arsenical copper.

SE1.13   Two beads

Carnelian; bored from both ends with conical drill.

SE1.14   Awl

Copper/copper alloy.

SE1.15   Ledge-handled storejar   (Pl. XIIIB)

Technique: Handmade with wheelmade rim. *Paste*: 2.5YR 'red' 5/6; many small-medium sand and lime; no core; hard. *Surface* (Interior): as paste. (Exterior): 5Y 'white' 8/2 wash; irregular diagonal combing on body.

TOMB SE1A

Very little investigation could be undertaken with regard to this tomb chamber, other than could be accomplished by reaching through the 'window' from the north wall of tomb SE1 and by probing in a limited way the space beyond. Apart from a narrow channel following the perimeter of the walls, the remainder of the chamber was filled with a heavy deposit of marl blocks and debris, indicating that the roof had completely collapsed.

As far as could be judged, the chamber appeared to be smaller than that of tomb SE1, and was probably circular in plan, with a diameter of about 2.5 m. Immediately beyond the 'window', on the west side, against the south wall, was found a four-spouted lamp (SE1A.3), and next to it a ledge-handled storejar (SE1A.4). The lamp was found to contain four disc-shaped carnelian beads (SE1A.2), similar to the two from SE1, and a fifth bead (also numbered SE1A.2) was found close by on the floor. A few small bone fragments were retrieved, but these could only be identified as human.

Tombs in the south-east sector

The relationship between the two chambers (SE1 and SE1A) is puzzling, for it is certain that the tiny window linking them could never have served as a connecting entrance-way. Nor was any trace of such an entrance found at any point along the north wall of tomb SE1. The chamber of tomb SE1A must therefore have had its own entrance and shaft, the latter presumably cut from the hilltop, somewhere to the north of that of tomb SE1. Nevertheless, it is clear that the two chambers had been conceived of as elements of an integral structure, for the window connecting both chambers at exactly floor level argues for a carefully planned construction, rather than the accidental intrusion of a niche into a pre-existing adjacent chamber. The unusual lamp, SE1.7 (=SE1A.1), had obviously been carefully placed to provide illumination for both chambers.

Contents

SE1A.2   Five beads

Carnelian; bored from both ends with conical drill.

SE1A.3   Four-spouted lamp

Technique: Handmade. *Paste*: 7.5YR 'pink' 7/4; many small-medium sand, ceramic and lime; no core; hard. *Surface* (Interior and Exterior): 2.5Y 'white' 8/2 wash; no blackening.

SE1A.4   Ledge-handled storejar

Technique: Handmade with wheelmade rim. *Paste*: 10YR 'grey' 6/1; very many medium sand, wadi gravel, ceramic and lime; no core; hard. *Surface* (Interior): as paste. (Exterior): 2.5Y 'light grey' 7/2 wash; band of tooth impression at base of neck; coarse and irregular combing on body.

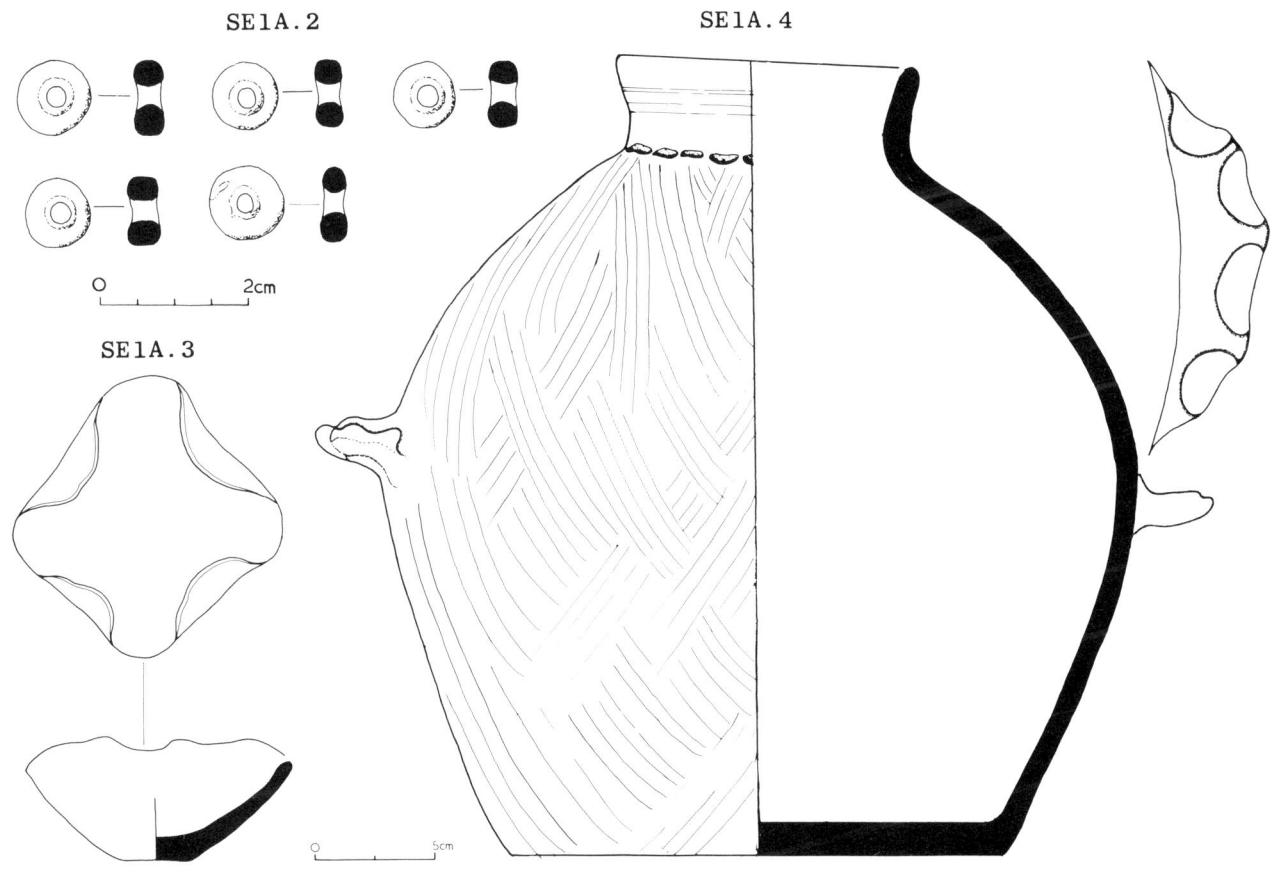

Fig. 41

TOMB SE2   Pls VIIIA–B and IXA
West slope Hill 114
Orientation: E–W Phase 1; W–E Phase 2

Tomb SE2, lying to the south of tomb SE1, provides one of the clearest and yet most unusual examples of re-use found during the 1984 season. It was discovered during the surface scraping operation of the west slope of Hill 114, when an interruption in the marl strata revealed the presence of a tomb shaft. Excavation of the relatively loose fill of eroded marl debris and topsoil produced the complete ground plan of a rectangular shaft, measuring 1.25 m east-west by 95 cm north-south. The upper part of the shaft had been truncated by erosion, and it was only preserved to a depth of 56 cm on the western (downslope) side. On the eastern side it was preserved to a depth of 2.30 m, and close to the south-east corner, on the south side of the shaft, at a height of 1.50 m above the base, was found a small and shallow niche-like depression. This had most probably been cut to provide a foothold, and its presence in this position suggests that the original depth of the shaft might have been quite substantial.

The entrance to the chamber was on the eastern side of the shaft. At first it appeared to be filled with collapsed debris but otherwise unsealed, with the obvious implication that the tomb had been disturbed and possibly robbed. Closer examination, however, revealed that the filling was in fact a type of densely compacted cement, composed of crushed marl mixed with clay, deliberately applied as a blocking. The cement had been applied to lie within the entrance-way rather than to cover it, beginning some 27 cm back from the external face. It had been applied in three roughly horizontal layers, the lowermost consisting of large blocks of clay mixed with pieces of broken marl. This extended from the base to a height of about 35 cm. Above this had been laid a 12 cm band of very fine clay and marl chips, and above this, to the top of the entrance-way, the mixture consisted of medium-sized pieces of marl with very fine clay pieces.

The original cutting of the entrance-way had been undertaken rather carelessly. The southern side followed as a continuation the lower part of the shaft wall, and was consequently more or less vertical. The northern side, however, had been cut into the east wall of the shaft, and was irregular and slightly off vertical, sloping inwards towards the top. It also appeared that a mistake had occurred during the cutting of the low arched top, for this had been reasonably well executed on the south side, but on the north it had been started too low down, producing a step-like depression in the overall curve. As cut in this way, the entrance was quite wide – 85 cm across the base – and in height it measured exactly 1.0 m at its maximum on the south side.

Quite clearly, the poor cutting of the entrance-way had been considered unacceptable, for the northern side had been skilfully regularised using six courses of mud-brick. These had been carefully shaped and positioned to provide a vertical face on the northern side, and by setting the uppermost brick at an oblique angle, the irregularity in the arched top had been virtually removed. The overall effect of this construction had therefore been to produce a slightly narrower, but now almost perfectly symmetrical entrance-way, and it was this modified structure that had been sealed with the clay-marl cement.

As excavation proceeded to remove the clay/marl cement blocking, it became apparent that the mud-brick construction consisted of more than merely a vertical stack of single bricks, and that it in fact extended some 1.20 m along the north side of the entrance-way into the chamber itself. The lowermost course consisted of three very low bricks, each measuring 35–40 cm long by 22 cm wide and only 5 cm high. The second course had bricks of similar dimensions in plan, but thicker, measuring 13–15 cm in height. The third course had only two rather long bricks, each measuring about 50 cm in length: their widths and heights were similar to those of the bricks of the lower two courses. The three upper courses were each represented by only one brick, that held in the mouth of the entrance-way, but from pieces of mud-brick found within the chamber proper (see below), it may be assumed that these too originally extended as two-to-three brick courses along the northern wall. The surviving fourth-course brick measured 15 cm in height by 21 cm wide. Its eastern end had been broken, but its length must have been in excess of 25 cm. The fifth-course brick was similar but slightly thinner, measuring only 8 cm in height, and the uppermost brick was a rather odd shape, almost triangular in cross-section, and had obviously been made to fit into the space created by the irregular cutting of the entrance-way arch. The bricks themselves were of a deep red colour and appeared to contain very little straw temper. They were bonded

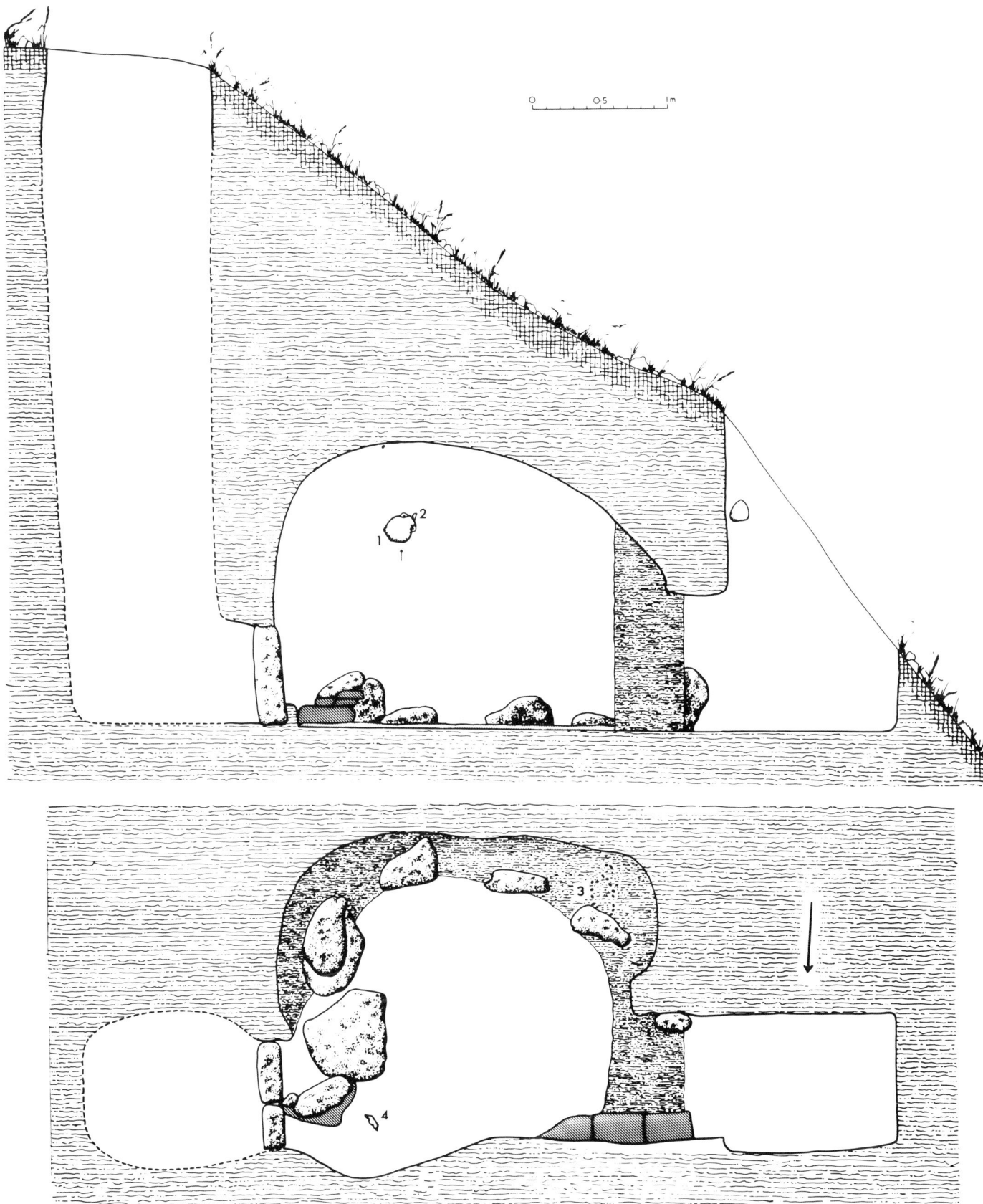

Fig. 42 Tomb SE2

together and to the side of the tomb by means of a cream-coloured mortar composed of finely crushed marl and shell. The final (easternmost) brick in each of the three fully preserved courses had been carefully shaped to give a smooth transition to the chamber wall.

The removal of the clay/marl blocking also fully uncovered a single stone (measuring approximately 45 × 30 × 15 cm), standing upright against the southern side of the entrance-way. This stone had been cemented into the blocking, but had been left partially protruding through the external face.

Beyond the clay-marl blocking, the chamber was seen to be completely filled with compact reddish-brown silt, which, to judge from the laminated nature of its structure, appeared to have been water-laid. Removal of this material from the top revealed that the chamber roof was in fact intact, if somewhat unstable, being heavily veined with a large number of extensive and quite wide cracks. These cracks had presumably facilitated the entry of water into the chamber, accounting perhaps for the substantial depth of silting. On the south-west side of the chamber, high up in the silt deposit, was found a loop-handled amphoriskos (SE2.1) with a small perforated cup or funnel (SE2.2) set in its mouth (Pl. IXB). These vessels had clearly been carried up to such a height (nearly 1.30 m above the floor surface) by the gradual elevation of the silt layer. The coincidence of a loop-handled amphoriskos and a perforated cup has been noted previously (see tombs NE10 and NE16 above). In the case of the pair from tomb SE2, when the vessels were separated, fugitive traces of a fibrous material were observed at their junction, indicating that a cloth had been placed between them. The possible function of these vessels is discussed in Chapter 3.

Further removal of the silt deposit revealed a number of surprising features. On the north side of the chamber, beyond the structural mud-brick mentioned above, the wall was easily defined, but on the south side considerable difficulty was experienced, for what initially appeared to be the chamber wall turned out to be a continuation of the clay/marl cement found in the entrance-way blocking. The cement had been applied in a broad semicircle, beginning at a point about mid-way along the back (eastern) wall, continuing along the south side, and then following the western wall to cover and seal the entrance-way. The blocking of the entrance-way was, in other words, only one element in a cementing operation which had been undertaken from *inside* the chamber. Excavation and removal of the cement uncovered the true chamber wall about 25–40 cm behind. It also revealed the manner in which the cement had been laid, showing that it had been founded on a row of large stones (average size 55 × 35 × 20 cm) which had been placed in a semicircle around the southern side of the chamber. The two northernmost stones on the east were beyond the limits of the clay/marl cement, and were effectively free-standing. The most northerly of these was found to be resting on a rather amorphous block of mud-brick, which was identical in nature to that which had been used on the north side of the entrance-way. As will be explained below, it is significant that neither this mud-brick 'lump', nor the large 'foundation' stones were lying directly upon the floor of the chamber, but were supported by a uniform level of silt which lay some 4 cm above it. On this same level, just to the west of the mud-brick block, was found a four-spouted lamp (SE2.4), lying on its side.

Behind the mud-brick 'lump', which, as stated above, lay beyond the limits of the clay/marl cement, the final removal of silt produced the most surprising result of all. For, instead of the anticipated east wall of the chamber, a second entrance-way was revealed. This was low and roughly rectangular in shape, measuring 55 cm in height and 75 cm in width. The base of this eastern entrance-way lay about 15 cm above the chamber floor, but as further investigations revealed, this apparent step was more in the nature of a sill, the bottom of the shaft being more or less on the same level as the chamber floor. The entrance-way was found to be blocked with two carefully selected and partially dressed rectangular stones, each measuring 70 × 36 × 20 cm. These had been positioned against the eastern side of the sill, resting on the base of the shaft, showing clearly, therefore, that the entrance had been sealed from the outside.

Because of the position in which the blocking stones had been laid, it was impossible to remove them from inside the chamber. By removing the clay sealing which had been applied to fill the gap between them, however, it was possible to probe the space beyond. This was sufficient to establish there the presence of a shaft, and to define the level of its base. Further investigation of the shaft could not be undertaken, nor could its top be located on the surface of Hill 114.

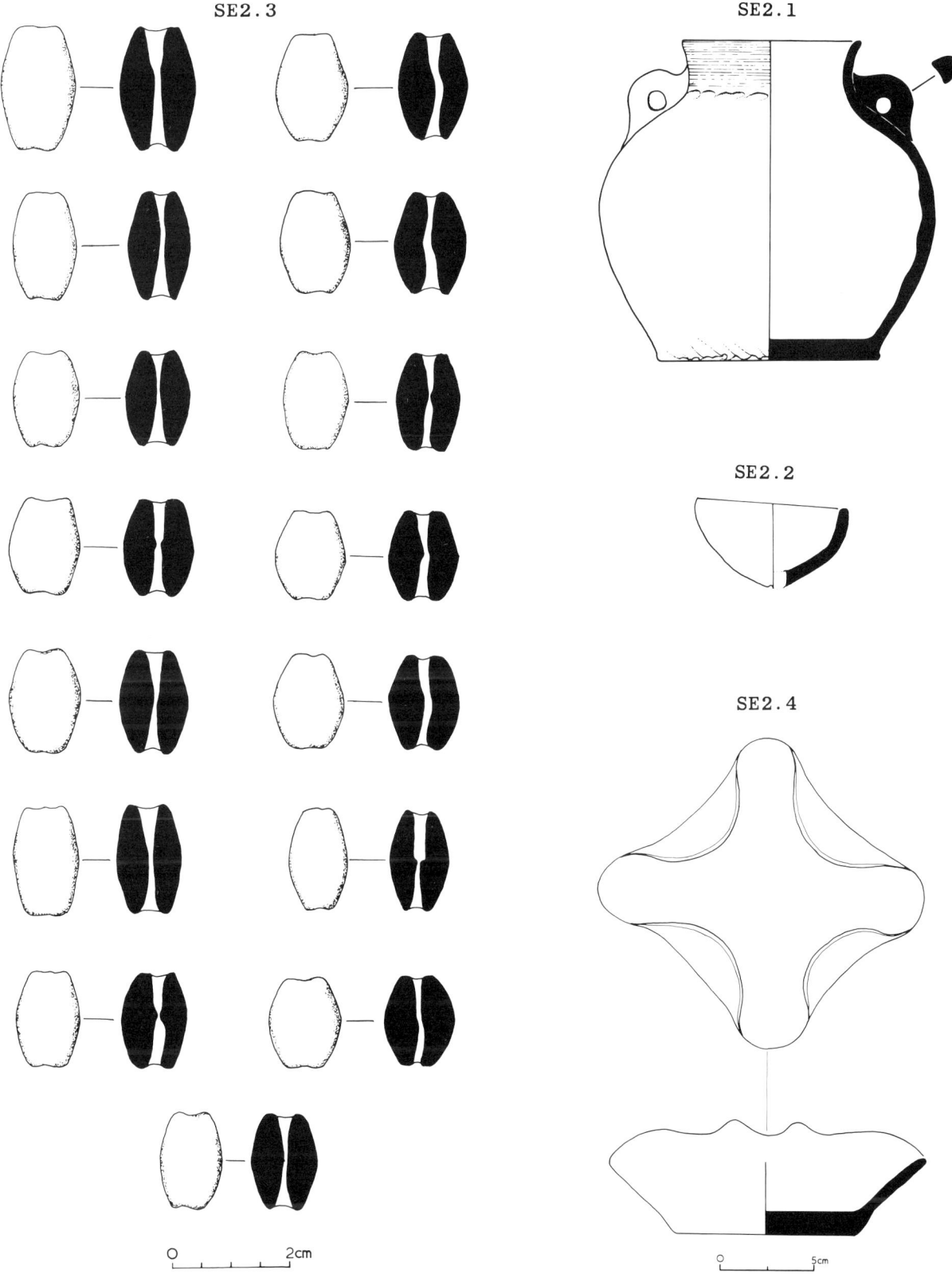

Fig. 43

The final operation in tomb SE2 was to remove the 4 cm silt layer which separated the level on which the semicircle of stones had been placed from the chamber floor. This revealed on the south-west side of the chamber, between the westernmost 'foundation' stone and the chamber wall and below the clay/marl cement, a necklace of fifteen reddish-tinged quartzite beads (SE2.3). These were found resting directly upon the floor surface, and were associated with a few small fragments of bone which could only be identified as of human origin.

The unusual findings in tomb SE2 clearly require explanation, and the problems raised by the excavation can only be resolved on the assumption that two phases of usage occurred. In phase 1, the tomb consisted of a simple and somewhat irregular chamber, sub-rectangular in plan and measuring 2.30 m north-south by 2.55 m east-west. The roof was domed towards the rear (east), achieving a maximum height of 2.05 m. The entrance, approached by a rectangular shaft, was on the western side and consisted of a poorly executed opening which had been regularised using mud-brick. It may be assumed that the original blocking of this western entrance-way consisted of large stones which were re-used in phase 2 (below). The only surviving funerary deposits relating to phase 1 consisted of a few bone fragments and the necklace, SE2.3, which were found lying directly upon the floor surface.

At a later period, which was represented in the tomb chamber by a 4 cm thick accumulation of silt, tomb SE2 was re-used. A second shaft was dug, which gave access to the chamber on the eastern side by means of a low, rectangular entrance. It would seem that the blocking stones were then removed from the western entrance-way and placed in a semicircle around the south side of the chamber. During this operation, part of the mud-brick from the north side of the entrance-way was damaged and became dislodged. A block of this material was also moved to the east side of the chamber, where it was used to support one of the stones. The semicircle of stones appears to have been used as the foundation for a thick skim of clay-marl cement which was applied around the southern side of the chamber, and which was continued across and into the earliest western entrance-way, forming an effective sealing.

The purpose of this cementing operation is difficult to understand. It could be suggested that it had been undertaken in order to seal away all traces of the previous (phase 1) interment. Certainly, it is true that the only remains of phase 1 were recovered from behind the semicircle of stones, below the cement, but it is also possible that this represents the original position of their interment and that the placement of the stones in phase 2 was purely coincidental. Indeed, the necklace (SE2.3) was found directly upon the floor surface, below the 4 cm layer of silt, and would not, therefore, have been visible at the time of construction of phase 2. Alternatively, therefore, the cementing might have been undertaken simply to add structural stability to the southern side of the chamber. The removal of the cement revealed many substantial cracks in the wall on this side, and it is possible that some of these had developed between phases 1 and 2, and that the need had been felt for some degree of reinforcement. In all events, the effect of the operation was to reduce the size of the chamber to approximately 2.20 m east-west by 1.90 m north-south. The funerary deposits of phase 2 had been severely disturbed by intrusive water and associated silting. Only a few tiny fragments of bone were found scattered throughout the silt deposit (identifiable as human only), but since they were contained within the reduced chamber, they cannot be related to those found beneath the cement on the south side of the chamber (phase 1) and must therefore represent a second individual buried in phase 2. The loop-handled amphoriskos with perforated cup (SE2.1 and SE2.2) and the four-spouted lamp (SE2.4), also found within the silt deposit of the reduced chamber, must similarly be assigned to phase 2.

Contents

PHASE 1

SE2.3   Necklace of 15 beads   (Pl. XID)

Reddish-tinged quartzite; bored from both ends with conical drill.

PHASE 2

SE2.1   Loop-handled amphoriskos

Technique: Handmade with wheelmade rim. *Paste*: 10YR 'very pale brown' 7/3; many small-medium sand, ceramic and lime; no core; hard. *Surface* (Interior): as paste. (Exterior): as paste; wet-smoothed.

SE2.2   Perforated cup

Technique: Handmade. *Paste*: 7.5YR 'reddish yellow' 7/6; many medium sand and ceramic, few medium lime; no core; hard. *Surface* (Interior and Exterior): as paste.

SE2.4   Four-spouted lamp

Technique: Handmade. *Paste*: 2.5YR 'light red' 6/6; many small-large sand, ceramic and lime; no core; hard. *Surface* (Interior and Exterior): as paste; no blackening.

TOMB SE3   Pl. XA
West slope Hill 114
Orientation: W–E

Investigation of an interruption in the marl strata to the south of tomb SE2 revealed the presence of a tomb shaft of substantial dimensions. As excavations proceeded, it became clear that the most fully preserved (east) face represented the rear of the shaft, and that the chamber had been situated on the west side, having been, in consequence, totally lost through erosion. In view of the unusually large proportions of the shaft, however, excavations were continued, and the interior fill was completely removed. This fill, below the upper 20 cm of topsoil, consisted of alternating layers of fine silt and gravelly clay. It contained, however, virtually no broken marl, strongly suggesting that the shaft had not been back-filled with the material removed from its excavation, but instead had filled up naturally over a period of time.

In plan, the shaft was roughly rectangular, measuring 2.80 m by 1.40 m at the base. The long sides on the north and south were slightly irregular but more or less vertical. The shorter eastern side, preserved to a height of 5.20 m, had been provided with two shallow steps (12–15 cm deep), one at 1.0 m and the other at 2.50 m above the base. The surface dimensions of the shaft must consequently have been slightly larger east-west. The western side of the shaft was only preserved as two narrow strips flanking either side of the entrance-way, but all three of the other sides showed well-preserved tool marks. These appeared as straight furrows, up to 30 cm in length and 2–3 cm wide, semicircular in section and running almost vertically (Pl. IXc). As mentioned in Chapter 1, it is probable that these marks represent spikes or rods which were hammered down into the rock and then used as levers to prise away blocks or fragments of marl.

The entrance to the chamber was on the western side of the shaft. Unlike those of any of the other tombs examined, this entrance-way was very large, and had been cut in the manner of a true doorway with superbly executed vertical sides. In width, the entrance-way measured 98 cm, and although the upper part had been lost through erosion, the preserved height of 1.80 m clearly indicates that it would have allowed access to an individual at full standing height.

Beyond the entrance-way to the west, a tunnel or passage gave access to the chamber proper. From the doorway, the dimensions of which it initially preserved, this passage gradually widened towards the west, achieving a maximum width of 1.20 m at a distance of 1.60 m. At this point a marked outcurving of the side walls indicated the transition to the chamber proper. Unfortunately, no traces of the chamber were preserved, but from the dimensions of the entrance-way and passage, and from the angle of curvature of the side walls at the point where they were truncated by erosion, it can be assumed that it had been very large.

As mentioned previously (see tomb SE1 above), the collapse of the chamber of tomb SE3, assuming it was of substantial size, was probably responsible in part for the formation of the wadi which now separates Hill 114 from Hill 113. How soon after construction this collapse occurred is, of course, impossible to determine, but it is just conceivable that the tomb builders, in the case of tomb SE3, had been over-ambitious in the scale of their design, and that the chamber had in fact collapsed before the tomb was ever used or even perhaps completed. Slight evidence for this suggestion comes from the fact that the entrance-way was found without any sort of blocking: neither were any stones, nor traces of any other potential sealing materials found within the fills of either the shaft or the chamber passage. It would surely seem inconceivable that a chamber which had been provided with such an impressive and carefully carved entrance-way had been left open, more especially since the shaft had not, apparently, been back-filled.

(For tomb plan and elevation, see overleaf.)

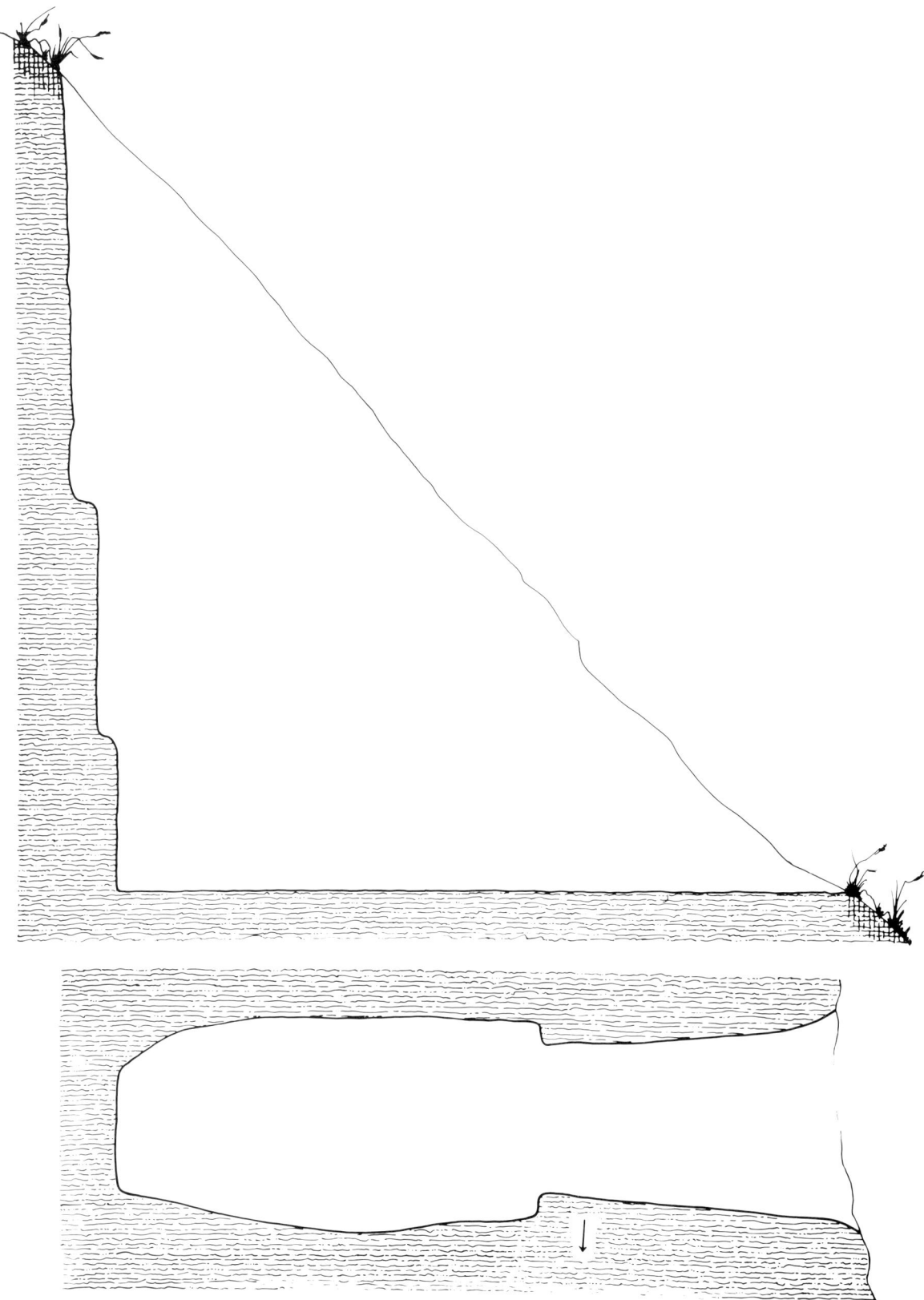

Fig. 44 Tomb SE3

TOMB SE4
West slope Hill 111
Orientation: E–W

From the disposition and orientation of the tombs discovered on both the west slope of Hill 111 (SE4, 5, 6 and 10) and the east slope of Hill 102 (SE7, 8, 9 and 11), it is clear that the shallow wadi at present separating the two hills did not exist in antiquity. At the time of tomb cutting, the two hills must have formed a single coherent whole. As in other cases (see, for example, tombs SE1–3, above) it can be suggested that the formation of the wadi might in part have been due to the collapse of tomb chambers with resultant subsidence. Subsequent erosion of the slopes on either side has been responsible for the exposure (and destruction) of tombs which had originally been dug down from a level surface. In the case of Hills 102 and 111 these effects have been made worse by a bulldozing operation undertaken in recent times to widen and level the wadi in order to create a trackway. The levelling had partly been accomplished by removing material from the top of Hill 111 and dumping it into the wadi bed. With regard to the tombs, this has had the effect of cutting off most of the upper parts of the chambers, shafts and entrance-ways. Hill 102 does not seem to have been lowered in the same way, and so the tombs situated there were found to be generally better and more fully preserved (see below).

Tomb SE4 was first recognised by the presence on the hill slope of four large stones. Just to the east of these was found a large and low depression which, on examination, proved to be the heavily eroded chamber of a tomb. The shaft had been situated on the west side, and had been completely destroyed by erosion. The entrance-way, of which the four stones had clearly formed the blocking, had also been largely lost through erosion. Just enough (approximately 15 cm) remained of the sides, however, to allow for its width to be recorded. This was 65 cm across the base, suggesting that the entrance-way had been quite small. The entrance-way width had been continued for a distance of 70 cm eastwards, suggesting that there had been a short tunnel giving access to the chamber proper.

The fill from within the eroded chamber consisted of soil, decayed marl-rubble and silt, together with large blocks of marl, these last indicating that the roof had collapsed before the tomb became damaged by the recent processes of bulldozing and slope erosion. Furthermore, below this mixed deposit, only a very thin layer of silt was encountered (3–4 cm), suggesting that only a short period of time had elapsed between interment and the collapse of the roof. The silt was, nevertheless, very hard and compact, and had been water-laid, its tightly banded structure showing evidence for seasonal intrusion of rainwater into the chamber.

Removal of the upper debris and excavation of the silt layer revealed the plan of the chamber and uncovered the funerary deposits. The chamber was large and oval in plan, measuring 4.70 m north-south by 2.65 m east-west. The rear (eastern) wall was preserved to a height of 1.90 m, and a change in angle of curvature towards the top, representing the transition to the roof, suggests that this must have been in the order of 2.20–2.50 m above the floor surface.

The funerary deposits were quite extensive. The fragmentary and poorly preserved remains of three individuals were found. The skeletal remains had clearly been badly damaged, not only by exposure to water but also through having been crushed by the collapse of the chamber roof. Skeleton A, identified as that of a male, aged 25–35 years, was found in the south-central part of the chamber in what was judged to be a flexed position with head towards the north. Skeleton B was found close to the north wall. This appeared to have been buried in an extended position with head towards the west, and was identified as probably that of a female, aged between 25 and 35 years. Skeleton C was represented by a scatter of bones on the north-west side of the chamber. The degree of preservation was insufficient in this case to allow for disposition or orientation to be determined, and the bones could only be identified as those of a human adult.

Tomb SE4 produced a fine collection of pottery vessels as grave goods. As mentioned above, the silt layer in this case was very shallow, indicating that only a short period of time had elapsed between interment and collapse. Consequently, it is unlikely that the pottery vessels had moved substantially (by the action of water) from the positions in which they had been placed. Indeed, although some of the larger vessels had been broken by the roof collapse, most were found standing upright and all were lying directly upon the floor surface. The vessels could be attributed with reasonable confidence, therefore, to the individual skeletons.

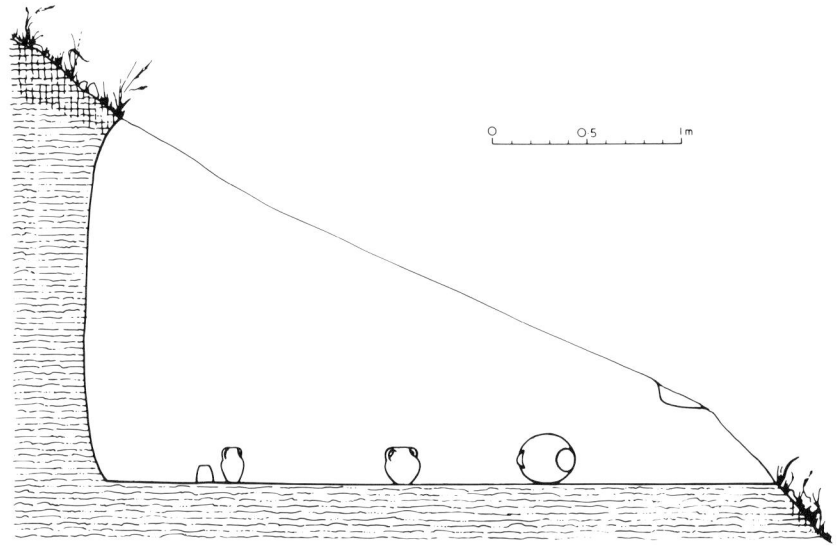
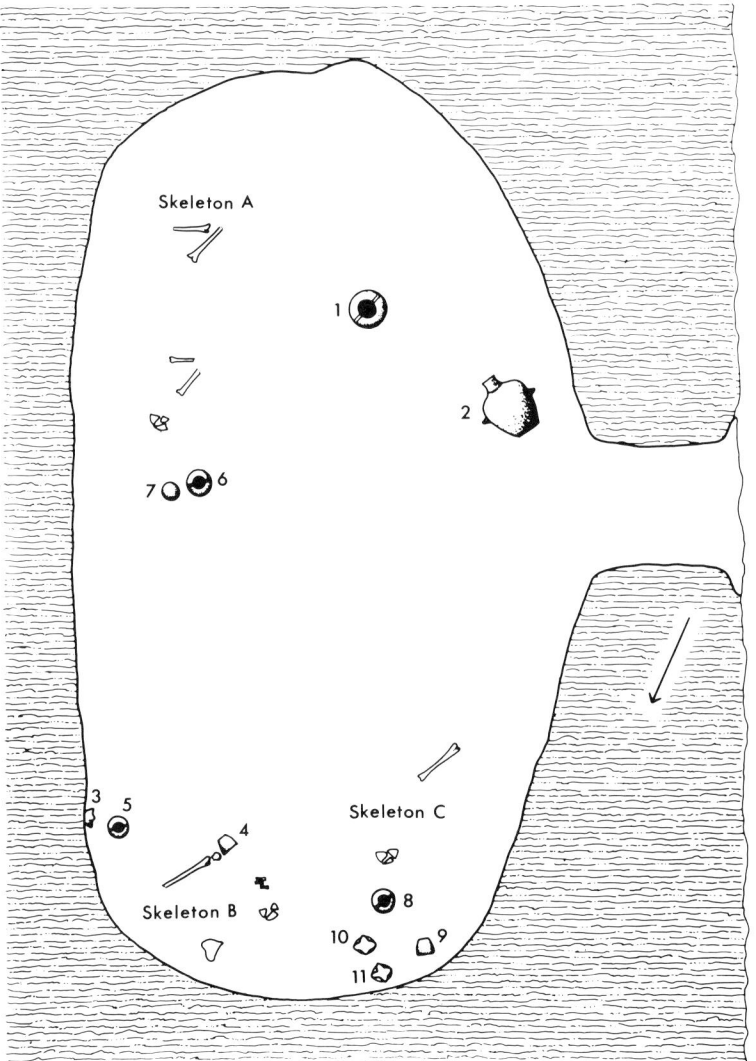

Fig. 45 Tomb SE4

A ledge-handled storejar was found close to the west wall of the chamber, just to the south of the entrance-way (SE4.2), and to the east of this vessel was a loop-handled amphoriskos (SE4.1). In these positions it would seem appropriate to attribute the two vessels to skeleton A. More closely associated with this individual were two further vessels, a small cup (SE4.7) and another loop-handled amphoriskos (SE4.6), both of which were found in close proximity to the fragmentary skull. Close to skeleton B on the north side of the chamber were found three vessels – a four-spouted lamp (SE4.3), which was pressed hard up against the east wall, a cup (SE4.4) and a loop-handled amphoriskos (SE4.5). Associated with the bone scatter of skeleton C on the north-west side of the chamber were four vessels – two four-spouted lamps (SE4.10 and 11), a loop-handled amphoriskos (SE4.8) and a cup (SE4.9).

Contents

SE4.1   Loop-handled amphoriskos

Technique: Handmade with wheelmade rim. *Paste*: 10R 'red' 4/8; very many very small sand and ceramic, few medium lime; no core; hard. *Surface* (Interior): as paste. (Exterior): as paste, incised line at base of neck; diagonal combing on body.

SE4.2   Ledge-handled storejar

Technique: Handmade (coil-built) with wheelmade rim. *Paste*: 10YR 'very pale brown' 7/4; very many small-medium sand and lime; no core; hard. *Surface* (Interior): as paste. (Exterior): 10YR 'white' 8/2 wash; band of diagonal incisions at base of neck.

SE4.3   Four-spouted lamp

Technique: Handmade. *Paste*: 7.5YR 'light brown' 6/4; many small-medium sand, few medium ceramic and lime; no core; hard. *Surface* (Interior and Exterior): as paste; blackened on all four spouts.

SE4.4   Cup

Technique: Handmade, upper part finished on wheel. *Paste*: 7.5YR 'reddish yellow' 7/6; very many small sand and lime, some medium sand and ceramic; no core; hard. *Surface* (Interior and Exterior): as paste.

SE4.5   Loop-handled amphoriskos

Technique: Handmade with wheelmade rim. *Paste*: 7.5YR 'light brown' 6/4; many very small-small sand and ceramic, some small lime; no core; hard. *Surface* (Interior): as paste. (Exterior): 2.5Y 'white' 8/2 wash.

SE4.6   Loop-handled amphoriskos

Technique: Handmade with wheelmade rim. *Paste*: 2.5YR 'light red' 6/6; many small-medium sand and ceramic, few large wadi gravel; no core; hard. *Surface* (Interior): as paste. (Exterior): 10YR 'white' 8/2 wash; diagonal combing on body.

SE4.7   Cup

Technique: Handmade. *Paste*: 5YR 'reddish yellow' 6/6; many medium-large sand, wadi gravel, ceramic and lime, few large ceramic; no core; hard. *Surface* (Interior and Exterior): as paste.

SE4.8   Loop-handled amphoriskos

Technique: Handmade with wheelmade rim. *Paste*: 7.5YR 'reddish yellow' 6/6; many very small-small sand, ceramic and lime; no core; hard. *Surface* (Interior): as paste. (Exterior): 10YR 'white' 8/2 wash.

SE4.9   Cup

Technique: Handmade, upper part finished on wheel. *Paste*: 10YR 'greyish brown' 5/2; very many small-medium sand, ceramic and lime; no core; hard. *Surface* (Interior): 10YR 'very pale brown' 8/3 wash. (Exterior): as interior; wet-smoothed.

SE4.10   Four-spouted lamp

Technique: Handmade. *Paste*: 5YR 'reddish yellow' 7/6; very many very small sand; no core; hard. *Surface* (Interior and Exterior): as paste; blackened on one spout only.

SE4.11   Four-spouted lamp

Technique: Handmade. *Paste*: 5YR 'reddish yellow' 7/6; few medium-large wadi gravel, ceramic and lime; no core; hard. *Surface* (Interior and Exterior): as paste; blackened on all four spouts.

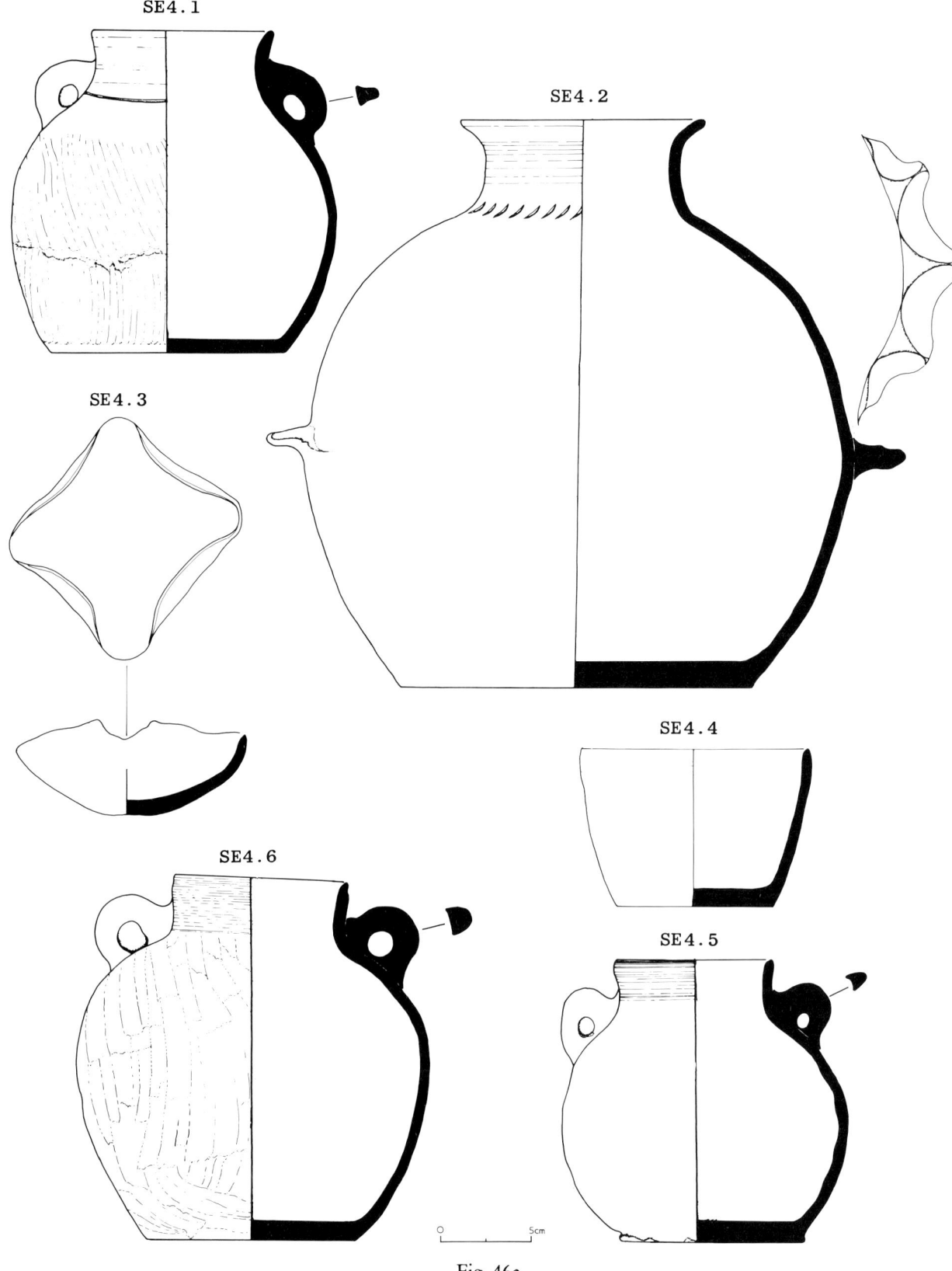

Fig. 46a

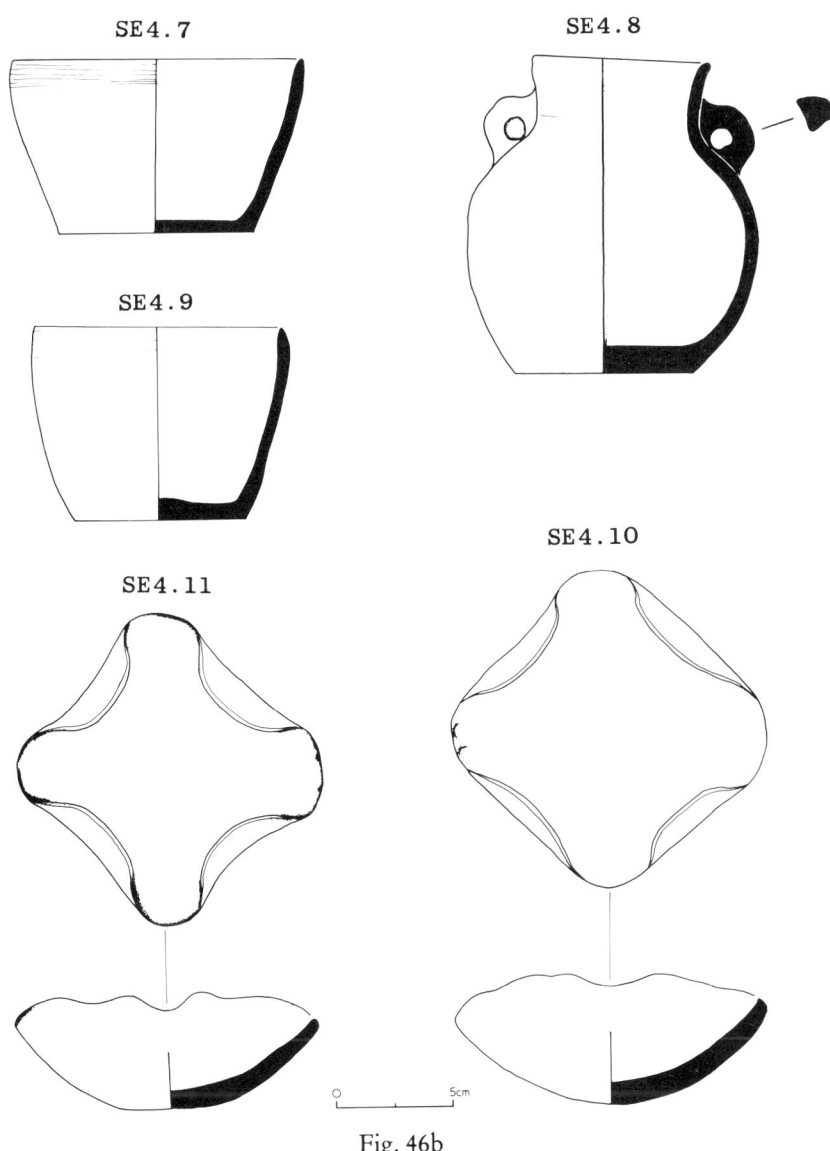

Fig. 46b

TOMB SE5
West slope Hill 111
Orientation: not establishable

(The plan and elevation of this partial tomb are shown on Fig. 54, with those of tomb SE10)

This extensively eroded tomb was found just to the south of tomb SE4. Only a small part of the chamber floor and associated wall had survived. No traces of the shaft, nor of the entrance-way had been preserved, and since the surviving portion of the chamber represented perhaps less than 20 per cent of the original, it was impossible to establish on which side (other than east) the access had been situated.

Excavation of the weathered fill of marl debris and silt produced a partial plan which suggests that the chamber might originally have been quite large, perhaps in the order of 2.50 m in diameter. The easternmost part of the chamber had been cut into the chamber of tomb SE10 (see below), the floor of which lay approximately 25 cm below that of tomb SE5. The chamber wall at the point of interruption had been made by cutting and smoothing the interior fill of tomb SE10, clearly showing, therefore, that the latter tomb had not only existed prior to the cutting of tomb SE5, but also that it had at least partially collapsed, creating a sufficient level of debris to allow for the completion of the wall of tomb SE5.

Despite the very limited area of the chamber which survived, the fragmentary and partial remains of two individuals were found. The bones, which were scattered amongst the debris on the floor of the chamber, were in extremely poor condition, having been both crushed and weathered, and no details regarding disposition, orientation or practice could be established. The bones were attributed to two skeletons, one (skeleton A) that of an adult (sex indeterminable) aged 25–35 years, and the other (skeleton B) that of a juvenile (sex indeterminable). No grave goods were found.

TOMB SE6
West slope Hill 111
Orientation: S–N

This partially preserved tomb was found to the north of tomb SE4, where it was recognised by an elongated depression on the hill slope. Removal of the dense filling of topsoil, decayed marl debris and silt revealed that slightly more than 50 per cent of the tomb had been lost through erosion. Since, however, the tomb had been orientated approximately north-south, the surviving portion provided an almost perfectly bisected ground plan, allowing for some details of the shaft and entrance-way to be established.

Based on the plan of the surviving half, and assuming of course a symmetrical arrangement, the chamber would appear to have been long and narrow, oval in shape, measuring approximately 2.80m north-south by 1.60m east-west. The east wall was preserved to a height of 1.0m, and the angle of curvature at the top suggests that the height of the chamber might have been in the order of 1.20–1.30m. Access was on the north side. The shaft was roughly rectangular in plan and very narrow, measuring only 50cm in width. The northern side of the shaft had been lost through erosion, and so the length could not be established. The lower part of the entrance-way on the eastern side was preserved, and again, assuming a symmetrical pattern, the opening had been formed by a slight constriction of the shaft walls, and would have been roughly 40cm wide. A single stone of its blocking remained, resting on the floor and attached to the side by means of a clay cement. A second stone found immediately to the north had clearly fallen out of position (see plan).

Although nearly half the area of the chamber floor was preserved, neither skeletal remains nor grave goods were encountered.

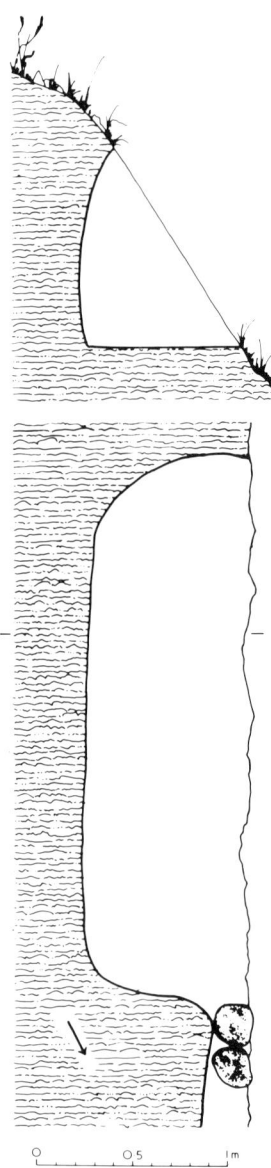

Fig. 47 Tomb SE6

TOMB SE7
East slope Hill 102
Orientation: N–S

As mentioned above (see tomb SE4), the tombs situated on the east slope of Hill 102 (tombs SE7, 8, 9 and 11) had suffered less from the effects of deliberate levelling and erosion than those on the opposite side of the wadi. In the case of tomb SE7, erosion had

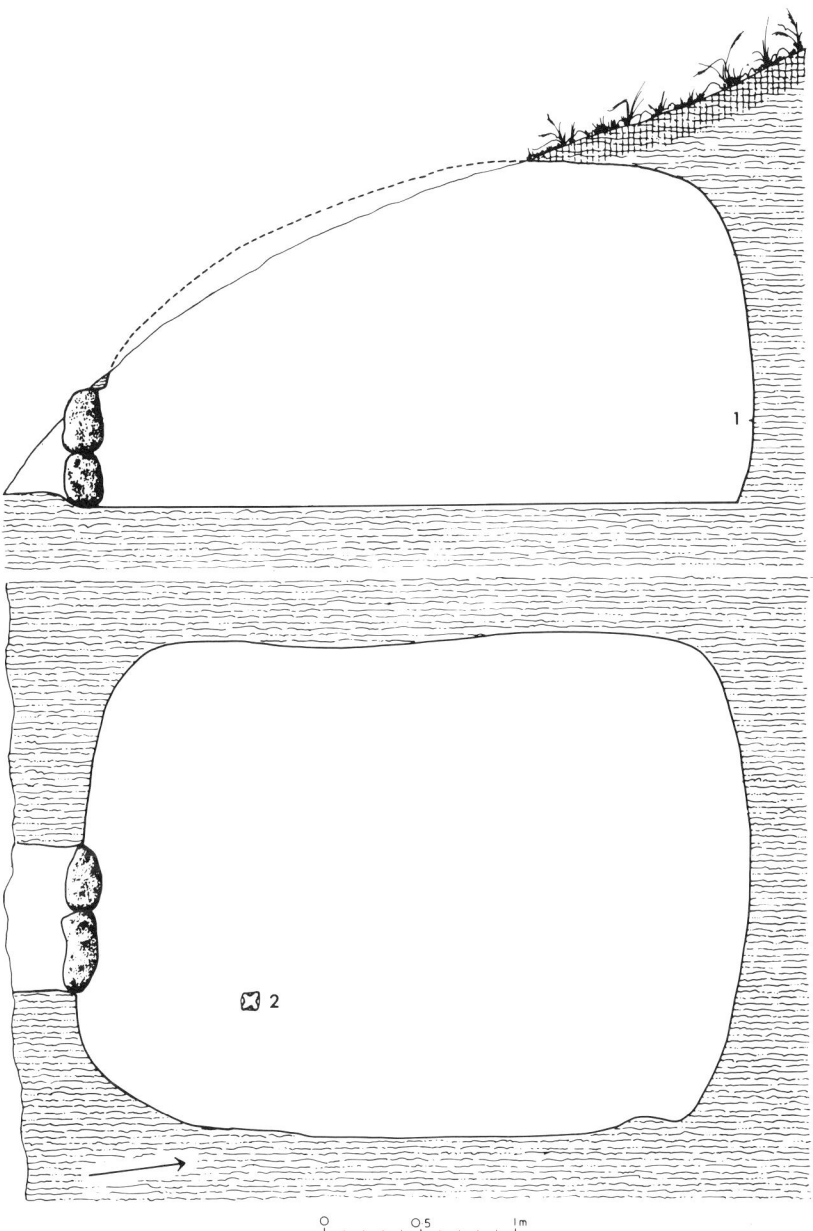

Fig. 48 Tomb SE7

removed most of the chamber roof and had truncated the southern part of the shaft, but otherwise this tomb was found to be relatively well preserved.

The existence of tomb SE7 was indicated by an interruption in the marl strata which, on cleaning, revealed a large oval feature showing as dull greyish-orange against the pale brownish-cream solid marl. Excavation demonstrated that this oval feature was composed of topsoil mixed with weathered and decayed marl, the removal of which uncovered the fully preserved lower part of the tomb chamber. Below the decayed marl rubble, large slabs of marl were found, these having derived from the collapse of the chamber roof. Separating this deposit of heavy blocks from the chamber floor was a very thin (less than 1 cm) layer of water-laid silt, the shallow depth of which suggests that only a short period of time had elapsed between interment and the collapse of the roof.

The chamber itself was oval to sub-rectangular in

plan, measuring 3.45 m north-south by 2.55 m east-west. A portion of the roof was preserved at the rear (north side) of the chamber, and this suggested that the roof must originally have been gently domed, with a maximum height of about 1.70 m towards the centre. The entrance was found on the south side, and consisted of a low, almost semicircular opening, 60 cm high and 75 cm wide across the base. Access was directly to the chamber with no linking tunnel, the entrance-way blocking being therefore almost flush with the south wall of the chamber. The blocking, which was found intact, consisted of three river boulders, laid in triangular fashion and cemented in place using a thick clay packing, reddish-brown in colour.

Although orientated north-south, parallel that is with the direction of the wadi between Hills 102 and 111, the tomb had lost the southern part of its shaft through the erosion of a small drainage gully which feeds into the main wadi from the west. Only a small portion was found to be preserved on the steep down-slope of this gully. This comprised a small area of floor and remnants of the east and west walls. From the preserved fragments, the shaft would appear to have been rectangular, or possibly square, and the same width as the entrance-way, that is 75 cm east-west. The base of the shaft was slightly higher than the floor of the chamber, the transition being marked by a low rounded step, 7 cm high.

The funerary deposits of tomb SE7 were found to be in extremely poor condition, having suffered not only from water damage but also more severely from the effects of the roof collapse. The fragmentary and partial remains of a single individual were found, concentrated on the north side of the chamber, close to the wall. The bones could only be identified as those of an adult, and no information could be obtained regarding disposition, orientation or practice. A single four-spouted lamp (SE7.2) was found on the south-east side of the chamber. This was lying on the floor, and had been badly crushed by the overlying debris. More interestingly, a small copper point (SE7.1) was found inserted into the north wall of the chamber, at a height of about 45 cm above the floor. This placement was obviously deliberate, suggesting that the point had served as some kind of hook.

Contents

SE7.1   Point (awl?)

Copper/copper alloy (fragmentary).

SE7.2   Four-spouted lamp

Technique: Handmade. *Paste*: 10YR 'very pale brown' 6/3; many small sand, some medium-large sand and lime; no core; hard. *Surface* (Interior): as paste. (Exterior): as paste; diagonal combing on sides; blackened all around rim.

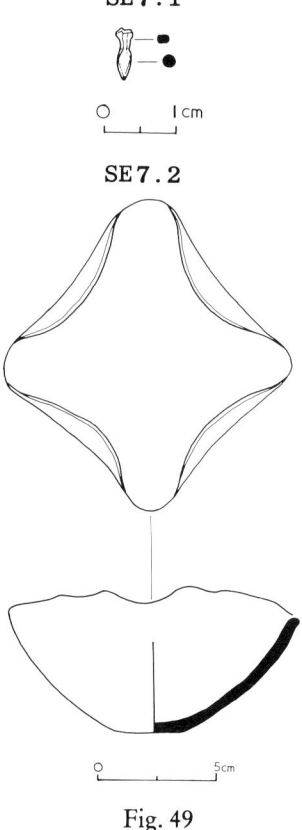

Fig. 49

TOMB SE8
East slope Hill 102
Orientation: N–S

Following the completion of the excavation of tomb SE7 (above), a surface scraping operation in the area just to the north of that tomb revealed an elongated rectangular feature, orientated north-south, which, on excavation, proved to be the shaft of tomb SE8.

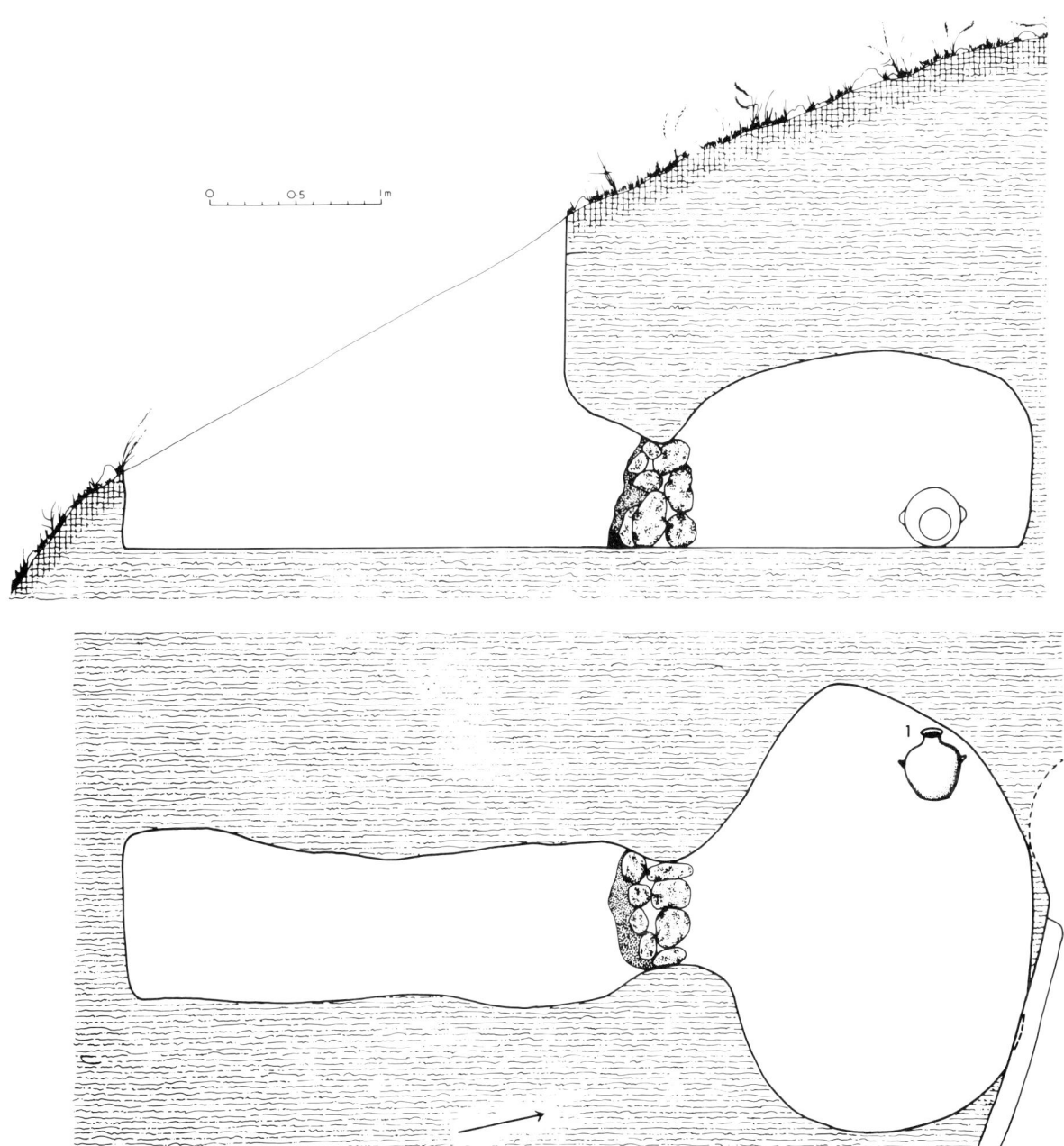

Fig. 50 Tomb SE8

The fill consisted of light reddish-brown soil containing a large number of small white marl chips. The material was homogeneous from top to bottom, suggesting that the shaft had been deliberately backfilled using the spoil removed from its excavation. The shaft was preserved to a depth of almost 2.0 m on the north side, but on the south side, where erosion had been more severe, the preserved depth was only 45 cm. In plan it was rectangular, long and narrow, and had been cut somewhat irregularly. The upper dimensions were 2.60 m north-south by 80–95 cm east-west. The northern side had been undercut, starting at a point 95 cm above the base, providing in effect a low sloping approach 60 cm long, leading to the entrance-way proper.

The entrance to the chamber, on the north side of

Tombs in the south-east sector

the shaft, was found with its sealing intact. This consisted of a dense, greenish-grey clay packing which, on removal, was seen to have been applied over the vertical face of a stone blocking. Unlike most of the other tombs, which employed a few large boulders for this purpose, tomb SE8 used a blocking which consisted of a larger number of quite small stones (average size 20–25 cm in diameter).

Removal of the blocking showed that the entrance-way itself had been roughly cut, the sides having been formed from a slight constriction of the lower shaft side walls. These were more or less vertical, but the arched top was extremely irregular and poorly executed. The entrance-way measured 58 cm across the base, and reached a maximum height of 60 cm at a point just east of centre. The removal of the blocking also allowed the interior of the chamber to be examined. The roof was found to be intact, only a few small blocks of marl having become detached from it. These were seen to be resting on top of a substantial silt deposit, between which and the roof of the chamber was a 50–70 cm air space.

Excavation of the silt layer revealed a laminated structure, indicative of seasonal deposition by intrusive rainwater over a prolonged period of time. The silt itself was deep reddish-brown in colour, and was extremely hard and compact. Its removal allowed for the plan and dimensions of the chamber to be established. The chamber was roughly circular in plan, measuring 2.0 m north-south by 2.55 m east-west. The roof was low and gently domed, reaching a maximum height of 1.14 m towards the rear of the chamber. The north wall, when fully cleaned, revealed a small 'window', approximately 45 cm in diameter. The fill of this feature consisted of greyish-brown, fairly loose soil, containing many small white marl chips. Subsequent investigations demonstrated that this 'window' had been produced as a result of the chamber of tomb SE8 having been cut into the shaft of a pre-existing adjacent tomb (tomb SE11 below), the exposed fill representing the in-filled shaft material of that tomb.

The skeletal remains of tomb SE8 were found to be in extremely poor condition, having suffered exten-

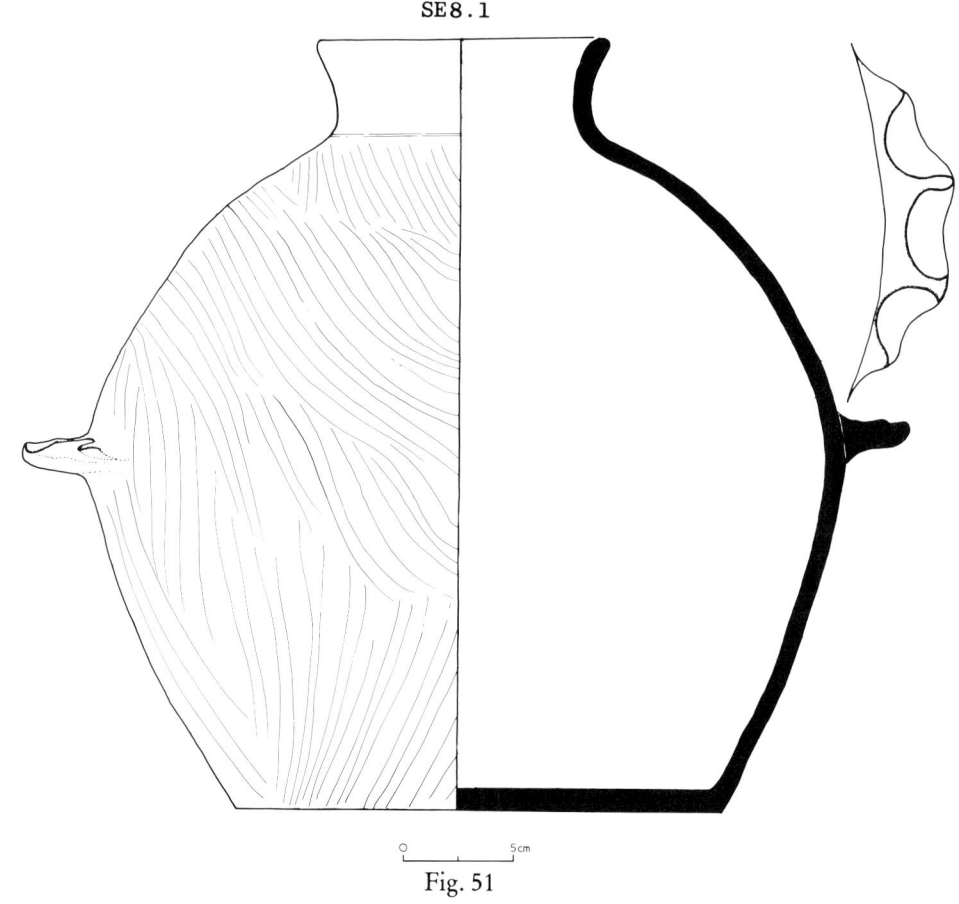

SE8.1

Fig. 51

sively from the effects of seasonal and prolonged inundation. Small bone fragments were found scattered throughout the chamber, below and within the silt layer. A slightly denser concentration of larger bones, including some skull fragments, was encountered on the north side of the chamber, on the floor, close to the wall, and it is possible that this position represents the site of the original interment. Clearly, no details could be adduced regarding disposition, orientation or practice, and the bones could only be identified as those of a single adult.

On the north-west side of the chamber, immediately north of the main concentration of skeletal remains, a large ledge-handled storejar was found. This was probably in more or less its original position, but had been displaced slightly so that it was found leaning against the chamber wall.

Contents

SE8.1   Ledge-handled storejar

Technique: Handmade with wheelmade rim. *Paste*: 5YR 'reddish yellow' 6/8; many small-medium sand, ceramic and lime; no core; hard. *Surface* (Interior): as paste. (Exterior): 2.5Y 'yellow' 7/6 wash; diagonal combing on body.

TOMB SE9
East slope Hill 102
Orientation: N–S

This poorly preserved tomb was found low down on the slope of Hill 102, immediately to the west of tomb SE8 and, in terms of orientation, almost precisely parallel to it. Erosion had been responsible for the loss of the chamber roof and all but the smallest traces of the shaft, but, surprisingly, the entrance-way was well preserved.

The tomb was recognised during the surface scraping operation of Hill 102 referred to above (see tomb SE8), when an oval depression was revealed, showing as dull greyish-brown against the pale brownish-cream marl. The depression represented the eroded chamber of tomb SE9, and was filled with a compact mixture of soil and decayed marl debris. Beneath this was a layer of large blocks of fairly clean marl which had presumably derived from the collapse of the chamber roof. Their position, below the decayed

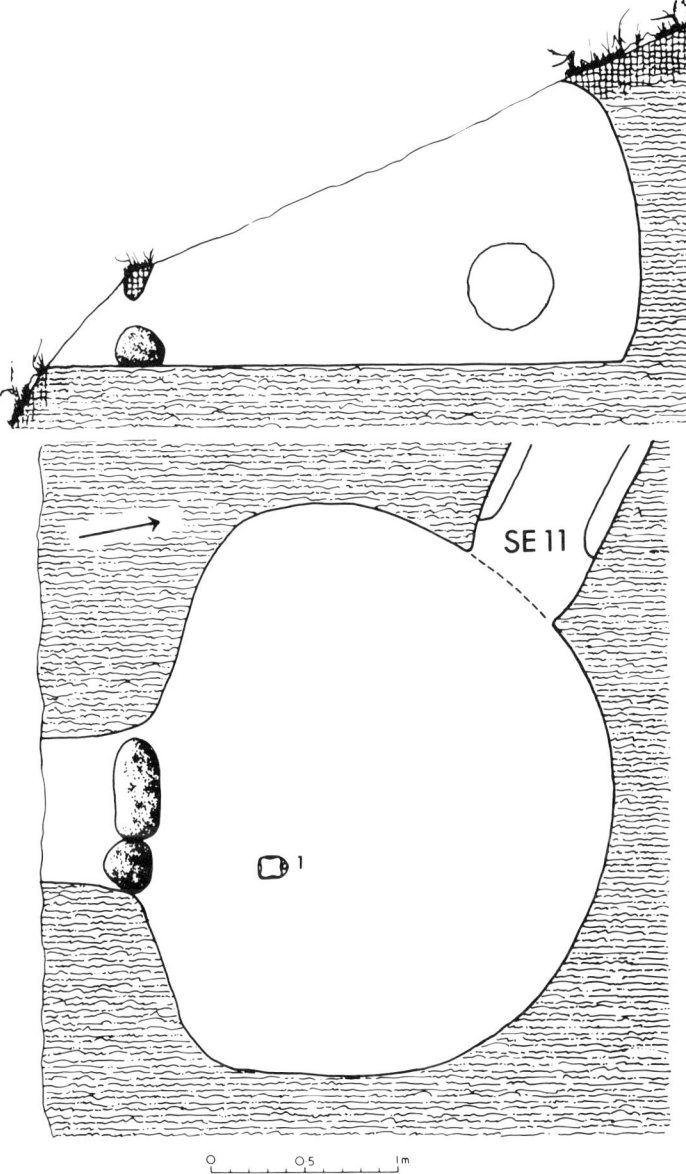

Fig. 52 Tomb SE9

marl rubble and directly above a 20–25 cm silt layer, suggests that the roof of the chamber had collapsed in antiquity, before the more recent processes of erosion had removed the overlying marl strata. The 20–25 cm accumulation of silt suggests that the chamber of the tomb had remained intact for a relatively long period of time before the roof gave way. The silt, which was reddish-brown in colour, was water-laid, indicating seasonal intrusion of water over a prolonged period.

The chamber itself was oval in plan, measuring 2.40 m north-south by 2.95 m east-west. Only a small portion of the roof was preserved on the north side, but from this it could be estimated that it would have been quite low and gently domed, with a maximum height of perhaps 1.40–1.50 m towards the rear of the chamber. As in the case of tomb SE8 (above), a small circular 'window' (about 40 cm in diameter) was found in the chamber wall on the north-west side, beginning at approximately 18 cm above the floor. This feature had again resulted from the cutting of tomb SE9's chamber into the south-eastern side of the pre-existing shaft of tomb SE11 (see below).

Access to the chamber was on the south side. The entrance-way was very low and semicircular in shape, measuring 85 cm across the base and only 35 cm high at the centre. Two blocking stones were found in position at the base. At least one other stone would have been necessary in order to close the opening, but this (or these) had become dislodged and had presumably rolled down into the wadi below.

Only a very small part of the shaft was preserved. This suggested, however, that it had been narrow (75 cm east-west), and would most probably have been rectangular or possibly square in plan.

The skeletal remains of tomb SE9 were found to be in exceptionally poor condition. A few bone fragments, mostly extremely small, were found scattered throughout the chamber. These were contained within the silt layer, and were insufficient to allow for any identification other than 'probably human'.

Only one object, a lamp (SE9.1), was found in tomb SE9, just south of the centre of the chamber and lying directly upon the floor surface. This lamp was of the highly unusual 'side-spouted' type, having, in addition to a four-spouted upper part, a lower hollow chamber connecting to a side-mounted spout. Another example of this otherwise unknown lamp type was found in tomb SE1 (see SE1.7 above, and further discussion in Chapter 3 below).

Contents

SE9.1   Side-spouted lamp

Technique: Handmade. *Paste*: 2.5YR 'light red' 6/6; many small-medium sand and lime, some medium ceramic; no core; hard. *Surface* (Interior and Exterior): as paste; blackened all around rim of upper bowl.

TOMB SE10
West slope Hill 111
Orientation: N–S

Tomb SE10 was found on the west slope of Hill 111, immediately to the east of tomb SE5. In fact, this latter tomb had been partially cut into the western side of tomb SE10 (see above, tomb SE5). Erosion and levelling had removed most of the roof of the chamber, and presumably also most of the upper shaft, although this was not excavated. The entrance-way, however, was found to be intact.

The tomb was recognised by a fairly small circular depression on the hill slope. Excavation revealed the presence of an eroded tomb chamber, the fill consisting of heavily weathered and decayed greyish-brown marl rubble, which persisted almost to floor level. This deposit overlay a very thin (less than 1.0 cm) silt layer, the insubstantial depth of which suggested that the roof of the chamber had collapsed very soon after the tomb had been sealed. Further confirmation of this is provided by the intrusion of tomb SE5, part of the western wall of which had been created by the shaping and smoothing of the interior rubble fill of tomb SE10, thereby demonstrating that this collapsed material must have existed when tomb SE5 was dug.

The chamber of tomb SE10 was somewhat

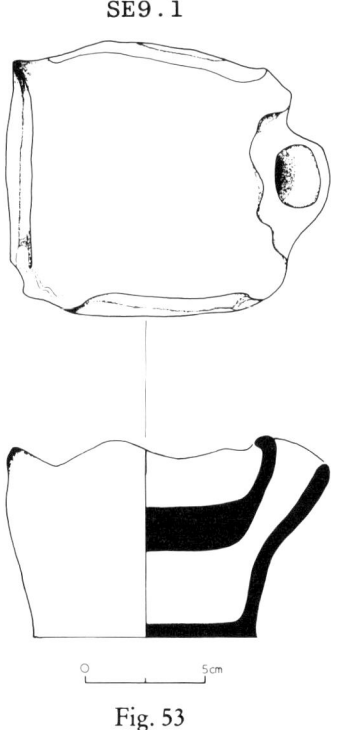

Fig. 53

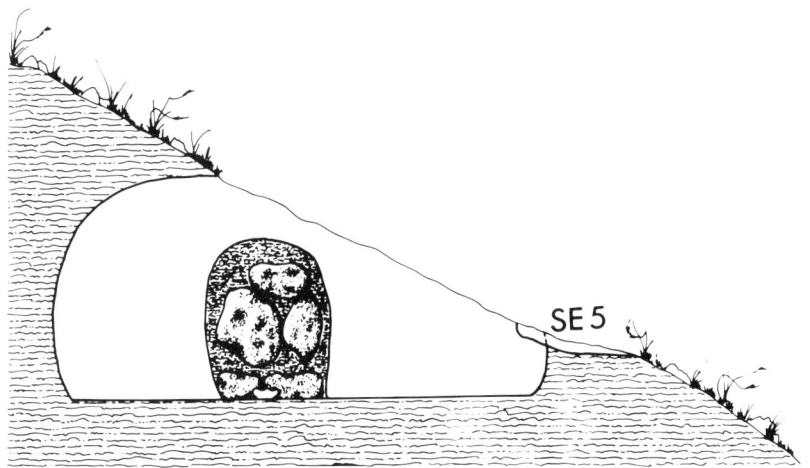

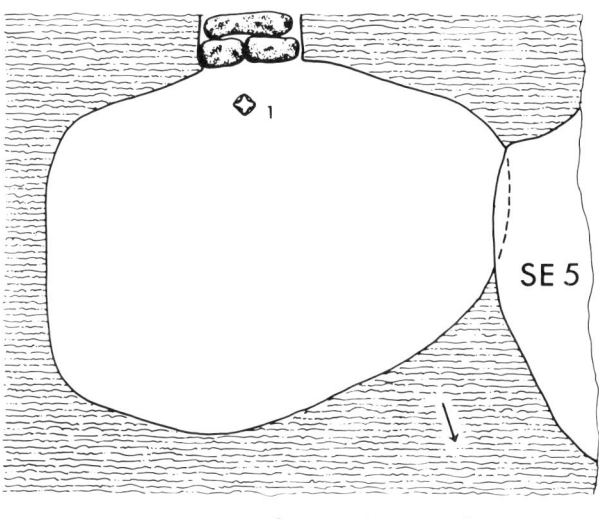

Fig. 54 Tomb SE10

irregular, but roughly oval in plan, measuring 1.85 m north-south by 2.40 m east-west. A part of the roof had survived on the most fully preserved (western) side, and these remains indicated that it had been low and only slightly domed, with a maximum height of approximately 1.15 m.

Access to the chamber was on the south side, where the entrance-way, which was only examined from the interior, was found to be fully preserved. It consisted of a neatly cut, almost oval opening, 80 cm high and 50 cm wide across the base (the widest point, however, was some 40 cm above the base, where the width was 65 cm). The blocking was intact, and consisted of six stones which had been 'floated' in a dense matrix of crushed marl and clay. This blocking could not be removed without causing a severe collapse, and consequently no investigation of the shaft could be undertaken.

The skeletal remains of tomb SE10 were found to be in extremely poor condition, having suffered not only from water damage but also from having been badly crushed by the collapse of the chamber roof. A concentration of bone fragments, mostly small, was found on the north side of the chamber, close to the wall. These appeared to represent the remains of a single individual, but could only be identified as adult. The only object in the tomb was a rather coarse and heavy four-spouted lamp (SE10.1), which was found lying upside-down on the south side of the chamber, just north of the entrance-way.

Contents

SE10.1   Four-spouted lamp

Technique: Handmade. *Paste*: 7.5YR 'light brown' 6/4; many small sand, many medium-large wadi gravel, sand and lime; no core; hard. *Surface* (Interior and Exterior): as paste; blackened all round rim.

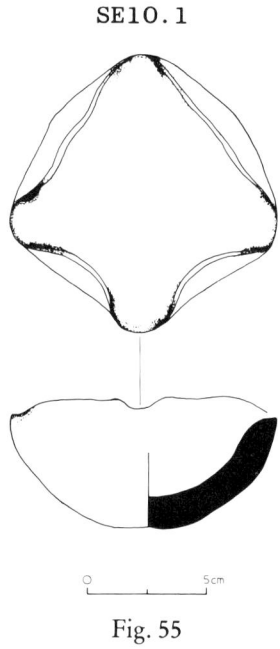

Fig. 55

TOMB SE11
East slope Hill 102
Orientation: W–E

This tomb was discovered during the surface scraping operation of Hill 102, when a rectangular feature, showing as dull greyish-brown against the brownish-cream marl, appeared on the slope immediately to the north of tomb SE8. Excavation revealed the presence of a fairly small and neatly cut tomb shaft, the interior fill of which consisted of loose greyish-brown soil containing many small white marl chips. The nature of the fill, which was homogeneous from top to bottom, suggested that the tomb shaft had been deliberately back-filled, using the material removed from its excavation.

The shaft of tomb SE11 was preserved to a depth of 2.80 m on the western side, but only to 55 cm on the eastern (down-slope) side. In plan it was roughly rectangular, measuring 70 cm north-south by 1.85 m east-west. Projecting ledges had been left during the cutting of the shaft on the north and south sides. These were 10–12 cm deep and 48 cm high, and extended from the western end of the shaft, where they flanked the lower part of the entrance-way, for distances of 1.40 m along the north side and 1.45 m along the south side. All four corners had been carefully cut and rounded to produce vertical jambs. As in the cases of tombs NE14 and NE20 (above), where similar features were encountered, it is suggested that these ledges served as supports for a covering of timber or reeds, producing in effect a low

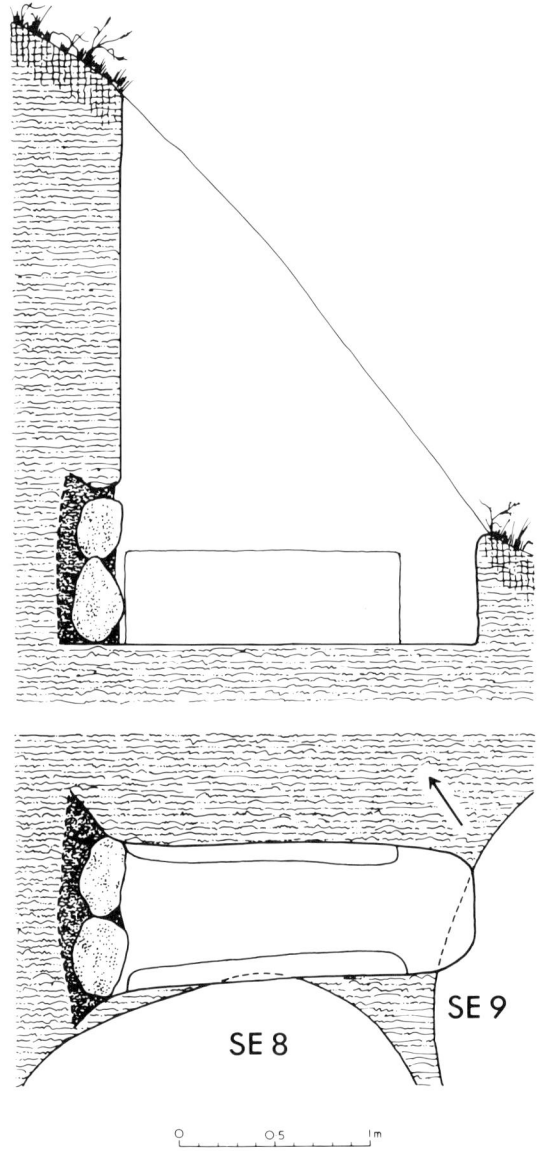

Fig. 56   Tomb SE11

tunnel linking the eastern end of the shaft to the chamber entrance.

As noted previously, the south-eastern side of the shaft had been cut into by the chamber of tomb SE9, and a second interruption in the southern wall had resulted from the cutting through of the chamber of tomb SE8 (see the relevant tomb descriptions above). The base of the shaft of tomb SE11 was more or less on the same level as the floor of tomb SE9's chamber, and the intrusion of the latter into the shaft had effectively, therefore, removed most of the poorly preserved south-eastern side. In the case of tomb SE8, however, the chamber floor was much higher than that of tomb SE9, and the circular 'window' caused by the interruption appeared quite high up in the shaft wall, its bottom beginning at a height of 60 cm above the base, that is above the top of the southern ledge.

The entrance to the chamber was on the western side. It consisted of a fairly wide opening, occupying the whole width of the shaft (75 cm). The sides were vertical to the height of the flanking ledges (48 cm from the base), above which a smoothly curving arch had been cut. The maximum height of the entrance-way was 80 cm at the centre.

The blocking was found to be intact, and consisted of three large stones arranged in triangular fashion. The spaces between and around them had been sealed using a dense cement composed of crushed marl and clay. Removal of the blocking revealed that the roof of the chamber had completely collapsed, the interior showing a massive fill of large blocks of marl, clayey soil and decayed marl rubble. Although a start was made on the clearance of this material, the work was interrupted by a sudden and heavy rain-storm. The shaft became flooded to above waist height, rendering further excavation impossible. Unfortunately, by the time the water had receded, there was insufficient time left in the season to return to the excavation of tomb SE11, and, regrettably, it had to be abandoned. No skeletal remains or other finds were recovered.

TOMB SE12
West slope Hill 102
Orientation: N–S

It is difficult to judge whether the wadi which at present runs between Hills 102 and 100/101 existed at the time of tomb cutting. On balance, it would seem likely that it did, for both of the tombs (SE12 and SE13) found on the shallow western slope of Hill 102 were orientated in the same direction, with chambers cut into the hill and shafts on the down-slope. This could of course be purely coincidental, but more significant is the fact that both of these tombs showed clear evidence for having been re-used, suggesting that, at the time of their re-use, their approaches must have been relatively easily accessible. This would certainly have been the case had the tombs been situated on a hill slope and approached by means of either a semi-shaft or a horizontally cut threshold. Had the tombs been cut down from a level surface and approached by means of a vertical shaft, the process of re-use would have been extremely difficult.

A surface examination and scraping of the western slope of Hill 102 revealed two rectangular features, showing as deep greyish-brown against the pale brownish-cream top-marl. The more northerly of the two was the approach to tomb SE12. As in other cases where tombs had been cut into existing hill slopes, the method of approach would have been by means of either a semi-shaft or a horizontally cut threshold (see, for example, tombs NE4, NE10 and NE14 above). In the case of tomb SE12, the distinction between these two functionally similar approach methods had been lost through erosion, the plan resulting from the excavation showing a rectangular area, truncated by the hill slope at the southern end. There would seem to be little doubt, however, that the method of approach employed for tomb SE12 would have been of the semi-shaft type, having, that is, a fourth low side on the down-slope. For, not only would the semi-shaft have been a more appropriate construction for a tomb of this scale, but also, as is noted below, the approach had been deliberately back-filled using the material removed from its excavation. Such a process would have been virtually impossible had the approach been of the horizontally cut threshold type with no southern retaining wall to contain the fill.

The excavated fill from the approach to tomb SE12 showed two clearly differentiated components. That from the southern end consisted of light greyish-brown soil containing many small white marl chips. The nature of this fill, which was homogeneous from top to bottom, suggested, as stated above, that the shaft had been deliberately back-filled. The fill from the northern end of the shaft was of a completely different character, orange-brown in colour, finely

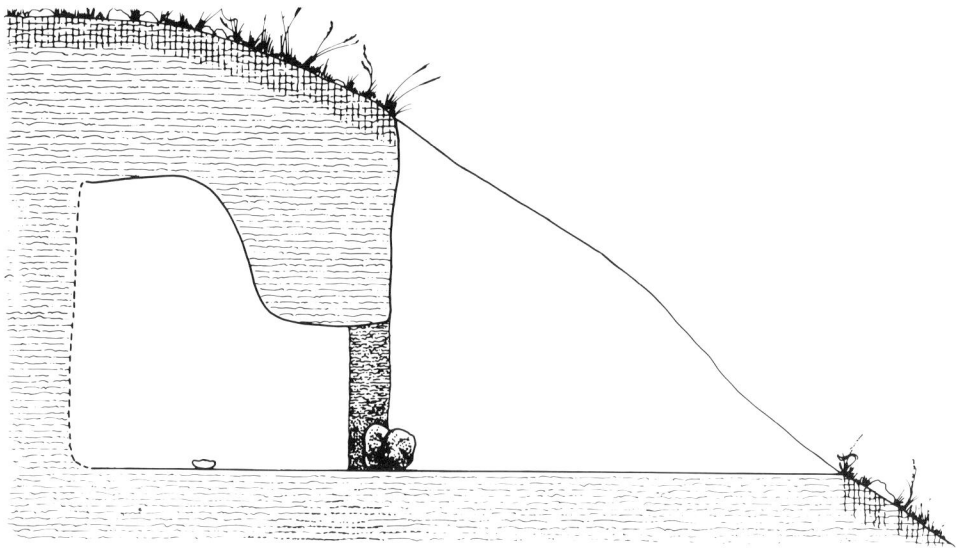

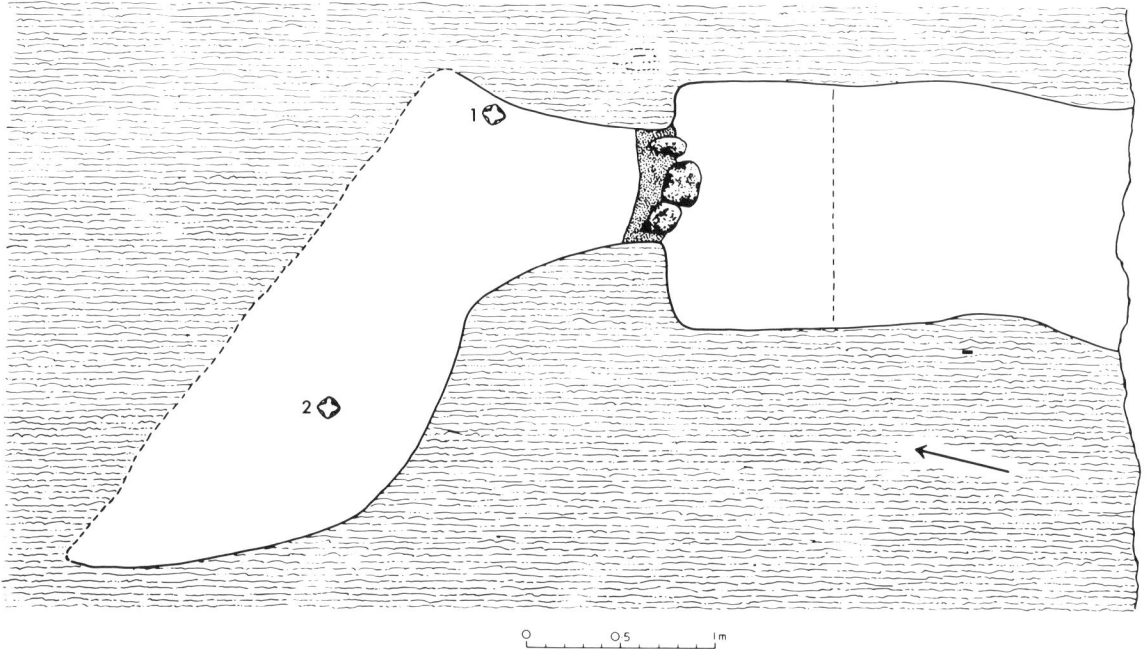

Fig. 57 Tomb SE12

divided but densely compacted. Examination of this material showed that it consisted of water-laid silt. On excavation, it was found that this silt had been deposited north of the line of a vertical cut which ran east-west across the shaft, beginning at a distance of 1.50 m from the southern end. Beneath the silt, at the base of the northern part of the shaft, were found a number of stones and lumps of hard bluish-grey clay which, as subsequent investigation showed, had derived from the blocking of the entrance-way.

Complete clearance of both fills revealed the surviving remains of the semi-shaft. It was rectangular in plan, measuring 2.35 m north-south by 1.25 m east-west. The northern side was preserved to a height of 1.80 m. As mentioned above, the southern side had disappeared completely through erosion, and therefore the north-south dimension given above may not represent the original length of the shaft. The chamber entrance was situated on the north side. It consisted of a neatly cut opening, almost triangular in shape, measuring 60cm across the base and 75cm high at the centre. The blocking showed evidence of having been disturbed. Three stones were found resting on the base, and these appeared to have been pushed out of position slightly southwards (back into the shaft). The stones were held together and to the sides of the entrance-way by means of a compact clay packing, bluish-grey in colour. Between the top of the stones (about 25 cm from the base) and the top of the entrance-way, the space had been sealed using a pale brown cement of crushed marl and clay.

Removal of the blocking revealed that the height of the entrance-way had been preserved for a distance of 1.05 m northwards, in the form of a low tunnel leading to the chamber proper. Over this distance, the width gradually increased to a maximum of 1.20m at the northern end. This tunnel was relatively free of debris, and the floor was overlaid only by a deposit of water-laid silt, approximately 8–10 cm deep. Beneath the silt, on the eastern side of the tunnel and close to the transition to the chamber, was found a four-spouted lamp (SE12.1), lying upright on the floor surface.

Beyond the tunnel, the chamber itself was seen to be filled with clayey soil, decayed marl rubble and large blocks of marl, indicating that the roof had collapsed. Removal of this heavy deposit began on the western side, and an estimated 50 per cent of the chamber was cleared down to the silt layer overlying the floor. A second four-spouted lamp (SE12.2) was found on the south-west side of the chamber, lying on top of the silt layer. This was associated with a few tiny fragments of bone which could only be identified as human. Unfortunately, before the remaining half of the chamber could be cleared, and before the exposed portion of the silt layer could be excavated, a major collapse occurred, and, for reasons of safety, no further work could be undertaken inside the chamber.

From the retrieved data, it would appear that the chamber of tomb SE12 had been roughly circular in plan, with a diameter of approximately 3.60–4.0m. A small part of the roof had survived on the southern side, above the exit from the tunnel, and from this it was seen to have been quite low, and almost flat rather than domed, with a height of approximately 1.45 m.

The evidence presented above demonstrates clearly that tomb SE12 witnessed two phases of usage. During phase 1, immediately following construction, the entrance-way had been blocked using stones, held in place by means of a clay packing. To this period of usage must be attributed the lamp, SE12.1, which was found directly upon the floor surface. Following interment and sealing of the entrance, the shaft was back-filled using the excavated material. After a certain period of time, represented in the tomb by an 8–10 cm accumulation of silt, the northern part of the shaft fill was dug out, and the chamber was re-entered by removing the upper part of the original blocking. A second interment was made on top of the accumulated silt layer, and this was also accompanied by a four-spouted lamp (SE12.2). The entrance-way was resealed using a cement of crushed marl and clay,

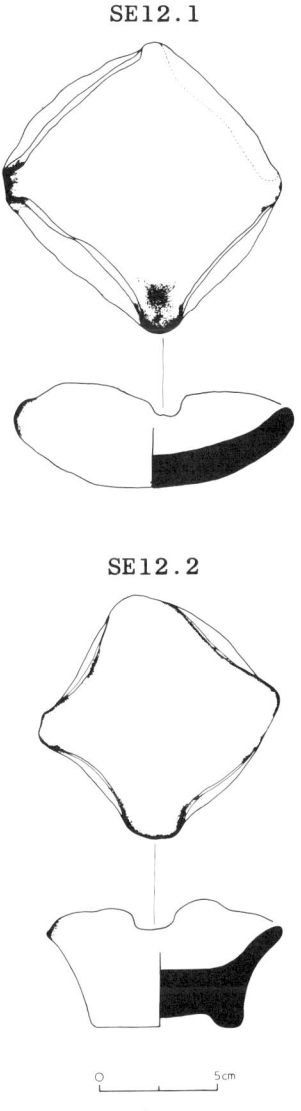

Fig. 58

but the exposed northern end of the shaft was not filled in again, and had apparently been left to silt up naturally.

Contents

PHASE 1

SE12.1   Four-spouted lamp

Technique: Handmade. *Paste*: 2.5YR 'red' 5/6; very many very small sand, some small-large ceramic; grey core; hard. *Surface* (Interior and Exterior): as paste; blackened on all four spouts.

PHASE 2

SE12.2   Four-spouted lamp

Technique: Handmade. *Paste*: 5YR 'reddish yellow' 6/6; many small-medium sand, ceramic and lime, some large ceramic; no core; hard. *Surface* (Interior and Exterior): as paste; blackened all around rim.

TOMB SE13
West slope Hill 102
Orientation: N–S

The approach to tomb SE13 was the more southerly of the two rectangular features revealed during the surface scraping operation of the west slope of Hill 102 (see above, tomb SE12). Excavation uncovered the remains of what was almost certainly a semi-shaft, similar in many respects to that of the adjacent tomb SE12. As in the case of that tomb, clear and similar evidence was found for some type of re-entry, again in the form of a vertical cut, appearing in the shaft fill, along an east-west line, at a distance of about 75 cm from the northern shaft wall. South of the line of this cut, the material consisted of greyish-brown soil containing many small white marl chips, representing the original back-filling of the shaft following the first usage of the tomb. The material from within the cut consisted of compact orange-brown water-laid silt, indicating that the northern part of the shaft, having been re-excavated, had been left open to silt up naturally; this following, presumably, a re-entry of the tomb chamber. At the base of the silt in the northern part of the shaft, a number of stones were encountered, which, as subsequent investigations showed, had come from the entrance-way blocking.

Complete clearance of the shaft enabled its plan

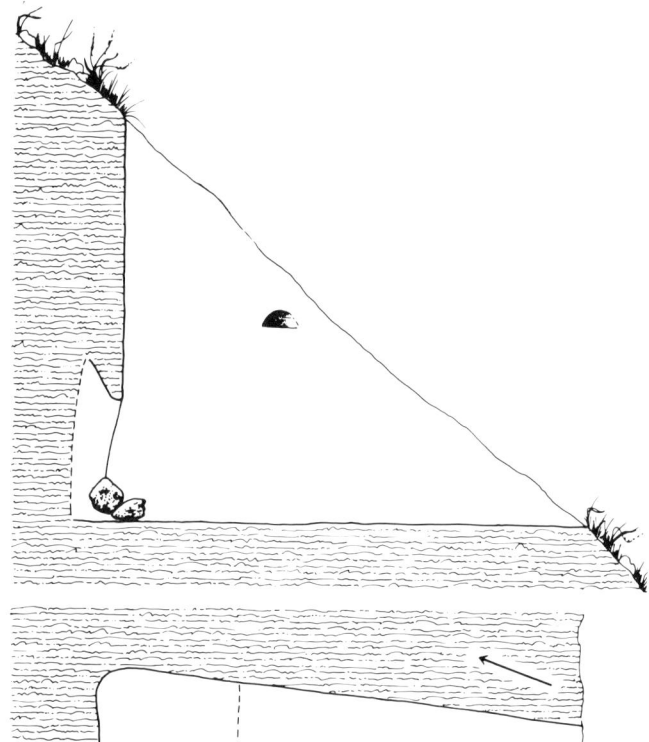

Fig. 59 Tomb SE13

and dimensions to be recorded. It was sub-rectangular in plan (as preserved), measuring 1.48 m east-west at the northern end and gradually narrowing towards the south, where it measured 1.15 m along the eroded (hill slope) edge. The southern side had been truncated by the erosion of the slope, the preserved length (north-south) being 2.55 m. The most fully preserved northern wall had survived to a depth of 2.05 m. A small, roughly cut foothold was found in the eastern wall, 1.0 m above the base and 70 cm south of the corner with the north wall. That this feature should exist at all is interesting in view of the semi-shaft method of approach. Clearly, the southern shaft wall, although undoubtedly lower than the northern, must still have been high enough to prevent direct access from the hill slope side.

The entrance to the chamber was on the north side, and took the form of a low, roughly executed, almost square opening, measuring 62 cm high by 58 cm across the base. The blocking had been disturbed: only two stones were found in position at the base, and these were held to the sides of the entrance-way by means of a dense, deep greyish-brown clay packing. A third stone was found lying immediately in front, but this had clearly fallen out of position. Unlike that of tomb SE12 (above), the entrance to tomb SE13 had not been sealed again following re-entry, and the 40 cm or so space above the undisturbed blocking stones was seen to be filled with water-laid silt, identical to, and indeed continuous with, that encountered in the northern part of the shaft. It is hard to conceive of the entrance-way having been left open had the chamber been reused, and it would seem more likely that in the case of tomb SE13, the chamber had simply been robbed. Whether this occurred in antiquity or in more recent times is impossible to determine.

Excavation proceeded with the removal of the silt from above and behind the blocking stones. Immediately behind them, at a height of approximately 2 cm above the floor surface, a small deposit of animal coprolites was found, together with a fragment of an animal jaw-bone which was identified as possibly that of a camel. Clearly, the reopened chamber had served as the den for a wild dog or similar carnivore, before silting up had been completed. Given the position of the deposit, at the base of the silt, it seems likely that this occurred soon after the tomb had been re-entered.

From the initial clearance of the silt, it appeared that the chamber opened directly from the entrance-way with no linking tunnel as in tomb SE12. As excavation continued into the chamber, however, it became clear that the roof was dangerously unstable, and, regrettably, the work had to be terminated before further details could be recorded.

TOMB SE14   Pl. XB
Surface Hill 9
Orientation: W–E

SE14 was the final tomb to be excavated during the 1984 season, and it also provided the second example of a stone-built grave (see tomb NE8 above for the other similar grave). It was discovered during a surface survey of Hill 9, when a large flat stone was found on the relatively level surface of the top of the hill. Clearance of the surrounding area revealed three further flat limestone slabs, somewhat smaller in size, lying to the east of the first one. The two easternmost slabs, which lay side by side, appeared to be parts of a single stone which had been broken in antiquity. Indeed, excavation showed that the crack between the two slabs had been reinforced by a further smaller slab which had been set upright against the eastern wall of the grave. It would seem, therefore, that the original intention had been to cover the grave with three slabs, as in the case of NE8.

The westernmost slab was the largest, measuring 2.0 m north-south by 1.02 m (maximum) east-west. The southern and eastern sides had been carefully cut to be more or less straight and at right angles to each other, but the other two sides had been left rounded and irregular. The central slab was somewhat smaller, measuring 1.80 m north-south by 0.88 m (maximum) east-west. The western side of this slab had been cut straight to produce a close fit with the westernmost slab, and the north and south sides had been cut at right angles to this side, and were roughly straight also. Assuming that the two easternmost slabs had originally been one, this would have measured about 1.60 m north-south by 0.75 m (maximum) east-west. The shape would have been roughly rectangular, but with a slight irregularity on the western side, conforming to that of the eastern side of the central slab.

Spaces between the slabs had been carefully filled using small stones. This was most apparent between the westernmost and central slabs. On removal, all the slabs were found to be of approximately the same thickness, between 20 and 28 cm. The removal of the slabs, because of their substantial sizes and weights, proved to be a lengthy process, and was not fully accomplished until the very end of the working day. Unfortunately, despite the presence of a guard, SE14 was damaged and robbed during the night. The following morning it was seen that a quite neat, rectangular trench had been dug into the centre of the grave, the bottom of this cut being well below the floor of the grave itself. Although some items of grave goods might have been removed by the robbers, careful excavation of the area around their cut, and exhaustive sieving of the spoil left by them on the edge of the grave, allowed many details of this interesting grave to be retrieved.

The interior fill of the grave (around the robbers'

Tombs in the south-east sector

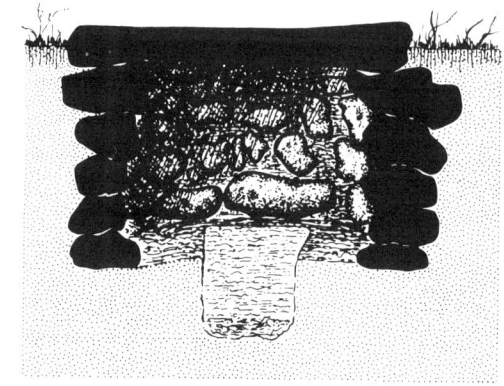

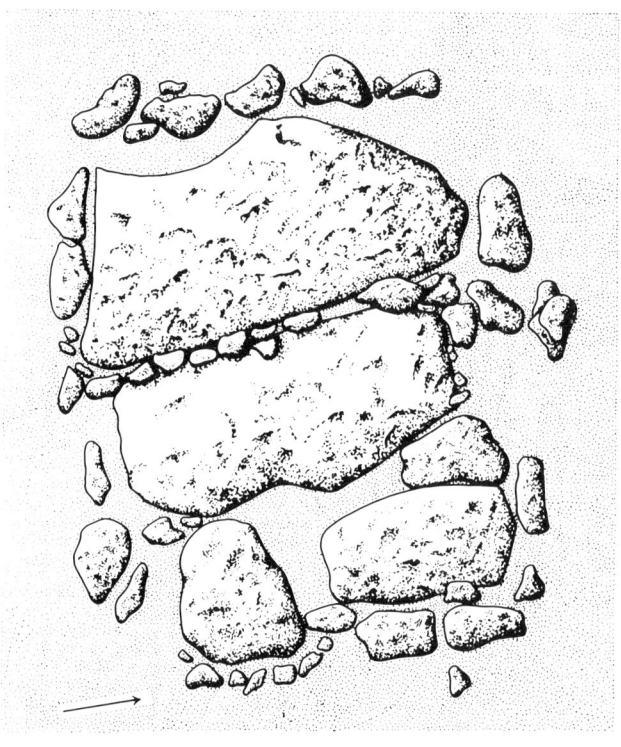
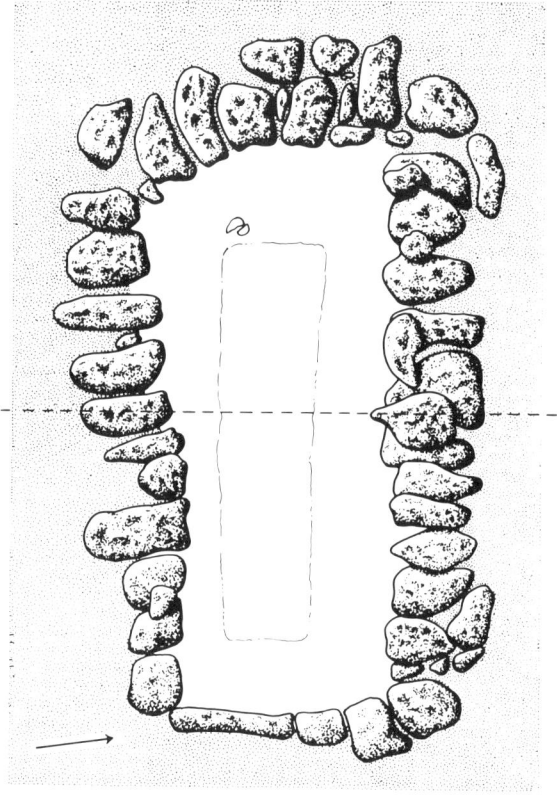

Fig. 60 Tomb SE14

trench) consisted of extremely hard and dense water-laid silt which persisted to the well-levelled base. Clearly no back-filling had occurred subsequent to interment, and the laminated structure of the silt indicated seasonal intrusion of water, puddling and sedimentation over a prolonged period of time. Removal of the silt revealed the structure of the grave itself. As in the case of tomb NE8 (above), SE14 was, in essence, a stone-lined grave, with wadi stones set into the sides of a neatly cut rectangular pit. This pit, as far as could be judged, would have measured roughly 3.0 m by 1.50 m. The stones, which were undressed but which had obviously been carefully selected, had been pressed, and presumably hammered, into the sides of the pit by as much as 50 per cent. Since it was a process of lining, and not one of producing a free-standing structure, the stones had been arranged rather than truly laid, and were only approximately in courses, five altogether, with many inconsistencies and gaps.

With regard to the funerary deposits, only a few details could be obtained. Immediately to the west of the robbers' trench, on the floor of the grave below the undisturbed silt, were found a number of small skull fragments. Further bones were recovered from the sieving of the robbers' spoil heap, and together with the skull fragments, they indicate that SE14 contained the remains of a single individual, adult (sex indeterminable), aged 25–35 years. From the position of the skull fragments, it would seem that the body had been buried with its head towards the west, and possibly on its back. The sieving also produced three finds, a single stone bead (SE14.2), the 'lip' of a cassid shell (SE14.3), and a copper riveted dagger (SE14.1), broken into five pieces but almost complete, including its four rivets.

Contents

SE14.1   Dagger   (Pl. XIIb)

Arsenical copper; four rivets in position on hilt.

SE14.2   Bead

Orange banded quartzite; bored from both ends with cylindrical drill.

SE14.3   Pendant (?)   (Pl. XIIId)

Shell; cassid lip.

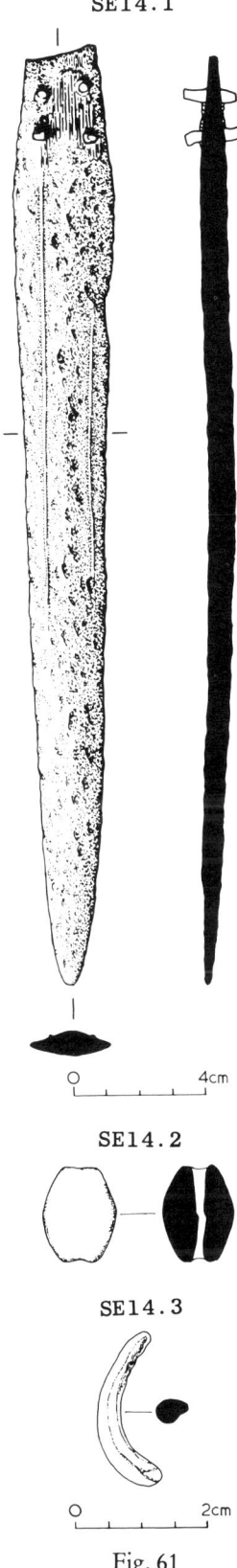

Fig. 61

CHAPTER 3

DISCUSSION

Altogether, thirty-seven tombs were examined during the 1984 season; that is, excluding NW1–3 (see Chapter 1), NE1 (a feature of non-funerary function), and treating NE16/17 as a single unit. Of these, twenty-three contained grave goods. On the basis of the associated finds, only one tomb, NE22, can definitely be assigned to the Proto-Urban period. Nineteen can, without doubt, be attributed to the Early Bronze IV (EBIV) period, including the two stone-built graves, NE8 and SE14. Three tombs (NE4, NE11 and NE12) contained only beads which, as noted below, are, in themselves insufficiently diagnostic to allow for an accurate chronological attribution. However, these tombs, together with the majority of those containing no grave goods whatever, can also be assigned to the EBIV period on the basis not only of formal and stylistic architectural comparisons with tombs containing well-dated deposits, but also, in some cases, by consideration of their locations and spatial relationships with known EBIV tombs. Thus, the close similarity of tomb NE4, which contained a single, rather undistinctive bead, to the immediately adjacent tomb NE2, which is well dated by two EBIV pottery vessels, would strongly indicate a comparable dating. Indeed, the remaining tombs found on the east slope of Hill 6 (NE5, NE6, NE7 and NE24), which contained no grave goods at all, also share this close similarity in terms of form, scale and construction method, and an EBIV dating can likewise be assumed for them.

The same argument can also be employed to suggest that the three small and heavily eroded tombs found on the west slope of Hill 4 (NE11, NE12 and NE13) also belong to the EBIV period. Tomb NE13 contained no grave goods, but tomb NE11 contained two stone pendants and NE12 a rather delicate necklace of beads and shells. Again, however, these finds are insufficiently characteristic of a particular period to permit an unequivocal attribution (see p. 97 below, however, on the beads from tomb NE12).

If the evidence for dating these three tombs to EBIV on the basis of tomb architecture (albeit scanty) seems somewhat tenuous, it should be pointed out that the only tomb clearly belonging to a period other than EBIV, the Proto-Urban tomb NE22, demonstrates a completely different manner of construction and form, showing an almost rectangular groundplan with accurately cut vertical walls, and also possibly a different method of entrance approach (see Chapter 2, tomb NE22).

No such reservations can, however, apply to the attribution of tombs NE14 and NE18 to the EBIV period, for these tombs, although only partially excavated, so closely resemble, in their semi-shaft approaches and entrance-ways, the adjacent tomb NE10, that their dating can be in no doubt. In addition, tomb NE14 showed the distinctive 'side-ledges' flanking the entrance-way, a feature found also in the shafts of tombs NE20 (well dated to EBIV) and SE11 (no finds).

Tomb SE3 was represented only by its shaft and

entrance-way, the chamber itself having been lost through erosion. The large rectangular and beautifully cut entrance-way was quite unlike that of any of the other tombs examined, and this could well be adduced as evidence for a non-EBIV dating. In support of an EBIV dating, however, should be mentioned the well-preserved tool-marks found on three sides of the shaft (see Chapter 2, tomb SE3, for details). These were identical in size and form to the tool-marks observed in several other tombs, including tombs NE15 and SE8.

The extensively eroded tomb SE5 contained the remains of two individuals but no associated grave goods. Too little of the structure was preserved to allow for architectural comparisons with other dated tombs, but a *terminus post quem* can be established on the basis of its cutting into tomb SE10, a tomb containing a typical EBIV four-spouted lamp.

Tomb SE6, only about half of which was found to be preserved, contained neither skeletal remains nor grave goods. In this case, however, erosion had cut the tomb along its long axis, preserving significant elements of its shaft, entrance-way and chamber. These suggest that tomb SE6 conforms, in terms of construction method and architectural form, very closely to the other tombs on the west slope of Hill 111, including the well-dated EBIV tomb, SE4. An EBIV dating for tomb SE6 would therefore seem appropriate.

Tomb SE11 was not investigated beyond the excavation of its shaft. This revealed, however, the distinctive 'side-ledges', found also in tombs NE20 (well dated to EBIV) and NE14 (see above). An EBIV dating for tomb SE11 can therefore be suggested. Further support for this dating comes from the *terminus ante quem* provided by the intrusion into the shaft of tombs SE8 and SE9, both of which contained well-dated EBIV deposits.

Finally, tomb SE13, lying immediately adjacent to tomb SE12 on the west slope of Hill 102, although again not examined beyond the clearance of the shaft, shows such a formal similarity to the latter tomb that an EBIV attribution would seem undeniable.

Proto-Urban Group: Tomb NE22

Tomb NE22 contained the remains of three individuals, representing two phases of interment. The best-preserved skeleton (A), belonging to the later phase, was associated with two juglets with high loop-handles (NE22.5–6), and a group of fifteen conical calcite beads (NE22.1, 2, 4, 7–18). The poor condition of the fourth find, a fragmentary ledge-handled jar (NE22.3), suggests that it might have been related to the earlier phase of interment, represented by skeletons B and C.

All three of the pottery vessels have a red burnished slip, and are typical of the Proto-Urban A culture. The juglets with exaggeratedly high loop-handles are characteristic of the more northerly aspect of this culture, and close parallels, showing the same rather squat form with broad flat base, can be found at Tell el-Farʿah in tombs 3, 11 and 15 (De Vaux and Stève 1949: fig. 2:12; De Vaux 1951: fig. 7:7; 1955: fig. 1:4).

The fragmentary jar with simple semicircular ledge-handles (NE22.3) again has a rather squat form, and a slightly concave base. This can also be paralleled at Tell el-Farʿah in tomb 5 (De Vaux and Stève 1949: fig. 8:8).

No parallels can be adduced for the unusual group of conical calcite beads. As mentioned above (Chapter 2, NE22), the position of these beads, close to the pelvis of skeleton A, and their closely interlocking configuration would seem to suggest that they formed a type of waist ornament, perhaps intended to cover the genitals.

Tombs of the Early Bronze IV Period

Taken together, the tombs which can be assigned to EBIV require, in themselves, little further comment. The most remarkable find of the 1984 season at Tiwal esh-Sharqi was the two stone-built graves (NE8 and SE14) which appear to have been fully integrated into the cemetery of otherwise shaft tombs, more typical of the period. These two graves are discussed more fully below. Otherwise, given that any interesting individual architectural features have already been highlighted in Chapter 2, it remains only to make a few remarks about the tombs in general.

With regard to the orientation of the tombs, no clear pattern can be discerned. For those tombs dug into the sides of hills, the orientation was determined by the pre-existing topography. Even when choice was available, however, in cases where tombs were dug down from level surfaces, no clear preference can be detected.

Discussion

Tomb	Orientation
NE9	S–N
NE15	W–E
NE16/17	W–E
NE20	W–E
NE25	NE–SW
SE1	W–E
SE2	E–W (phase 1)
	W–E (phase 2)
(SE3)	(W–E)
SE4	E–W
SE5	not establishable
SE6	S–N
SE7	N–S
SE8	N–S
SE9	N–S
SE10	N–S
SE11	W–E

The orientation of the deceased within the tomb might be considered to be of greater significance than that of the tomb itself. Unfortunately, as detailed in Appendix A below, the state of preservation of the skeletal remains was such that only in a very few cases could such an orientation be established with any degree of reliability.

Tomb	Orientation	Facing	Posture
NE2	W–E	N	flexed
NE4	W–E	N	flexed
NE8 (A)	S–N	E	flexed
(B)	S–N	E	flexed
NE11	S–N	W	flexed
NE12	S–N	W	flexed
NE21	W–E	?	?
NE24	N–S	E	?
SE4 (A)	N–S	?	flexed
(B)	W–E	?	extended
SE14	W–E	up (?)	on back (?)

The above tabulation obviously represents too restricted a sample to allow for statistically significant conclusions to be drawn. Despite the limited number of individuals for consideration, however, a lack of consistency is immediately apparent, not only overall, but even within the same tomb (see tomb SE4).

As far as the burial practice is concerned, the poor state of preservation of the skeletal remains again prevents any detailed discussion as to whether this might have been primary or secondary. Only in tomb NE8, one of the stone-built graves, was there clear evidence to suggest that skeleton B represented a secondary burial (see Appendix A below), albeit apparently interred contemporaneously with the individual represented by skeleton A (see Chapter 2). Otherwise, it can only be said that no evidence was found to suggest that the practice was other than primary.

The finds from the Early Bronze IV tombs

The pottery and other objects recovered from the Early Bronze IV tombs at Tiwal esh-Sharqi during the 1984 season appear to be chronologically homogeneous, and in terms of the tripartite system proposed for the period by Dever (1980: 35–64) relate most clearly to those assemblages that characterise the central sub-phase, EBIVB (see below for further discussion).

Pottery

The repertoire of pottery vessels is quite restricted, and can be classified under only eight types. The distribution of these types throughout the various tomb deposits is shown in the table opposite.

Generally, the pottery is technically well made. The clay was well prepared, uniformly tempered with small to medium sand, ceramic and lime grits, and the vessels were evenly fired. Many of the vessels were provided with a cream wash, and an additional decorative treatment is found in the body combing seen on many of the ledge-handled storejars and loop-handled amphoriskoi.

LEDGE-HANDLED STOREJARS

All the storejars are characterised by a wide-bodied, rather squat form with a broad, flat or slightly indented base. The ledge-handles are of the 'envelope-folded' variety (typical of EBIVB), in the most developed case of which, NE10.4, the folds have become fused together to form a continuous lip. Necks are either slightly flaring with simple rims (SE1.15, SE1A.4 and SE8.1), or vertical with out-turned rims (NE2.1, NE10.4, SE1.1, SE1.2 and SE4.2). Four of the vessels show a discrete decoration at the base of the neck: a single band of impressions on NE10.4, SE1A.4 and SE4.2, and a band of rope moulding on SE1.1. NE10.4 has additionally two incised lines on the shoulder. The bodies of six of the storejars

Distribution of pottery types in Early Bronze IV tombs

TOMB	NE2	NE8	NE9	NE10	NE10A	NE15	NE16	NE17	NE20	NE21	NE23	SE1	SE1A	SE2	SE4	SE7	SE8	SE9	SE10	SE12
TYPE																				
Ledge-handled storejar	NE2.1			NE10.4								SE1.1 SE1.2 SE1.15	SE1A.4		SE4.2		SE8.1			
Loop-handled amphoriskos		NE8.2		NE10.3 NE10.5 NE10.9	NE10A.1		NE16.1 NE16.2 NE16.7	NE17.4	NE20.2	NE21.1		SE1.4		SE2.1	SE4.1 SE4.5 SE4.6 SE4.8					
Round-based storejar				NE10.7																
Bowl				NE10.6 NE10.8			NE16.5													
Cup	NE2.2		NE9.2				NE16.6		NE20.1		NE23.1	SE1.3 SE1.5			SE4.4 SE4.7 SE4.9					
Perforated cup				NE10.10		NE15.1 NE15.8	NE16.4							SE2.2						
Four-spouted lamp				NE10.1 NE10.2		NE15.3 NE15.4 NE15.6	NE16.3	NE17.3	NE20.3			SE1.8 SE1.11	SE1A.3	SE2.4	SE4.3 SE4.10 SE4.11	SE7.2			SE10.1	SE12.1 SE12.2
Side-spouted lamp												SE1.7						SE9.1		

Discussion

(NE2.1, SE1.1, SE1.2, SE1.15, SE1A.4 and SE8.1) are ornamented by combing (note that in the case of SE1.1, the combing is so faint that it could not be accurately recorded for the drawing). In all instances, this decoration appears to have been executed using a comb of five teeth, each tooth being approximately 3 mm wide and the space between them (represented by the raised ridges) being 1.0–1.5 mm.

Parallels for the Tiwal esh-Sharqi storejars are numerous, and the following list concentrates, therefore, only on those that are particularly close.

El Husn	tomb (Harding 1953: fig. 4:60)	cf. SE8.1, SE1.15
Jericho	tomb P22 (Kenyon 1965: fig. 53:9)	SE4.2
	tomb O1 (Kenyon 1965: fig. 63:5)	✗ SE1A.4
	tomb P24 (Kenyon 1965: fig. 68:1)	SE1.1
	tomb G8 (Kenyon 1960: fig. 86:1)	NE10.4
Beth Shan	tomb 89 (Oren 1973: fig. 18.1)	SE1.2, NE2.1

Similar body combing has been recorded at Beth Shan (Oren 1973: 35), and from the el-Husn tomb (Harding 1953: 2). Directly comparable ledge-handled storejars were also found during Helms' excavations at Tiwal esh-Sharqi in 1983 (see especially Helms 1983: figs 17:1 and 19:2–4 from tomb 14, and fig. 21:15 from tomb 5).

ROUND-BASED HANDLELESS STOREJAR

Only one example of this type was found, in tomb NE10 (NE10.7). It has an ovoid, somewhat irregularly fashioned body with a short, slightly flaring neck and everted rim. A virtually identical jar was found by Helms in 1983 (see Helms 1983: fig. 16:9 from tomb 14). Elsewhere, similar but rather more globular jars were found in the el-Husn tomb (Harding 1953: fig. 3:48, 50), there decorated at the base of the neck with a band of incisions. An incomplete, but apparently similar vessel was found in tomb 58 at Megiddo (Guy and Engberg 1938: pl. 88:10). The closest external parallel in terms of body shape, however, is probably an example from tomb 110 at Beth Shan (Oren 1973: fig. 22:1), although this piece has an applied cordon at the base of the neck.

LOOP-HANDLED AMPHORISKOI

Next only to four-spouted lamps, loop-handled amphoriskoi were the most numerous element within the repertoire of vessels found at Tiwal esh-Sharqi (seventeen examples). They show great variety with regard to specific shape and size (from NE10.3 which is only 90 mm high to NE16.1 which is 218 mm high), but the majority (all but three) are characterised by a thin-walled, elegantly proportioned ovoid body with a flat or slightly indented base which, in some instances, is so pronounced as to give the impression of a true ring base (see especially NE10.5, NE16.1 and NE17.4). Two of the amphoriskoi, NE8.2 and NE20.2, are much heavier, with wide, squat bodies, and stand on rather broad bases. One of these, NE20.2, has what is probably a potters' mark incised on the shoulder.

Generally, the necks are either gently flaring or more or less vertical with a slight convexity towards the rim. One vessel, NE10.9, shows a quite different profile, with a disproportionately wide mouth and no true shoulder: it is here described as a 'mug-amphoriskos'.

The amphoriskoi show limited decoration. Most are covered with a pale cream wash, and a few (NE16.1, NE20.2, SE4.1 and SE4.6) show body combing similar to that found on the ledge-handled storejars. Otherwise, ornamentation is confined to the base of the neck: NE8.2 and SE4.1 with incised lines, and NE16.1 with a band of tooth impressions.

A number of similar amphoriskoi were found during Helms' excavations at Tiwal esh-Sharqi in 1983 (see especially Helms 1983: figs 18:4 and 12 from tomb 14, 21:3 from tomb 3, 21:8 from tomb 9 and 22:6 from tomb 25). Otherwise, since the loop-handled amphoriskos is one of the most ubiquitous EBIV forms, parallels are too numerous to permit a complete listing, and the following examples have been selected as being particularly close.

Beth Shan	tomb 89 (Oren 1973: fig. 18:10)
	tomb 26 (Oren 1973: fig. 19:15)
	tomb 262 (Oren 1973: fig. 23:9)
	tomb 108 (Oren 1973: fig. 24:7)
Megiddo	tomb 217B (Guy and Engberg 1938: pl. 10:19)

Discussion

	tomb 41
	(Guy and Engberg 1938: pl. 10:8)
	tomb 878A
	(Guy and Engberg 1938: pl. 20:19) – for
	'mug-amphoriskos' NE10.9
Jericho	tomb H5
	(Kenyon 1960: fig. 75:3–4)
	tomb G53
	(Kenyon 1960: fig. 86:15)
	tomb G40
	(Kenyon 1960: fig. 98:1
	tomb H11
	(Kenyon 1960: fig. 110:1)
	tomb M1
	(Kenyon 1965: fig. 36:4)
	tomb D1
	(Kenyon 1965: fig. 43:3)
	tomb O1
	(Kenyon 1965: fig. 63:1)
El-Husn	tomb
	(Harding 1953: figs 1–3 *passim*)

BOWLS

Bowls were poorly represented in the repertoire of vessels excavated in the 1984 season. Only three were found, two in tomb NE10 (NE10.6 and NE10.8), and one in tomb NE16 (NE16.5).

NE10.6 has gently curving walls, slightly inturned towards the top. NE10.8 is shallower and has a more open, slightly flaring form. NE16.5 is somewhat similar to both the above, but shows a marked incurving towards the top, and has two simple, semicircular ledge handles. All three bowls have broad flat bases, and all three show horizontal striations just below the rim (most pronounced on NE16.5), indicating that they were finished on a wheel.

Helms' 1983 excavations produced many more bowls, including several which closely parallel those under discussion (see Helms 1983: figs 16–22 *passim*). Elsewhere, close parallels to the Tiwal esh-Sharqi bowls are few. A bowl somewhat similar to NE10.6 was found at Megiddo in tomb 1101B Lower (Guy and Engberg 1938: pl. 6:29. Note, however, that this example is much larger). A close parallel for NE10.8, also showing wheel-finishing, was found at Jericho in tomb M17 (Kenyon 1965: fig. 89:10). Other examples from Megiddo (Guy and Engberg 1938: pl. 88:2 from tomb 41 and pl. 22:10 from tomb 1120A) and Jebel Qaʿaqīr (Gitin 1975: fig. 3:13) are generally similar to NE10.8, but lack the wheel-finishing. For NE16.5, the only close parallel that can be cited is a bowl from Iktanu, Phase 2 (Prag 1974: fig. 7:5), showing similar simple ledge handles.

CUPS

With only one exception (NE20.1), the cups from the 1984 season are of the straight-sided, slightly flaring type, sometimes with a very gently incurved mouth. Bases are flat and quite wide relative to the height of the vessel. NE20.1 is of a different form, again with a flat base, but with incurved walls and two upwardly projecting knob handles. This piece is decorated with three irregular horizontal incised lines at the point of handle attachment.

The straight-sided cups all show horizontal striations below the rim, resulting from wheel-finishing. Two of them have vertical combing on the body (NE2.2 and NE23.1), and the body of SE1.5 appears to have been shaved vertically.

A number of similar straight-sided cups were found during Helms' excavations at Tiwal esh-Sharqi in 1983 (see Helms 1983: figs 16–22 *passim*), and a directly comparable vessel to NE20.1, with similar knob handles and incised decoration, was found in tomb 25 (ibid: fig. 22:2).

Elsewhere, straight-sided cups have been found at Megiddo (Guy and Engberg 1938: pl. 10:2 from tomb 41, pl. 20:11 from the shaft of tomb 878, and pl. 22:12 from tomb 1120A), at Jebel Qaʿaqīr (Dever 1973: fig. 4:15) and at Khirbet el-Kirmil (Dever 1975: fig. 5:21–3). A fragmentary example showing similar vertical body combing was found at ʿArôʿer in level VIa (Olávarri 1969: fig. 4:15).

Parallels for NE20.1 are more elusive. A rather similar cup with incised decoration but lacking the knob handles was found at Jebel Qaʿaqīr in Cemetery C (Dever 1973: fig. 4:22), and an example, also incised, but with a more open profile and only one knob was found at Khirbet el-Kirmil (Dever 1975: fig. 5:18).

PERFORATED CUPS

Five examples of these little vessels, which are often described as 'funnels', were found during the 1984 season. All are very similar, with a hemispherical form, and a single hole, 4–6 mm in diameter, in the bottom. Three similar examples were recovered during Helms' excavations in 1983 (Helms 1983: fig. 16:3–4 from tomb 14, and fig. 21:4 from tomb 19).

Discussion

Comparable funnels have been found at the following sites, a listing which does not claim to be exhaustive.

Jericho	tomb M1
	(Kenyon 1965: fig. 36:6)
	tomb M9
	(Kenyon 1965: fig. 36:11)
	tomb P5
	(Kenyon 1965: fig. 47:15)
	tomb G83
	(Kenyon 1965: fig. 80:3)
Lachish	tomb 2015
	(Tufnell 1958: pl. 66:450)
	tomb 2114
	(Tufnell 1958: pl. 66:451)
Khirbet el-Kirmil	cemetery
	(Dever 1975: fig. 5:28)
Jebel Qaʿaqīr	cave G23
	(Gitin 1975: fig. 4:3)
	tombs
	(Dever 1972b: 233)
ʿAin es-Sâmiya	cemetery
	(Dever 1972a: fig. 3:7)

Dever has suggested that these perforated cups or funnels were in fact 'leben cups', designed to suspend (by means of strings) the fermenting agent in a large jar of milk (Dever 1973: 53, n.33; 1975: 30*). This idea seems very plausible in view of the findings at Tiwal esh-Sharqi. For in two cases, perforated cups were found resting in the mouths of loop-handled amphoriskoi (NE10.10 in NE10.5, and SE2.2 in SE2.1), and in a third instance the perforated cup was found right inside the amphoriskos (NE16.4 inside NE16.2). Most revealing was the pair from tomb SE2 (Pl. IXB), for when the perforated cup was removed from the mouth of the amphoriskos, fugitive white traces of a fibrous material were observed at the junction of the two vessels, suggesting that a cloth separator had been used between them. Not only would this cloth have provided a means of supporting the cup securely in the mouth of the amphoriskos (rather than by means of strings as proposed by Dever), but, more significantly, it would have permitted a slow and controlled dripping of the fermenting agent into the milk below.

FOUR-SPOUTED LAMPS

A wide variety of shapes, sizes and indeed qualities of four-spouted lamps were found during the 1984 season. They range from the superbly fashioned, thin-walled and wheel-finished examples from tomb NE10 (NE10.1–2) to the excessively crude lamp from tomb NE20 (NE20.1). This latter piece surely represents a 'home-made' attempt, for it is hard to imagine that this horrible lamp was the product of even the most incompetent potter! There is variation, too, in the degree of 'pinching', as created by the amount to which the side walls were folded in. This ranges from the near vertical-walled SE7.2, with spouts that are therefore almost right-angled in plan, to the elegantly inturned SE2.4 with wide semi-circular spouts. None of the lamps, however, show the exaggerated folding, leading to sharply pointed spouts, which seems to typify the latest in the series (see Richard 1978: 111–13).

One unusual type, worthy of note, is SE12.2, which has a high foot and stands on a true ring base. Otherwise bases are either flat or rounded, the two forms being found in roughly equal proportions. Interestingly, as the distribution list below shows, round-based and flat-based lamps were never found together in the same tomb (omitting, that is, the unusual SE12.2).

Flat base		Round base	
NE10	2 examples	SE1	2 examples
NE15	3 examples	SE1A	1 example
NE16	1 example	SE4	3 examples
NE17	1 example	SE7	1 example
NE20	1 example	SE10	1 example
SE2	1 example	SE12	1 example

This observation may not necessarily have chronological significance, however, for at Jericho lamps with flat and rounded bases were frequently found together in the same tomb deposits (see Kenyon 1960: figs 75–100 *passim*, and Kenyon 1965: figs 28–90 *passim*). Perhaps at Tiwal esh-Sharqi the differentiation could be related to family or tribal preferences, since, with the single exception of SE2.4, all the flat-based lamps were found in the north-east sector, and all the round-based lamps came from the south-east sector.

The four-spouted lamp is such a well-known and widespread EBIV type that it seems unnecessary to present a full listing of parallels (for convenience see Pritchard 1963:67, supplemented by Richard 1978: 161–2).

SIDE-SPOUTED LAMP

Two examples of this highly unusual lamp type were

Discussion

found in different tombs (SE1.7 and SE9.1). This vessel has the normal four-spouted saucer on top, but it is set on a tall base which has an internal hollow chamber connecting to the exterior by means of a spout of roughly square cross-section. In other words, there is no direct connection between the lamp saucer and the lower chamber. Both SE1.7 (Pl. XIV) and SE9.1 show extensive blackening on the four spouts of the lamp saucer, and had clearly been used. No such blackening is found, however, on the side-spouts, indicating that the function of these must be unrelated to the burning process.

It is possible that the lower chamber was used to contain water, perhaps in an attempt to cool the oil and prolong the length of burning. A more attractive, if somewhat fanciful suggestion would be that the lower chamber contained an aromatic or perfumed substance, the scent of which would issue through the side-spout as the lamp heated up.

As far as the writer is aware, this lamp type is without parallel.

Metal objects

DAGGERS

Four daggers were found during the 1984 season. NE25.1 has a simple, rather small blade, with the hilt narrowing to a slightly rounded end, and four rivets. NE8.1 is somewhat similar in shape, but larger, in both width and length. Both daggers conform closely to Kenyon's type A at Jericho (1965: fig. 22:1). The dagger from tomb SE1 (SE1.6, Pl. XIIc) is also similar, but has a midrib running along the centre of each blade face and can be related, therefore, to Kenyon's type D (ibid: fig. 22:7). Slightly narrower and longer, with just the hint of a shoulder, is the dagger from tomb SE14 (SE14.1, Pl. XIIB). The blade in this case has two low ribs or veins, on one side only, running parallel with the edge. The hilt of the dagger had been broken, and the end section was not found (see Chapter 2: SE14). It is just possible, therefore, that SE14.1 had originally been secured to its handle using six rivets rather than four. In terms of its overall shape, however, SE14.1 is most closely similar to Kenyon's type C at Jericho (1965: fig. 22:6).

The veining on the blade of SE14.1 may be a feature that has not previously been noted, but in terms of the overall shape and proportions, this dagger and the other three are all typical of the EBIV period, and indeed they would all be included in Richard's type 1, the commonest and most widespread type for the period (see Richard 1978: 228–30 and pls XXII-XXIII, 'Narrow-Bladed Daggers', for parallels and associated references).

Three of the daggers, NE8, NE25.1 and SE1.6, showed an interesting feature in that in each case, in addition to the four rivets in position on the hilt, two further rivets were found side by side a short distance away. This observation leads to the suggestion that the handles of these daggers were attached in two sections, sandwiching the blade between them, and held at the distal end by the two additional rivets.

All four of the daggers showed traces of organic material, preserved by the corrosion products of the copper, adhering to the hilt and representing the remains of the handles. Two of the daggers, NE8.1 and NE25.1, were kindly examined by Jacqui Watson of the Ancient Monuments Laboratory (Historic Buildings and Monuments Commission for England), London, using the Scanning Electron Microscope. The results demonstrated that in both cases the material used for the handle was horn.

The same two daggers (NE8.1 and NE25.1) were analysed by X-ray Fluorescence (energy-dispersive), again at the Ancient Monuments Laboratory. The results indicated that they were both composed of arsenical copper, containing less than 5% arsenic.

The remaining two daggers (SE14.1 and SE1.6) and the javelin (SE1.12, see below) were analysed, also by X-ray Fluorescence (energy-dispersive), by Michael Hughes of the British Museum Research Laboratory. For SE14.1, the results were:

Copper	95.8%
Iron	0.5%
Arsenic	3.5%
Lead	0.1%
Tin	None detected

This dagger is again, therefore, composed of arsenical copper. For SE1.6, the results were more unusual:

Copper	87.0%
Iron	0.1%
Arsenic	0.2%
Lead	0.05%
Tin	12.0%

This demonstrates that SE1.6 is made of true tin bronze. The occurrence of a bronze weapon in EBIV is unusual, but not otherwise unknown. A number of bronze fenestrated axes have been reported, and a bronze dagger was found at Jericho in a group of otherwise identical daggers composed of arsenical copper (see Prag 1974: 91 and note 63). The results for the javelin are given below.

SMALL BLADE

Tomb NE15 contained a small blade with rounded butt and no rivet attachment (NE15.7). Two rivets were, however, found in close proximity (NE15.5), and on analogy with the daggers above, it might be suggested that this little blade was placed between two organic handle elements and secured at two points by means of the rivets.

JAVELIN

A single example of this typical EBIV weapon was found in tomb SE1 (SE1.12, Pl. XIIA). It has a leaf-shaped blade with a midrib on either face, a long square-section shaft which becomes flattened and rounded towards the blade, and a hooked tang. Parallels for this type of javelin are relatively few, and are listed below:

Tell el-'Ajjûl	tomb 227
	(Petrie 1931: pl. XIX:49)
	tomb 275
	(Petrie 1931: pl. XIX:48)
Gibeon	tomb 13
	(Pritchard 1963: fig. 18:9)
Jericho	tomb G83
	(Kenyon 1965: fig. 41:11)
	tomb M13
	(Kenyon 1965: fig. 41:13)
Jebel Qa'aqīr	cemetery
	(Dever 1972b: 233)
Khirbet el-Kirmil	cemetery
	(Dever 1975: fig. 6:6–7)
Lachish	tomb 2111
	(Tufnell 1958: pl. 22:1)
	tomb 2032
	(Tufnell 1958: pl. 22:2)
	tomb 2100
	(Tufnell 1958: pl. 22:3)
'Ain es-Sâmiya	cemetery
	(Dever 1972a: fig. 5:1–3)

As the list shows, and as previously noted by Dever (1972a: 103), this type of javelin shows a central and southern distribution in Palestine. SE1.12 provides the first published example from Transjordan.

Analysis of the javelin gave the following result:

Copper	97.4%
Arsenic	2.0%
Iron	0.4%
Lead	0.1%
Tin	None detected

This weapon is again, therefore, composed of arsenical copper. (Note that the javelin was found in the same deposit as the bronze dagger, SE1.6.)

AWLS

Two copper/copper alloy awls were found, NE17.1 and SE1.14, both with square-section shafts and gently tapering points. The top of SE1.14 shows a swelling which, on examination, proved to be a deposit of mineralised organic material, most probably wood.

Awls are fairly common in EBIV deposits, but most tend to show a circular cross-section. According to Dever (1973: 55 and note 39), the square-section awls represent a continuation of EBII–III traditions. Awls similar to those excavated at Tiwal esh-Sharqi have been found at Jericho in tomb P5 (Kenyon 1965: fig. 45:5) and at Lachish in tomb 6031 (Tufnell 1958: pl. 22:8).

It is possible that the copper/copper alloy object used as a hook in tomb SE7 (SE7.1; see Chapter 2, tomb SE7) might also have been part of a similar awl, but unfortunately the fragmentary and poor condition of this piece does not permit a definite identification.

Objects of stone and shell

BEADS

Several tombs contained beads, either as necklaces (NE12.1 and SE2.3) or as small groups or individual items (NE4.1, single bead; NE9.1, single bead; NE11.1–2, pendant and bead; NE17.2, single bead; SE1.13, two beads; SE1A.2, five beads). Tomb NE8 contained quite a large number of beads (twenty-seven), but in view of the fact that many of the quartz beads had not been completely drilled through, it would seem unlikely that they formed part of a necklace. In the cases of NE12.1 and SE2.3, however, the positions in which the beads were found made it quite clear that they had been strung together as necklaces.

For the most part, the beads are unremarkable, and most of the types, the majority of which are simple disc and barrel shaped, can be paralleled at Jericho and Lachish (see especially Kenyon 1960: fig. 90; 1965: figs 25, 33, 51 and 82, and Tufnell 1958: pl. 29). The pendant from tomb NE11 (NE11.1, Pl. XIA) is closely similar to two examples from Qedesh (Tadmor 1978: fig. 11:20–21).

The finest piece is undoubtedly the delicate necklace from tomb NE12 (NE12.1, Pl. XIc), consisting of tiny pale bluish-green faience beads, interspersed with larger limestone disc beads, *conus* shells and finely carved, sub-rectangular limestone double spacers. Rather similar spacers were found in the vicinity of the tell of Beth Shan during the laying of a pipeline in 1951 (Israel Department of Antiquities, registration no. 51–7301), there associated with typical EBIV pottery vessels including four-spouted lamps and an envelope-folded ledge-handled storejar (the writer is extremely grateful to Miriam Tadmor of the Israel Museum for supplying this information).

DIGGING-STICK WEIGHT

A complete digging-stick weight was found in the chamber of tomb NE25 (NE25.4). Although such purely functional objects, which were used in the construction of the tombs, would not normally be considered as grave offerings, NE25.4, which was found in good condition and in close proximity to the other grave goods, might possibly have served as such. NE25.4 is annular in shape, and is made of orange sandstone, with the central hole bored from either side.

Similar digging-stick weights have been found in EBIV contexts at Jericho in tombs N4, M5 and A92 (Kenyon 1965: fig. 19:1–2; 1960: fig. 70:12), and at Jebel Qa'aqīr (Dever 1973: fig. 5:18), but the type, showing little or no typological difference, appears to go back to the Late Chalcolithic period (see Richard 1978: 249 and pl. XXXI).

SHELLS

The shells were kindly identified by David S. Reese of the Field Museum of Natural History, Chicago.

The *conus* shells included in the necklace from tomb NE12 (NE12.1) have been referred to above (see under beads). More interesting perhaps was the occurrence in tomb SE14 of a cassid lip (the thickened outer, palatal or apertural lip of the Mediterranean Helmet shell – superfamily *Tonnacea*, family *Cassidae*). This cassid lip was almost certainly intended for use as a pendant, for a similar but later (twelfth century BC) lip, pierced for suspension, was found at Ta'anach (Lapp 1967: fig. 24). Unpierced lips from Late Bronze and Iron Age contexts have also been found at Megiddo (Guy and Engberg 1938: pl. 130:3, tomb 912B; pl. 94:6, tomb 877A1; and pl. 166:12, tomb 39).

The stone-built graves

Perhaps the most significant discovery of the 1984 season of excavations at Tiwal esh-Sharqi was that of two stone-built graves, NE8 and SE14. In each case, they consisted of a sub-rectangular pit, lined on all four sides with four or five courses of stones and capped by three limestone slabs. Both NE8 and SE14 contained deposits which can clearly be dated to the EBIV period (see above).

Stone-built graves of this type, characterised by a general uniformity of constructional method, have been found at a number of sites in Palestine and Syria, but are most usually associated with the following MBIIA period. Well-known Syrian examples are from Baghouz on the Euphrates (Mesnil du Buisson 1948), Tell et-Tin in the Lake of Homs (Gautier 1895) and Yabrud in south-central Syria (Assaf 1967). In Palestine, MBIIA stone-built graves have been found at Ras el-'Ain (Ory 1937) and Gezer (Macalister 1912: fig. 158). In all of these cases, the grave goods are purely local to the area, but tend to be richer in nature (weapons at Baghouz and Tell et-Tin, elaborately decorated pottery at Ras el-'Ain and Gezer), suggesting perhaps that these were the graves of a social élite (but not necessarily a warrior class as proposed by Oren in 1971: 111–39). Only at Yabrud is there evidence that the stone-built graves were first used in EBIV (see, however, below with regard to cairn burials): two painted 'teapots' were found in one of the graves, dating to late in the period (Assaf 1967: pl. 3:23–4).

At Tiwal esh-Sharqi, two points are relevant. Firstly, the material from tombs NE8 and SE14 is identical in nature and date to that of the other shaft tombs, belonging, that is, to EBIVB (see below), indicating that these two graves formed an integral and contemporary element of the cemetery. Secondly, the grave goods found in NE8 and SE14 are not especially remarkable. Indeed, compared with some of the larger shaft tomb deposits such as NE10 or SE1, they are rather poor. In other words, there is no evidence at Tiwal esh-Sharqi, on the basis of the grave goods, to suggest that the stone-built graves, although conceptually very different from the shaft tombs, represent the graves of people of an elevated social status in the EBIV period, unless, of course, this type of grave is, in itself, an indication of such a differentiation.

So different are the stone-built graves in concept, that it might be argued that they provide evidence for a minority intrusive element within the population; one which was fully integrated into the EBIV society and only in the following MBIIA period attained some degree of social elevation. This is certainly possible, but, on the other hand, there are several examples in Syria, Palestine and Transjordan of EBIV cairn and cist burials which, although slightly different in construction method and overall execution, are clearly related to the stone-built graves (see Richard 1978: 255–8). It is possible, therefore, that although the Tiwal esh-Sharqi stone-built graves most clearly resemble the later MBIIA examples (especially those of Ras el-'Ain), their ancestry lies instead in the contemporary and earlier cist and cairn burials, the local development of which can be traced back to the EBI and possibly Chalcolithic periods (see Prag 1974: 101–2 and associated references).

Chronology and Conclusions

As shown above, with regard to the EBIV period the repertoire of pottery vessels and other objects recovered from the 1984 excavations at Tiwal esh-Sharqi is quite restricted. It can be expanded only very slightly by consideration of the finds from Helms' excavations at the site in 1983. Found in that season were a number of cups with incurved walls (Helms 1983: figs 16:2, 18:7–10, 20:5–6 – there termed 'goblets'), a single example of the typical EBIV wide-mouthed jug (ibid: fig. 26:5), two loop-handled teapot amphoriskoi (ibid: figs 18:1 and 21:6), and two 'poker-headed' javelins (ibid: fig. 18:2–3). In addition, it should be noted that one of the loop-handled amphoriskoi (ibid: fig. 22:3) was decorated with red paint.

The addition of Helms' 1983 material to that excavated in 1984 does not alter the opinion expressed previously, which is that the Tiwal esh-Sharqi cemetery (or at least that part of it so far examined) should be placed chronologically in the middle of the EBIV period. Within the tripartite system established by Dever (1980: 35–64) this would be classified as EBIVB, but here a slight reservation must be expressed. For if there is a fault in Dever's generally excellent analysis of the period, it lies in an over-rigidity of classification which fails to take sufficient account of chronological overlaps, both internally with regard to the various regional 'families' of EBIV, and at either end in relation to EBIII and MBIIA. In other words, for reasons of purely regional conservatism, the cultural attributes that define EBIVB might well have persisted much longer in some areas than in others which had already adopted features which would be expressed as EBIVC.

Nevertheless, even allowing for quite substantial chronological overlaps, it is clear that the Tiwal esh-Sharqi repertoire shows none of those features which define the earliest phase of the period, EBIVA, as represented for example by tomb A54 at Bâb edh-Dhrâ' (Schaub 1973: 2–19) and phase 1 at Iktanu (Prag 1974: 77–8). The details of this initial phase of EBIV, which marks the transition from EBIII, are discussed in considerable detail in Richard 1978.

It is equally clear that the Tiwal esh-Sharqi assemblage includes none of those features which define the latest phase of EBIV, EBIVC. The storejars have well-defined envelope-folding ledge handles which show no tendency towards becoming vestigial. Band and wavy-line incised decoration, a characteristic feature of amphoriskoi, storejars, teapots and goblets of EBIVC, is absent, and none of the lamps, whether flat- or round-based, show the sharply pinched spouts and concavity of body wall typical of the latest in the series.

The cemetery of Tiwal esh-Sharqi undoubtedly served the occupation site of Tell Umm Hammad, where excavations by Helms in 1982–4 have revealed an extensive occupation during the EBIV period (see especially Helms 1986: 25–50). Stratigraphically, four phases ('stages') of occupation were isolated at Tell Umm Hammad el-Gharbiya, all of which appear to fall within EBIVB, although the latest (8), which includes examples of wavy-line incised decoration, may extend into EBIVC (see Helms 1986: fig 18:8). It would, of course, be premature, in advance of Helms' final report, to discuss the possibility of an EBIVC horizon at the site. Suffice it to say that if such an occupation is present, the tombs related to it have not yet been found, but indeed they could well be present in the large areas of the cemetery which have not so far been explored.

REFERENCES

Assaf, A.A.
   1967 Der Friedhof von Yabrud. *Annales archéologiques arabes syriennes* 17: 55–68.

Dever, W.A.
   1972a Middle Bronze I Cemeteries at Mirzâbaneh and ʿAin es-Sâmiya. *Israel Exploration Journal* 22: 95–112.
   1972b A Middle Bronze I Site on the West Bank of the Jordan. *Archaeology* 25: 231–3.
   1973 The EBIV-MBI Horizon in Transjordan and Southern Palestine. *Bulletin of the American Schools of Oriental Research* 210: 37–63.
   1975 A Middle Bronze I Cemetery at Khirbet el-Kirmil. *Eretz Israel* 12 (Glueck volume): 13*–18*.
   1980 New Vistas on the EBIV ('MBI') Horizon in Syria-Palestine. *Bulletin of the American Schools of Oriental Research* 237: 35–64.

Gautier, J.-E.
   1895 Note sur les fouilles entreprises dans la haute vallée de l'Oronte. *Comptes rendus de l'Académie des inscriptions et belles lettres* 23, 4th series: 441–64.

Gitin, S.
   1975 Middle Bronze I 'Domestic' Pottery at Jebel Qaʿaqīr: A Ceramic Inventory of Cave G23. *Eretz Israel* 12 (Glueck volume): 46*–62*.

Glueck, N.
   1951 *Explorations in Eastern Palestine IV*. Annual of the American Schools of Oriental Research 25–8. New Haven: American Schools of Oriental Research.

Guy, P.L.O. and Engberg, R.M.
   1938 *Megiddo Tombs*. Oriental Institute Publications 33. Chicago: University of Chicago.

Harding, G.L.
   1953 An Early Bronze Age Cave at El Husn. *Palestine Exploration Fund Annual* 6: 1–13.

Helms, S.W.
   1983 The EBIV (EB-MB) Cemetery at Tiwal esh-Sharqi in the Jordan Valley, 1983. *Annual of the Department of Antiquities of Jordan* 27: 55–85.
   1984 Excavations at Tell Um Hammad esh-Sharqiya in the Jordan Valley, 1982. *Levant* 16: 35–54.
   1986 Excavations at Tell Um Hammad, 1984. *Levant* 18: 25–50.

Kenyon, K.M.
   1960 *Excavations at Jericho I: The Tombs Excavated in 1952–4*. London: British School of Archaeology in Jerusalem.
   1965 *Excavations at Jericho II: The Tombs Excavated in 1955–8*. London: British School of Archaeology in Jerusalem.

Lapp, P.W.
   1967 The 1966 Excavations at Tell Taʿannek. *Bulletin of the American Schools of Oriental Research* 185: 2–39.

Macalister, R.A.S.
   1912 *The Excavation of Gezer, Vol. I*. London: John Murray.

Mellaart, J.
   1962 Preliminary Report of the Archaeological Survey in the Yarmuk and Jordan Valley. *Annual of the Department of Antiquities of Jordan* 6–7: 126–57.

Mesnil du Buisson, R. du
   1948 *Baghouz, l'ancienne Corsôtê – le tell archaïque et la nécropole de l'âge du bronze*. Leiden: Brill.

Olávarri, E.
   1969 Fouilles à ʿArôʿer sur l'Arnon. *Revue biblique* 76: 230–59.

Oren, E.D.
   1971 A Middle Bronze Age I Warrior Tomb at Beth-Shan. *Zeitschrift des deutschen Palästina-Vereins* 87: 107–39.

References

1973 *The Northern Cemetery of Beth Shan*. Museum Monograph of the University Museum, University of Pennsylvania. Leiden: Brill.

Ory, J.
1937 Excavations at Ras el-'Ain II. *Quarterly of the Department of Antiquities of Palestine* 6: 99–120.

Petrie, W.M.F.
1931 *Ancient Gaza I: Tell el-Ajjūl*. London: British School of Archaeology in Egypt.

Prag, K.
1974 The Intermediate Early Bronze – Middle Bronze Age: An Interpretation of the Evidence from Transjordan, Syria and Lebanon. *Levant* 6: 69–116.

Pritchard, J.B.
1963 *The Bronze Age Cemetery at Gibeon*. Museum Monograph of the University Museum, University of Pennsylvania. Philadelphia: University of Pennsylvania.

Richard, S.
1978 *The End of the Early Bronze Age in Palestine-Transjordan: A Study of the Post-EBIII Cultural Complex*. Unpublished PhD dissertation, Johns Hopkins University.

Schaub, R.T.
1973 An Early Bronze IV Tomb from Bâb edh-Dhrâ'. *Bulletin of the American Schools of Oriental Research* 210: 2–19.

Tadmor, M.
1978 A Cult Cave of the Middle Bronze I near Qedesh. *Israel Exploration Journal* 28: 1–30.

Tubb, J.N.
1985 Excavations in the Early Bronze Age Cemetery of Tiwal esh-Sharqi: A Preliminary Report. *Annual of the Department of Antiquities of Jordan* 29: 115–28.

Tufnell, O.
1958 *Lachish IV: The Bronze Age*. London: Oxford University Press.

Vaux, R. de
1951 La troisième campagne de fouilles à Tell el-Far'ah près Naplouse. *Revue biblique* 58: 393–430, 566–90.
1955 Les fouilles de Tell el-Far'ah près Naplouse: cinquième campagne. *Revue biblique* 62: 541–89.

Vaux, R. de and Stève, A.M.-A.
1949 La deuxième campagne de fouilles à Tell el-Far'ah près Naplouse. *Revue biblique* 56: 102–38.

APPENDIX A

THE HUMAN BONES FROM TIWAL ESH-SHARQI

JANET D. HENDERSON

Examination of the human skeletal remains from the site was undertaken both *in situ* and after excavation. A minimum number of forty-one individuals were found to be present. Bone preservation was extremely poor throughout and this necessarily restricted the analysis. Observations were attempted for age, sex, stature, anthropology and pathology. Details of the results by tomb are given in the sub-appendices A1–3, with the exception of the archive inventory of bones and teeth present which is held by the author.

Demography

The results for sex are summarised in Table 1. Sex is given as either 'Male', '?Male', '?Female', 'Female' or '–' (not known). Since attributions of sex cannot be made with certainty, these are essentially statements of probability, representing respectively probably male, possibly male, possibly female and probably female. No attempt was made to sex infants, juveniles or sub-adults since it is generally accepted that sexual dimorphism in the skeletons of young individuals is insufficiently marked for attributions of sex to be made with any degree of confidence (see, for example, Krogman 1962 or El-Najjar and McWilliams 1978). For adults, standard methods were used (all cited in Stewart 1979).

As only fifteen out of a possible total of forty-one individuals could be assigned an attribution of sex, very little could be said about these results. On the evidence available there was no apparent discrimination in burial by sex (for example, all male burials). Whether or not there was any bias in the distribution between male and female is uncertain, given that ten adults could not be sexed at all.

An initial age assessment was made for each individual as infant (*c.* birth to 6 months), juvenile (*c.* 6 months to 12 years), sub-adult (*c.* 12–20 years) or adult (older than 20 years). Where possible, a closer estimate (in months or years) was then made. As with sex, standard techniques were used (ibid.). The results for the preliminary estimates are given in Table 2.

With the exception of the four individuals identified only as 'human', ageing was possible for the whole sample. As with sex it was clear that there was no overall bias (for example, towards adults only). The two largest groups were the adults and juveniles respectively. With the exception of one individual (Tomb SE5, skeleton B) more precise estimates were made for all the juveniles. This showed that

TABLE 1. *Results – sex*

Sex	Number
Female	4
?Female	5
?Male	1
Male	5
Unsexed: Adult	10
Unsexed: Infants, Juveniles, Sub-adults	12
Identifiable as 'human' only	4
Total sexed:	15
Total:	41

Appendix A: Human bones

TABLE 2. *Results – age*

Age	Number
Infant	–
Juvenile	10
Sub-adult	2
Adult	25
Identifiable as 'human' only	4
Total:	41

there was a more or less even split between those aged at less than 5 years (five individuals) and those at more than 5 years (four individuals). Only eight of the adults were given closer age estimates. These were all 'young' (less than 35 years). However, it must be stressed that ageing of adults is susceptible to a far greater degree of error than that of juveniles and that these estimates should be treated with caution.

Overall, it was noticeable that there was an apparent absence of infants and older adults. In the case of the infants, possible explanations of this would include: under-representation of infants owing to increased post-mortem loss (infant bones may be very fragile); differential burial practice (infants may have been buried in another unexcavated part of the site or may not have been regarded as worthy of burial in a cemetery at all), and a genuine absence of infants due to survival in the population beyond infancy. With the adults, comment is complicated by the difficulties involved in estimating age in individuals where skeletal growth and development is complete (in other words, some of these adults aged as 'young' may, in fact, have been 'old'). Further, the greater proportion of those recovered were aged as 'adult' only (seventeen out of twenty-five). If the absence of older adults were to be found to have been real, then differential burial practice (as with the infants) and early mortality in the sample would have to be considered. However, with both the infants and the adults three factors preclude any conclusions on the pattern seen: firstly that the sample is extremely small, secondly that only part of the known area of the cemetery was excavated, and thirdly, and most importantly, that this is a cemetery population sample and therefore does not necessarily equate with the biological population using the cemetery at any point in time.

Anthropology and pathology

With regard to the analysis of normal and abnormal skeletal variability, so few observations could be made that comment would not be justified on the results as a whole. Individual details are given below, under headings A1 (pathology) and A3 (anthropology).

Burial practice

In all, from the areas excavated, a total of thirty-one tombs produced human remains totalling a minimum number of forty-one individuals. The archaeological evidence for burial practice is discussed elsewhere. Comment here is confined to skeletal evidence for primary or secondary burial. Table 3 gives the figures for tombs with single, double or triple burial. Particular questions that may arise, given that nearly a third of the tombs produced more than one individual, include whether or not burial was primary or secondary and whether there was evidence for prolonged use of tombs over a period of time. For the most part, neither of these queries could be answered on the present sample, owing to tomb collapse and disturbance of tomb contents (see Chapter 2) and consequential poor bone preservation. In only one case (tomb NE8) was it possible to say that a skeleton represented evidence for secondary burial (skeleton B). In this case the bones were positioned approximately correctly but their articulation was such as to have been anatomically impossible. Whether or not this represented disturbance of the skeleton in the grave by the insertion of a later burial (skeleton A) or 'true' secondary burial could not be determined.

TABLE 3. *Multiple burial*

Area	Single	Double	Triple
NE	17	4	1
SE	6	2	1

Summary and conclusions

Excavation of a number of tombs at the cemetery site of Tiwal esh-Sharqi found that thirty-one tombs still contained human remains which represented a minimum number of forty-one individuals. Poor bone preservation of the whole sample meant that little could be said about these finds other than with respect to the distribution by age and sex. This last showed no apparent bias in the group; individuals of both sexes and all ages (except infants) were present. Given that burial took place over a period of approximately 150 years, further comment could not be justified.

A1. Human bone catalogue

In the following catalogue the results are listed by tomb, and observations are included as follows:

Bone condition

This is a summary of the condition of the skeleton with an estimate, given as a percentage, of the amount present. For example, 'Nearly complete skeleton in good condition,

Appendix A: Human bones

75%'. This means that most of the bones of the skeleton were represented (approximately 75%) and that they were well preserved. A more detailed inventory of the bones and teeth is kept in the site archive (held by the author).

Sex

Attributions of sex are quoted together with a brief comment on the method(s) used in making the attribution. For example, 'Female, based on skull and pelvic morphology and the dimensions of the humerus'.

Note: The phrase 'general skeletal morphology' is used to indicate a general assessment of the skeleton with particular reference to overall robustness or gracility.

Age

Age estimates are quoted together with an abbreviated statement of the method(s) employed. For example, '5–10 years: dental development'.

Stature

Estimates of stature are given in metres with the standard deviation of the estimate. An imperial equivalent is also given, together with details of the bone(s) used. For this sample all estimates were made using Steele's method (1970). For example, '1.70 m ± .0879, *c.* 5′7″, R femur – segment 1'.

Pathology

A reference to a tooth as 'unidentified' indicates that it was not possible to determine whether the tooth was maxilliary or mandibular, or whether it was from the right or left side of the dentition. Otherwise teeth are referred to by means of the FDI system (Fédération Dentaire Internationale – see, for example, Downer 1975 for details).

Tomb NE2

Fragmentary remains in poor condition, < 25%.
12–15 years: dental development, epiphyseal union.

DENTAL PATHOLOGY
Periodontal disease: slight.
Enamel hypoplasia: 2,3 only, lines present, estimated age 4–5 years.

Tomb NE3

Fragmentary remains in very poor condition, < 25%.
?Female, based on general skeletal morphology.
Adult.

Tomb NE4

Partial skeleton in poor condition, *c.* 30%.
Female, based on morphology of the skull and skeleton generally and the dimension of the femur, humerus and scapula.
Adult.

DENTAL PATHOLOGY
Ante-mortem tooth loss: molar, precise tooth identification not possible.

SKELETAL PATHOLOGY
Joint disease: there was some slight evidence for degenerative change to the heads of the proximal phalanges of the feet. None of the other bones were affected.

COMMENT
Bone preservation was such that it was not possible to suggest the cause either of the tooth loss or of the changes to the foot phalanges.

Tomb NE5

Fragmentary remains in very poor condition, < 25%.
2–3 years: dental development.

Tomb NE6

Fragmentary remains in very poor condition, < 25%.
6 months – 1 year: dental development.

SKELETAL PATHOLOGY
Metabolic
Cribra Orbitalia: moderately severe, left orbit only (right unavailable for examination).

Tomb NE7

This tomb was found to have contained a minimum number of two individuals. These were numbered A and B.

SKELETON A
Partial skeleton in poor condition, 30%.
Female, based on the dimensions of the femur and tibia.
Adult.

SKELETON B
Partial skeleton in poor condition, 30%.
?Female, based on general skeletal morphology and femoral dimensions.
Adult.

Tomb NE8

This tomb was found to have contained a minimum number of two individuals. These were numbered A and B.

SKELETON A
Partial skeleton in poor condition, 50%.
Male, based on pelvic and general skeletal morphology and the dimensions of the femur, talus and calcaneus.
Adult.
1.70 m ± .0879, *c.* 5′7″, R femur – segment 1.

Appendix A: Human bones

SKELETON B
Partial skeleton in very poor condition, 30%.
Male, based on skull and general skeletal morphology and femoral dimensions.
25–35 years: dental wear.

Tomb NE9

Fragmentary remains in very poor condition, < 25%.
Adult.

Tomb NE10

There were two skeletons in this tomb, numbered A and B.

SKELETON A
Fragmentary remains in poor condition, < 25%.
Male, based on general skeletal morphology and femoral dimensions.
20–25 years: dental wear.

SKELETON B
Fragmentary remains in very poor condition, < 25%.
5–10 years: bone size.

Tomb NE10A

Fragmentary remains in very poor condition, < 25%.
5–10 years: dental development.

Tomb NE11

Fragmentary remains in very poor condition, < 25%.
5–10 years: dental development, bone size.

DENTAL PATHOLOGY
Enamel Hypoplasia: incisor (unidentified), groove, age (approx.) 2–3 years.

Tomb NE12

Fragmentary remains in very poor condition, < 25%.
3–5 years: dental development.

Tomb NE13

This individual was represented by a few fragments of bone in very poor condition which could be identified as 'human' only.

Tomb NE15

This tomb was found to have contained a minimum number of two individuals. These were numbered A and B.

SKELETON A
Fragmentary remains in very poor condition, < 25%.
Female, based on femoral dimensions.
25–35 years: dental wear.

SKELETON B
Fragmentary remains in very poor condition, < 25%.
5–10 years: bone size.

Tomb NE16

Fragmentary remains in very poor condition, < 25%.
Adult.

Tomb NE17

Fragmentary remains in very poor condition, < 25%.
?Female, based on femoral dimensions.
Adult.

Tomb NE20

This individual was represented by a few fragments of bone in very poor condition which could be identified as 'human' only.

Tomb NE21

Fragmentary remains in very poor condition, < 25%.
1–2 years: dental development.

Tomb NE22

This tomb was found to have contained a minimum number of three individuals. These were numbered A, B and C.

SKELETON A
Partial skeleton in fair condition, 30%.
Male, based on general skeletal morphology and the dimensions of the femur, talus and calcaneus. 25–30 years: dental wear, epiphyseal union.
1.72 m ± .0879, *c.* 5′7½″, R femur – segment 1.

SKELETON B
Fragmentary remains in very poor condition, < 25%.
Female, based on general skeletal morphology and humeral dimensions.
Adult (young): dental wear.

SKELETON C
Fragmentary remains in very poor condition, < 25%.
10–15 years: bone size, epiphyseal union.

Tomb NE23

Fragmentary remains in very poor condition, < 25%.
<5 years: bone size.

Tomb NE24

Fragmentary remains in very poor condition, < 25%.
Adult.

Appendix A: Human bones

Tomb NE25

Fragmentary remains in very poor condition, < 25%.
Adult.

Tomb SE1

This tomb was found to have contained a minimum number of two individuals. These were numbered A and B.

SKELETON A
Fragmentary remains in very poor condition, < 25%.
?Female, based on general skeletal morphology.
Adult.

SKELETON B
Fragmentary remains in very poor condition, < 25%.
?Male, based on general skeleton morphology and femoral dimensions.
Adult.

Tomb SE1A

This individual was represented by a few fragments of bone in very poor condition which could be identified as 'human' only.

Tomb SE2

This individual was represented by a few fragments of bone in very poor condition which could be identified as 'human' only.

Tomb SE4

This tomb was found to have contained a minimum number of three individuals. These were numbered A, B and C.

SKELETON A
Fragmentary remains in very poor condition, < 25%.
Male, based on pelvic and general skeletal morphology and femoral dimensions.
25–35 years: dental wear.

SKELETON B
Fragmentary remains in very poor condition, < 25%.
?Female, based on skull morphology and femoral and humeral dimensions.
25–35 years: dental wear.

DENTAL PATHOLOGY
Periodontal disease: moderate.

SKELETON C
Fragmentary remains in very poor condition, < 25%.
Adult.

Tomb SE5

This tomb was found to have contained a minimum number of two individuals. These were numbered A and B.

SKELETON A
Fragmentary remains in very poor condition, < 25%.
25–35 years: dental wear.

SKELETON B
Fragmentary remains in very poor condition, < 25%.
Juvenile: bone size.

Tomb SE7

Fragmentary remains in very poor condition, < 25%.
Adult.

Tomb SE8

Fragmentary remains in very poor condition, < 25%.
Adult.

Tomb SE10

Fragmentary remains in very poor condition, < 25%.
Adult.

Tomb SE14

Fragmentary remains in very poor condition, < 25%.
25–35 years: dental wear.

A2. Results for sex, age and stature

Number	Sex		Age (in years)	Stature Metric	Imperial
NE2			12–15	–	–
NE3		?Female	Adult	–	–
NE4		Female	Adult	–	–
NE5			2–3	–	–
NE6			6 months–1 year	–	–
NE7	A	Female	Adult	–	–
	B	?Female	Adult	–	–

Appendix A: Human bones

A2. Results for sex, age and stature

Number		Sex	Age (in years)	Stature Metric	Imperial
NE8	A	Male	Adult	1.70m ± .0879	c. 5'7"
	B	Male	25–35	–	–
NE9		–	Adult	–	–
NE10	A	Male	20–25	–	–
	B	–	5–10	–	–
NE10A		–	5–10	–	–
NE11		–	5–10	–	–
NE12		–	3–5	–	–
NE13		–	–	–	–
NE15	A	Female	25–35	–	–
	B	–	5–10	–	–
NE16		–	Adult	–	–
NE17		?Female	Adult	–	–
NE20		–	–	–	–
NE21		–	1–2	–	–
NE22	A	Male	25–30	1.72m ± .0879	c. 5'7½"
	B	Female	Adult	–	–
	C	–	10–15	–	–
NE23		–	<5	–	–
NE24		–	Adult	–	–
NE25		–	Adult	–	–
SE1	A	?Female	Adult	–	–
	B	?Male	Adult	–	–
SE1A		–	–	–	–
SE2		–	–	–	–
SE4	A	Male	25–35	–	–
	B	?Female	25–35	–	–
	C	–	Adult	–	–
SE5	A	–	25–35	–	–
	B	–	Juvenile	–	–
SE7		–	Adult	–	–
SE8		–	Adult	–	–
SE10		–	Adult	–	–
SE14		–	25–35	–	–

A3. Anthropological results – morphology and metrics

Owing to the poor bone preservation, very few observations could be made. The results, where available, are listed below. Standard reference texts were used in assessing which variables should be recorded. Those used were: Berry and Berry 1967, Bass 1971, Grant 1972, El-Najjar and McWilliams 1978, Finnegan 1978.

Tomb NE2

Skull	Torus maxillaris	Absent, R+L
	Torus palatinus	Absent
	Premaxillary suture	Absent, R+L
	Anterior palatine alveolar foramen	Absent, R+L
Mandible	Mental foramen – position	R only: PM 1/2
	Mental foramen – number	R only: single
Femur	Third trochanter	R only: absent
Talus	Os trigonum	Absent, R+L
Calcaneus	Calcaneal facet	R only: double

Tomb NE8, Skeleton A

Patella	Patella spurs	Absent, R+L
	Vastus notch	Absent, R+L
	Bipartite patella	Absent, R+L
Calcaneus	Calcaneal spurs	R only: absent
	Calcaneal facet	R only: double

Appendix A: Human bones

Tomb NE8, Skeleton B

Skull	Metopism	Absent
	Nasal junction (shape)	Rounded
	Malar tuberosity	L only: present, slight
	Marginal tubercle	L only: absent

Tomb NE22, Skeleton A

Humerus	Septal aperture	R only: absent
Radius	Distal facet	L only: single
Ulna	Olecranon spurs	Absent, R+L
Femur	Third trochanter	Absent, R+L
	Poirier's facet	R only: absent
Patella	Patella spurs	R only: absent
	Vastus notch	R only: absent
	Bipartite patella	R only: absent
Talus	Talar facet	Single, R+L
	Os trigonum	L only: present
Calcaneus	Calcaneal spurs	R only: present
	Calcaneal facet	R only: single

Metrics – femur

Tomb		FeL1		FeL2		FHD1		FeD1		FeD2		FeD3		FeD4		FeE1	
		R	L	R	L	R	L	R	L	R	L	R	L	R	L	R	L
NE8	A	–	–	–	–	46	–	–	–	–	–	–	–	–	–	–	–
NE8	B	–	–	–	–	50	–	–	–	–	–	–	–	–	–	–	–
NE22	A	–	–	–	–	51	50	28	29	33	36	–	–	–	–	–	–

Index of abbreviations

Note: 1. All measurements are given in millimetres (mm).
2. Various authors give definitions of the measurements used. The particular reference used for each measurement is cited below.
3. R = Right, L = Left.

FeL1	Maximum length (Brothwell 1981)
FeL2	Oblique length (Brothwell 1981)
FHD1	Maximum head diameter (Bass 1971)
FeD1	Sub-trochanteric antero-posterior diameter (Bass 1971)
FeD2	Sub-trochanteric medio-lateral diameter (Bass 1971)
FeD3	Mid-shaft antero-posterior diameter (Bass 1971)
FeD4	Mid-shaft medio-lateral diameter (Bass 1971)
FeE1	Bicondylar breadth (Giles 1970)

Metrics – talus and calcaneus

Tomb		TaL1		TaB1		TaH1		TaT1		TaT2		CaL1		CaB1		CaH1		CaL2		CaB2	
		R	L	R	L	R	L	R	L	R	L	R	L	R	L	R	L	R	L	R	L
NE8	A	–	–	45	–	32	–	33	–	30	–	85	–	26	–	44	–	46	–	53	–
NE22	A	–	54	–	44	–	35	–	–	–	–	81	–	29	–	47	–	50	–	39	–

Index of abbreviations

Note: 1. All measurements are given in millimetres (mm).
2. All measurements are taken from Steele (1976).
3. R = Right, L = Left.

Talus

TaL1	Maximum length
TaB1	Talar width
TaH1	Body height
TaT1	Maximum length of the trochlea for the tibia
TaT2	Maximum width of the trochlea for the tibia

Calcaneus

CaL1	Maximum length
CaB1	Minimum width
CaH1	Body height
CaL2	Load arm length
CaB2	Load arm width

Appendix A: Human bones

References

Bass, W.M.
    1971 *Human Osteology*. Columbia: Missouri Archaeological Society.

Berry, A.C. and R.J.
    1967 Epigenetic variation in the human cranium. *Journal of Anatomy* 101: 361–79.

Brothwell, D.R.
    1981 *Digging Up Bones*. London: British Museum (Natural History), 3rd ed.

Downer, G.C.
    1975 *Dental Morphology: An Illustrated Guide*. Bristol: John Wright and Sons Ltd.

El-Najjar, M.Y. and McWilliams, K.R.
    1978 *Forensic Anthropology*. Illinois: Charles C. Thomas.

Finnegan, M.
    1978 Nonmetric variation of the infracranial skeleton. *Journal of Anatomy* 125: 2337.

Giles, E.
    1970 Discriminant function sexing of the human skeleton. Pages 99–109 in Stewart, T.D. (ed.), *Personal Identification in Mass Disasters*. Washington: National Museum of Natural History.

Grant, J.C.B.
    1972 *An Atlas of Anatomy*. Baltimore: Williams and Wilkins, 6th ed.

Krogman, W.M.
    1962 *The Human Skeleton in Forensic Medicine*. Illinois: Charles C. Thomas.

Steele, D. Gentry.
    1970 Estimation of stature from fragmentary remains of long limb bones. Pages 85–97 in Stewart, T.D. (ed.), *Personal Identification in Mass Disasters*. Washington: National Museum of Natural History.
    1976 The estimation of sex on the basis of the talus and calcaneus. *American Journal of Physical Anthropology* 45: 581–8.

Stewart, T.D.
    1979 *Essentials of Forensic Anthropology*. Illinois: Charles C. Thomas.

APPENDIX B

CONSERVATION TREATMENTS EMPLOYED AT TIWAL ESH-SHARQI

MARGOT M. WRIGHT

The two major categories of material excavated from the site which required conservation were ceramic and copper alloy artefacts. Beads composed of stone, shell, alabaster or bone/teeth constituted a relatively minor category.

Ceramic vessels

At first appearance, the fabric of the vessels seemed to be quite robust but, in fact, upon closer examination, the fabric proved to be rather soft and friable, especially when the pottery contained many small inclusions as temper or when, as in some cases, it seemed to be made from a clay which, when fired, had the appearance of a fine red-orange fabric.

A standard form of conservation technique was adopted to treat the majority of the ceramics, both whole vessels and sherds.

1. Whole vessels were excavated and the fill examined.
2. The outer surface was cleaned gently by means of a variety of tools, such as dental picks, stencil cutters and cocktail sticks. The clay marl which adhered to the surface of the vessel was removed with extreme caution so as not to cause damage to the vessel. In some cases, because of the softness of the object, cleaning was terminated and the ingrained dirt left *in situ*.
3. Some vessels were found to have large crystals adhering to both inner and outer surfaces. These insoluble salt crystals tended to disfigure the artefacts and therefore, when possible, they were removed from the surface (outer) of the object by scalpel blade or, when the crystals were large and hard, they were ground down by mini-drill using a variety of metal bits. Often, the crystals were left *in situ* if their removal was considered to be damaging to the vessel. The crystals adhering to the interior surface of the vessel were not subjected to any such treatment.
4. The outer surface of the vessel or sherd was cleaned further by brushing the surface with tap water which, in the area where the conservation laboratory was established, appeared to be of good quality. Clay or marl adhering to the interior of the artefact was rinsed off when possible, but often the fine silt proved to be too difficult to remove and hence was left so as not to harm the fabric of the vessel.
5. The object was immersed in tap water for a period of about one hour to allow the fabric to become fully saturated with water and thus to prevent the body of the vessel from being affected by the dilute solution of

Appendix B: Conservation

acid which, in some cases, was used to remove carbonates from the surface (outer). The carbonates (insoluble salts) were removed by dripping 5–10% nitric acid from a Pasteur pipette on to the body of the object where they could be seen to have formed hard white deposits. The carbonates reacted with the acid, causing effervescence and forming nitrates, soluble in water.

6. The ceramic was immersed in tap water for a period of four days to remove the soluble salts from the fabric. During this time, the water was changed at least twice a day, and at all times care was taken to ensure that the object was submerged fully in the water to prevent areas appearing above the surface from which evaporation could occur, resulting in efflorescence and damage to the object. Certain artefacts were considered to be too delicate to be treated with acid and hence were subjected to a short period of soaking. The four-day period of immersion in tap water was judged to be sufficient to remove the majority of soluble salts present and ideally, under laboratory conditions, the final soaking would have been in distilled water, and the level of salts present in the distilled water after soaking monitored by conductivity meter to decide whether the treatments should be continued or terminated.
7. The object was removed from the tap water and allowed to dry in the shade.
8. When the sherds or vessel had dried completely, usually after two or three days, the fabric was inspected to discover whether it was strong or weak. Because they were in a highly weakened state, some objects had to be consolidated by immersing them in a solution of 10% Paraloid B-72 (ethyl acrylate-methyl methacrylate co-polymer, manufactured by Rohm & Haas) in toluene. Ideally, the artefact would be immersed in the consolidating solution and subjected to vacuum to ensure penetration of the co-polymer but, due to lack of facilities, the object was immersed for a period of approximately 20 hours. It was removed from the solution and the solvent allowed to evaporate slowly: toluene was selected as the solvent because it evaporates more slowly than acetone and therefore was less likely to cause the consolidant to migrate to the surface of the vessel or sherds.
9. Broken vessels were reconstructed and the sherds held in position with masking tape so that, when joined, they could be put together efficiently, without causing damage to the edges, and to prevent any sherds from being 'locked out'.
10. The sherds were joined with H.M.G. (cellulose nitrate adhesive). This adhesive is soluble in acetone or toluene and therefore the joins may be taken down at any point in the future.
11. Whenever necessary, in order to give the reconstructed vessel strength or to enhance its appearance, gaps were filled with dental plaster, and in some vessels small sherds were 'floated in'. The dental plaster was ground down to form a smooth surface with various grades of abrasive films and the surface was painted with powder colours in Rowney Cryla Matt Medium Number 2 or with Cryla Acrylic colours in water.

Copper alloy artefacts

1. Smaller objects such as rivets, points and blades were cleaned mechanically by mini-drill and scalpel blade under a binocular microscope.
2. Each object was degreased by immersion in acetone for 30–60 seconds.
3. The object was immersed in 3% benzotriazole in ethanol and subjected to vacuum for a period of approximately 12 hours, after which the vacuum was released and the object allowed to remain in the solution for a further 12 hours to try to obtain a stable state in which corrosion was inhibited.
4. Excess benzotriazole was removed by rinsing the object with ethanol, after which the solvent was allowed to evaporate.
5. The object was protected by the application of two coats of Incralac* (a solution of 20% in toluene), the first coat being allowed to dry before the application of the second.

Large objects, such as daggers and javelins, were wrapped in acid-free tissue and packed with Silica Gel in an air-tight box to reduce relative humidity (RH) and hence reduce corrosion. Most of the objects appeared to be relatively stable, but this was belied by the fact that when part of a dagger was mechanically cleaned, overnight the green corrosion products, indicative of active bronze disease, were observed to have developed. This observation is rather disturbing and emphasises the point that copper alloy objects should be stored under controlled environmental conditions, i.e. RH less than 45%, immediately after excavation and that they should be treated to try to obtain stabilisation by trained conservators, after which they should be maintained in a stable environment with low RH.

Beads

All the beads were cleaned by swabbing gently with cotton wool dampened with ethanol.

The beads excavated from Tomb NE8 (NE8.6), which appeared to have been manufactured from the roots and lower parts of teeth, were in a very poor state of preservation which necessitated immediate consolidation with 10% Paraloid B-72 in acetone so that they did not disintegrate; fragments were joined with H.M.G.

*methyl methacrylate co-polymer (Paraloid B-44), toluene, ethanol or butyl acrylate, benzotriazole, epoxidised soya bean oil.

APPENDIX C
DISTRIBUTION OF FINDS

Through the generosity of the Jordanian Department of Antiquities, the following tomb groups were granted to the British Museum: NE2, NE10/10A, NE12, NE15, NE16, NE17, NE20, NE23, SE1/1A, SE2, SE7, SE8, SE12 and SE14. The objects are in the Department of Western Asiatic Antiquities, and are registered as follows:

NE2.1	1984.6.11: 1
NE2.2	1984.6.11: 2
NE10.1	1984.6.11: 3
NE10.2	1984.6.11: 4
NE10.3	1984.6.11: 5
NE10.4	1984.6.11: 6
NE10.5	1984.6.11: 7
NE10.6	1984.6.11: 8
NE10.7	1984.6.11: 9
NE10.8	1984.6.11: 10
NE10.9	1984.6.11: 11
NE10.10	1984.6.11: 12
NE10A.1	1984.6.11: 13
NE12.1	1984.6.11: 14
NE15.1	1984.6.11: 15
NE15.2	1984.6.11: 16
NE15.3	1984.6.11: 17
NE15.4	1984.6.11: 18
NE15.5	1984.6.11: 19
NE15.6	1984.6.11: 20
NE15.7	1984.6.11: 21
NE15.8	1984.6.11: 22
NE16.1	1984.6.11: 23
NE16.2	1984.6.11: 24
NE16.3	1984.6.11: 25
NE16.4	1984.6.11: 26
NE16.5	1984.6.11: 27
NE16.6	1984.6.11: 28
NE16.7	1984.6.11: 29
NE17.1	1984.6.11: 31
NE17.2	1984.6.11: 32
NE17.3	1984.6.11: 30
NE17.4	1984.6.11: 33
NE20.1	1984.6.11: 34
NE20.2	1984.6.11: 35
NE20.3	1984.6.11: 36
NE23.1	1984.6.11: 37
SE1.1	1984.6.11: 38
SE1.2	1984.6.11: 39
SE1.3	1984.6.11: 40
SE1.4	1984.6.11: 41
SE1.5	1984.6.11: 42
SE1.6	1984.6.11: 43
SE1.7 (=SE1A.1)	1984.6.11: 44
SE1.8	1984.6.11: 45
SE1.11	1984.6.11: 46
SE1.12	1984.6.11: 47
SE1.13	1984.6.11: 48
SE1.14	1984.6.11: 49
SE1.15	1984.6.11: 50
SE1A.2 (=SE1.9)	1984.6.11: 51
SE1A.3 (=SE1.10)	1984.6.11: 52
SE1A.4	1984.6.11: 53
SE2.1	1984.6.11: 55
SE2.2	1984.6.11: 56
SE2.3	1984.6.11: 54
SE2.4	1984.6.11: 57
SE7.1	1984.6.11: 58
SE7.2	1984.6.11: 59
SE8.1	1984.6.11: 60
SE12.1	1984.6.11: 62
SE12.2	1984.6.11: 61
SE14.1	1984.6.11: 63
SE14.2	1984.6.11: 64
SE14.3	1984.6.11: 65

The remaining tomb groups (NE4, NE8, NE9, NE11, NE21, NE22, NE25, SE4, SE9 and SE10) were retained by the Jordanian Department of Antiquities, and the objects are in the Archaeological Museum at Salt.

PLATE I

View from the bed of the Zarqa across the northern part of the cemetery area. Hill 4 is on the right, showing tombs NE10, NE11, NE12, NE13, NE14 and NE18

PLATE II

a. Tomb NE2

b. Tomb NE22

PLATE III

a. Tomb (grave) NE8 during initial stages of excavation

b. Tomb (grave) NE8 at completion of excavation

PLATE IV

b. Tomb NE10, semi-shaft and entrance

a. Tomb NE9, shaft and entrance

PLATE V

b. Shaft and entrance of tomb NE15. The entrance to the small side-chamber, NE15A, is seen on the right, close to the scale

a. Interior of tomb NE10 during excavation, showing nature of collapsed marl fill

PLATE VI

a. Bilobate tomb NE15/16

b. West slope of Hill 114, showing, from left to right, tombs SE1, SE2 and SE3

PLATE VII

a. Tomb SE1. The 'window' connecting tomb SE1 with tomb SE1A is seen towards the centre of the picture

b. Entrance to tomb SE1

PLATE VIII

b. Tomb SE2. Phase 1 entrance, showing structural mud-brick on left

a. Tomb SE2. Phase 1 shaft and entrance

PLATE IX

a. Interior of tomb SE2 at completion of excavation, showing arrangement of stones in Phase 2. The Phase 2 entrance is seen on the left

b. Amphoriskos and perforated cup (funnel) found high up in the interior fill of tomb SE2

c. Tool marks on eastern shaft wall of tomb SE3

PLATE X

b. Tomb (grave) SE14 after initial surface clearance, with covering slabs still in position

a. Shaft and entrance of tomb SE3

PLATE XI

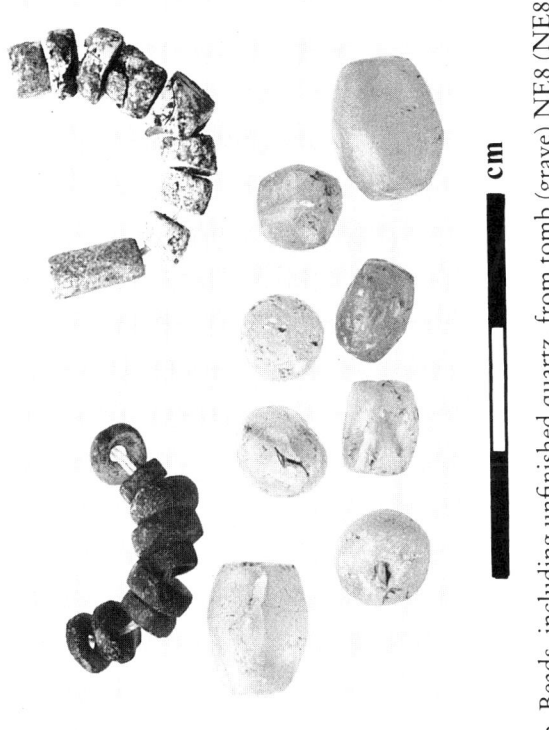

b. Beads, including unfinished quartz, from tomb (grave) NE8 (NE8.6)

d. Necklace of beads from tomb SE2 (SE2.3)

a. Stone pendant from tomb NE11 (NE11.1)

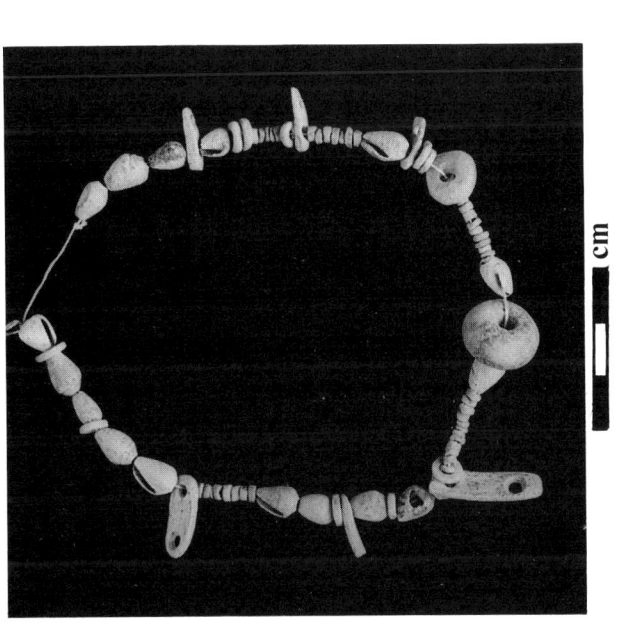

c. Necklace of beads, spacers and shells from tomb NE12 (NE12.1)

PLATE XII

a. Javelin from tomb SE1 (SE1.12)
b. Dagger from tomb SE14 (SE14.1)
c. Dagger from tomb SE1 (SE1.6). Note organic material (horn) on hilt

PLATE XIII

b. Ledge-handled storejar from tomb SE1 (SE1.15)

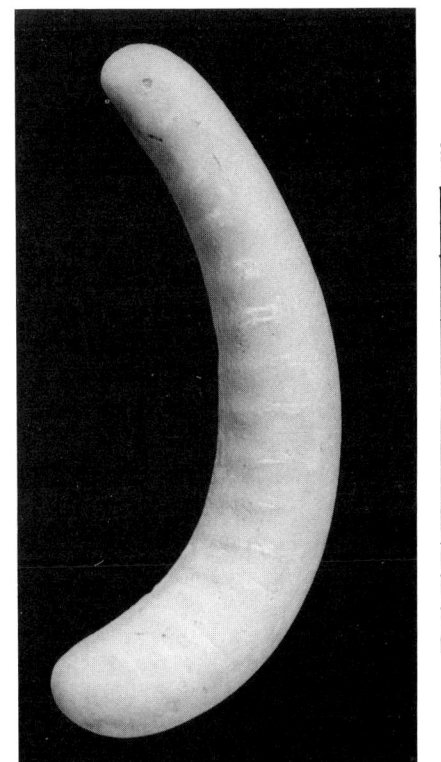

d. Cassid lip from tomb SE14 (SE14.3)

a. Juglet from tomb NE22 (NE22.6)

c. Group of vessels from tomb NE16

PLATE XIV

Side-spouted lamp from tomb SE1 (SE1.7)